THE UNMAKING OF AN AMERICAN

ALSO BY ROGER PULVERS

Liv
The Dream of Lafcadio Hearn
Half of Each Other
The Honey and the Fires
Peaceful Circumstances

Roger Pulvers

THE UNMAKING OF AN AMERICAN

A Memoir of Life in the United States, Europe, Japan and

Australia

BALESTIER PRESS
LONDON · SINGAPORE

Balestier Press
71-75 Shelton Street, London WC2H 9JQ
www.balestier.com

The Unmaking of an American
Copyright © Roger Pulvers, 2019

First published by Balestier Press in 2019

A CIP catalogue record for this book
is available from the British Library.

ISBN 978 1 911221 33 3

All translations appearing in this book are by the author. Japanese names follow standard Japanese order, with surnames before given names, except in cases where the people themselves have used the Western order, such as Taro Yashima and Harry Mimura.

Extracts from the following works are used with permission: *O Lost: A Story of the Buried Life*, Thomas Wolfe, University of South Carolina Press, 2000; *Onna Toshite, Joyu Toshite*, Koyama Akiko, 2011; *Toden Fukushima Genpatsu Jiko Soridaijin Toshite Kangaeta Koto*, Kan Naoto, Gentosha, 2012.

Edited by Holly Thompson
Cover illustration by Lucy Pulvers

Contents

Part Four: THE FIRE ON THE SHORE

Part Five: KENJI'S NET

Part Six: THE AMERICAN IN ME

LIFE ON A RIM

1

Webs of Memory

Can you look back on your life—objectively, honestly, truthfully—and discover the numberless elements that went into creating it? Or are we all destined to resign ourselves to our life's results—call them, taken together, "fate"—and pretend that we are not bothered one way or the other by the outcome?

Inheritance and personal experience may have endowed you with abilities and qualities that allow you to turn an instant of potential disaster into a stroke of fortune . . . but how do you enhance those skills and qualities to make them useful to you? When you find yourself in the sequential labyrinth of events that make up your life, how do you ensure that you are choosing the right paths for yourself? How do you sort the myriad events, encounters, accidents and experiences—from the banal to the intense, from the miniscule to the prodigious—and turn them into memories that become meaningful for your future life? By meaningful memories, I mean those that help you to access your confidence and genuinely complement your self-esteem.

A memoir is a personal chronicle that may be more about other people than yourself. It is just as much concerned with outside events far beyond your control as with the inner workings of your own heart and mind. We become the people we read about in novels; we react the way poets do in poems; we see ourselves in characters on the stage and on screens. We are made up of other people who we encounter in myriad ways that defy time and space: through the inheritance of DNA, through chance encounters in life and art, through our human innate ability to consider and treat the pain and joy of others as our own pain and joy. A memoir is an amalgam of the narratives of many people, real and fictional, who continue to live throughout the timespan of one's own life in the memory of the memoir's subject—the one that Miyazawa Kenji referred to as "the phenomenon called I."

No memory, however trivial and banal, is unimportant if it remains with you; no feeling that was once felt cannot be retrieved when you feel the absolute need to access it. And it is our memories that order the chaotic conglomeration of experience and sentiment that make up our selves. Stanislaw Ignacy Witkiewicz, Polish playwright and novelist, used the word *nienasycenie*, or insatiability, to describe life's essential dilemma: that you can never be sated with enough knowledge or pleasure, never plumb the depths of existence or understand its enigmas no matter how intense your need. American novelist Thomas Wolfe wrote that he wanted to "unweave the swarming web, unthread to its last filament the texture of a pattern which could have no end." Those two authors longed for nothing short of devouring the entire world of experience with no limit on location or time. Witkiewicz and Wolfe strove to create for themselves a semblance of meaning through their writing. The mind's saving grace was that ability to order the past into a semblance of meaning.

Our personal histories are no different. They are also composed of insatiable and unfathomable moments. They are collections of countless filaments of encounter, snippets of conversation, images that are suspended above us as if waiting for us to stretch out our arms and pluck them out of the air at will. It is our recollections of them that afford us the freedom to view ourselves in our present and live for another day. These recollections naturally come to take on a definite order. Without that order, we would not be able to live with ourselves, let alone with others.

Our memories implant themselves in arbitrary associations. When parting once with my then girlfriend Susan before we were married, I happened to be standing beside a white column outside a bus depot. I cannot for the life of me remember where the depot was but I can see the column clear as day. The tiny bumps of its surface texture appeared in my eyes as a mountain range. I rubbed my fingers over them. I can recall that texture in stark detail now, now forty years later. They seemed to be absorbing the sorrow and the anguish and the desolation of parting that I felt at the time. At an earlier time than that, a single venetian blind lifted into a V by a hand that appeared in the window of a house across the street from the embassy of North Vietnam came to symbolize for me a dramatic meeting inside the embassy (more on this later). Even before that, in August 1967, my own fist pounding on the wooden arm of a chair still signals for me a decision I made at that moment to leave the country of my birth for good. The fist and the leaving are one.

The white "mountains" on a column, the angle of the venetian blind in the sun, the clenched fingers of a fist striking wood—mundane images and trivial gestures, yet they came to take on an enormous personal significance and to be the spur of associations in some of the most momentous instants of my life.

Everyone's memory is no more than a rich collection of just such images, gestures and sounds.

2

Generations of Family Stories

It is strange in this century, thanks to technology, how we may come to learn things about ourselves. In some ways, the internet is a more reliable source than the talkative great-aunt or suddenly confessional grandparent. Old people confabulate: they are not always reliable sources as they pluck items from that web of their own memory.

When we are little we are told any number of stories about our parents, relatives and ancestors without the ability to verify their truthfulness. Occasionally we meet a relative who corroborates or, what is more likely, contradicts the stories in one or another of their facets. Old photographs may play a part in our vicarious recollection of our genetic past, but they merely freeze an instant of time, and one that, while being irrefutable in authenticity, may be dubious in its reflection of a more general truth.

As a little boy, I was told by my mother that there existed a photograph of five generations of our male ancestors in one picture, but mother had neither seen the photograph nor known which men were featured. It would be an unusual occurrence for five generations of a family to be alive simultaneously.

Many years later, thanks to the internet, I came into contact with Robert Krengel, a third cousin living in Belgium, who shared my intense interest in family history. Luckily one of the five people pictured in the photograph was related to him too, and he had a copy of the photo. He sent me a copy of the copy through the post, identifying the members of our family: the Krengels. And sure enough, five generations are there, beginning with my great-great-grandfather and beside him, his son, my great-grandfather. The man in the middle is an elder brother of my grandfather; then, beside him, his son; and beside him, his son. The youngest member of the five is the same generation as me. He looks to be about ten years old. The photo was taken in 1904. As I was born in 1944, I am probably about fifty years younger than my relative of my generation in the photo.

I immediately phoned my mother in Los Angeles to tell her that I was in possession of the photo and that I would have it copied and sent to her right away.

"Don't bother," she said. "I'm not interested in seeing those people."

Among the members of my immediate family I am the only one obsessed with who came before me. My parents, Louis and Miriam, who were both born in New York, had no interest whatsoever in the lives of their parents or ancestors in "the old country" (which was, in our case, three different countries, namely Russia, Poland and Lithuania). It wasn't the anger of rejection of their DNA that motivated my parents; it was simply the apathy of disinterest.

It is often said that an active disinterest in an older generation may form the basis of a passion for rediscovery in the next generation. Yet among my many Jewish friends, I am one of the few obsessive enthusiasts for lineage. In fact, with me, my interest goes beyond enthusiasm: I have always felt that I *needed* to know who my ancestors were and what they were like. I sensed them inside myself, right down to the marrow of my bones. The gene pool is vast, and we may inherit little or nothing from our ancestors save perhaps a genetic propensity for one malady or another. Our traits, quirks and the vagaries of our personalities are, I believe, our own—a conglomeration of characteristics that make us both exceedingly ordinary and yet unique at the same time. If we cannot get away from ourselves, we can blame it on no one but ourselves. And yet I could not escape my ancestors' stories because I was convinced that they were integral to my own narrative as it unfolded in the United States, Europe, Japan and Australia.

If my grandparents—the two paternal ones, who were born somewhere in the Pale of Settlement in Russia, and the two maternal ones, my grandmother in Vilnius and my grandfather in Krakow—made the journey at the end of the nineteenth century in search of a better life from their homelands to New York, and my parents, for a similar reason, moved from New York to Los Angeles in the year of my birth, 1944, then why was it so out of the ordinary that, years later, I went further west to Japan and south to Australia?

If the primary theme in the passage of time is motion, then I had to know the deep reasons behind this motion. Why do we make major decisions in our life? Why do we leave one place for another? Can we truly construct a "new life" elsewhere? Of course, we can, but I needed to know *why*.

This obsession with past narrative started very early on my part. As a child, I was constantly asking about ancestors and relatives and was invariably fobbed off with a wave of a hand and a word or two about how insignificant the past was. When I was thirteen, my mother showed me a thick notebook of short stories written by her father. I was immediately entranced, as I had been told little or nothing about my grandfather. When I asked about them later, she said, "Oh, I threw those out." Did she not realize, I recall thinking then, that they didn't belong to her? I was convinced at the time that they belonged to me, but now that I have my own children and grandchildren, I realize that those stories belong to them.

As for my studying Russian and Polish and traveling to the U.S.S.R. and Poland in the 1960s, this was only considered by my parents and their friends in terms of political convictions. "Is your son a Red, or what?" one of my father's friends said to him. That those countries boasted a rich cultural history and were the homelands of the vast majority of the Jews who had come to live in the U.S. were issues of no concern to them, despite their being Jewish and the descendants of people in those homelands. The profound fear of communism trumped all else, blinding most Americans to all humanity "behind the Iron Curtain," where every aspect of life was presumably gray, dour and devoid of joy.

* * *

There were three stories that I remember hearing vague details about. The first concerned my mother herself.

Mother, born in New York on December 1, 1912, was proud of her drawing and penmanship talent.

"When I was sixteen," she said to me, "I was written up in 'Ripley's Believe It or Not' for being able to draw the exact same picture at the same time with both hands and write the same words in perfect penmanship with both hands forward, backward and upside down."

The widely syndicated feature *Ripley's Believe It or Not!*, which the cartoonist Robert Ripley had begun in 1918, was still very popular when Mother told me this in the early 1950s. Ripley's colorfully illustrated column featured the uncanny and "unbelievable." Of course, even without the column in hand, I had all the proof I needed in my mother's demonstrations of her rare, if somewhat bizarre, gift. But it wasn't until 2015, more than eight years after Mother's death at age 94, that I discovered an article on the internet from the New York Evening Post of Friday, March 22, 1929, about some of the unbelievably talented people who had once appeared in Ripley's column: "Miss Miriam Krengel, Aged Sixteen—I can write just as quickly backward as forward!"

The citation was composed only of those fourteen words and did not detail my mother's ambidextrous abilities. But I had seen those talents demonstrated with my own eyes and did not doubt them. This was one family story, hardly a secret, that turned out to be authentic. And I'm sure that Mother, who had been uninterested in the old five-generation family photograph, would have loved to have seen her name mentioned in this old newspaper article on the internet, a medium that she never learned to use.

Another story from my mother's side of the family concerned her father and two of her uncles. My grandfather Samuel and his brothers David and Sidney had established a highly successful jewelry business in New York and Chicago. Samuel had apprenticed in diamond cutting as a young man after leaving his birthplace of Krakow for Antwerp and Vienna, two centers of diamond cutting and gem merchandizing. He arrived in the U.S. on a ship from Liverpool in the year 1900, and, in a matter of a decade, he and his two brothers were conducting a thriving trade in diamonds and other precious stones.

But as my mother once told me, her father and his brothers had lost a great deal of money and had to cope with a drastic reduction in lifestyle. My maternal grandparents, together with their four children, were compelled to move out of their lavish home in Flatbush, Brooklyn, and give up their two chauffeured automobiles. Mother, however, was never clear about the circumstances of this sudden change of fortune. Not long after I found the article about my mother's digital deftness, I discovered one from the *El Reno Daily Democrat* (El Reno, Oklahoma) from Saturday February 18, 1922. The same article, supplied by United Press, appears in several other newspapers found on the internet titled "BIG LOOT."

Sidney Krengel, New York jewelry salesman, reported to the police here today that his satchel containing $150,000 worth of diamonds was stolen from his berth on an Illinois Central train. Krengel said he left Chicago last night and upon arrival here the gems were missing.

Any calculation of this 1922 sum would put it well into millions of dollars today. Details provided in other newspapers divulge that Sidney had put the diamonds under the pillow in his Pullman car when he went to bed and that they were gone the next morning. The gems were not insured.

Great-uncle Sidney, who was no doubt transporting the gems from Great-uncle David in Chicago to Grandfather Samuel in New York, must have been devastated. Naturally, my mother, being only nine at the time, would not have been told in detail what happened. Children of that era were "protected" from facts of an unpleasant nature, and she probably never knew the truth.

But the most unpleasant of stories comes from my father's side of the family, whose members occupied the other extreme of the economic spectrum. My father, born the eighth of nine children on December 25, 1903, was brought up in a New York slum. His father, Morris, was born in Russia in 1862 (though some citations contradict this with dates of 1863 and 1864). Grandfather Morris Pulvers was an orphan and illiterate all his life, so it is not easy to establish an accurate date of his birth. No one knows where in Russia's part of the Pale of Settlement he was born, and it would be nigh on impossible to trace the actual place or date.

(If the Great Depression had not struck the U.S. and the world, my parents would have never met each other, my mother coming from wealth and my father from utter poverty. Thanks to the stolen diamonds and the stock market crash, my mother's family was reduced to a lower-middle-class existence and my parents were thrown together, like passengers finding themselves sharing a second-class train carriage.)

My paternal grandfather, Morris Pulvers, arrived in the United States in 1897 after having lived for some years in London with his first wife, with whom he had four children, and his second, my grandmother, who gave him five. He was a paraplegic. He had lost both his legs to frostbite while fleeing his hometown during winter months after being conscripted into the Tsar's army. Russian Jews were forced to spend twenty-five years in the army and could not rise above the rank of sergeant.

It speaks well for the immigration policy of the United States of the day that the country would accept such an uneducated man, burdened by disability and a large family. I, for one, am grateful for that open policy—the grandson of an illiterate disabled immigrant was able to attend Harvard Graduate School on a scholarship and become an author. My father, however, was not so lucky. He was forced to abandon his education upon graduation from elementary school and, at age twelve, find a job. He rarely spoke about his parents or siblings, and when he did, it was chiefly in a negative light.

One story that sticks in my mind concerned a lawsuit brought against my father's mother by her own daughter (my father's elder sister), Rose. Apparently, as I was told by my father, my aunt was suing her mother for possession of the family house in 1932. The name Rose was spoken in our household coupled, as if it were her title, with *gonif*—the Yiddish word for scoundrel, thief.

But an article I found on the internet told a somewhat different story. It appeared in *The Brooklyn Daily Eagle* on Friday, April 4, 1930, and dealt with the family house, two years before my father's version of the incident. And it wasn't about my aunt Rose at all. Ah, family stories!

The article in *The Brooklyn Daily Eagle* is titled "Wife and Five Children Driving Him Out, Says Legless Man":

> Morris Pulvers, 68, who has no legs and is minus some of his fingers, has brought suit in Supreme Court against his wife, Mrs. Esther Pulvers, asking that she be compelled to deed him a half interest in the house they occupy with their five grown children at 2363 85th St.
> In an affidavit submitted today . . . Pulvers declared that

the house was bought with their joint savings, each chipping in $1,000 and that he allowed his wife to put it in her name because she had promised that she would take good care of him.

'Several months ago my wife and children decided I had become a burden,' Pulvers swore, 'and decided to get rid of me. They evolved a plan of selling the house and taking the money and leaving me to take care of myself as well as I could. With this in mind they made life at home extremely miserable for me.' He added that he heard his wife talk to realtors about selling the place and it was then he said he demanded a deed for his half, which his wife refused.

. . . Mrs. Pulvers said the house was bought with her own savings, and that she never made any agreement to give her husband half. She said he brought this suit just to harass her and as a result she has been unable to renew the mortgage. Justice MacCrate reserved decision.

The Pulvers (*sic*) were married in London 38 years ago.

That's where the article ends. My grandfather died not long after that, and my grandmother followed him to the grave a couple years later. I never did find out what happened to the family home on 85th Street in Brooklyn, though my father insisted that "that mamzer Rose could never steal the house from our mother." *Mamzer* (Yiddish—bastard) is another term he applied to his sister, as if *mamzer* were her real first name. The truth was that it was my grandmother, backed by her children, who was behind the eviction of my illiterate legless grandfather. We are obliged to seek out and recompose the reality of our narratives from the fake, and frequently revised, family "news" that is handed down to us.

3

Rose Comes to Australia

My father had a reconciliation with Aunt "Gonif Mamzer" Rose in 1972, bringing her with him from Los Angeles when he and my mother visited me in Canberra, Australia, not long after I had moved there from Kyoto, Japan. I had been told as a child to despise this woman, my aunt, and now her gaping lips, smeared with chunky lipstick as thick as Van Gogh's oil paint, were rushing toward my face for a kiss-and-make-up. Her bouffy dyed hair brushed against my tautly squinted eyes, and her round rhinestone sunglasses nearly broke the ridge of my nose, but we managed to have our awkward kiss, and, I suppose, all was forgiven, though I personally had felt no enmity toward her for something that had allegedly happened long before I was born, and actually hadn't happened at all. As for my father, unbeknownst to me, he had forgiven her and withdrawn the Yiddish pejoratives stuck to her name. It's comforting to know that a strain of belated, if half-hearted, forgiveness, if not a grasp of facts or commitment to truth, runs in one's family.

All of these events, incidents and encounters from the past have now reformed in my memory and become a part of me, allowing me to travel in my mind down a vanishing avenue. It is not the incidents themselves that become significant; it is how we discover and come to terms with them that becomes significant.

The gap in the time between when they happened and when we find out about them closes and extends in a single line into our present.

4

Meeting Polish Film Director Andrzej Wajda

In mid-March 1970, I was sitting beside Polish film director Andrzej Wajda in the back seat of a Kyoto taxi. Andrzej and I were to become close friends, but at that time I was a star-struck budding author of twenty-five while Andrzej, eighteen years older than me, was already a household name in Poland and in any other country where the art of cinema was valued.

His first three films—his trilogy about the war: *A Generation, Kanal* and *Ashes and Diamonds*—had moved me deeply and taught me about the ravages that war inflicts on the psyche. Now I had met him and was asking him about the making of those films. I thought to myself in that taxi, "It is to have these moments that I learned Polish!"

He spoke that day, as I took him around the city of Kyoto where I had been living since November 1967, of his childhood.

"My father, Jakub Wajda, was a captain in the Polish Army. He was killed by the Soviets in the Katyn Massacre. Do you know about that, Roger?"

Of course, I had studied the history relating to the murder of some 26,000 Poles, approximately 14,700 of whom were serving in the military, and I knew from my time in Warsaw and Krakow that speaking about the massacre in public in Poland was strictly taboo. Stalin had personally signed the order, on March 5, 1940, to proceed with the mass execution. The Soviets, presumably Poland's allies and protectors from Western aggression, had perpetrated this atrocity on the Polish nation. They would not permit its merest mention. It would be as if the United States had forbidden Japanese people to "claim" that it was the Americans who had dropped the atomic bombs on Hiroshima and Nagasaki.

But I had no idea at the time that there was a link between Andrzej and me when it came to the massacre of 1940.

Though it is known worldwide as "the Katyn Massacre," the mass murder took place in a number of locations. The bodies of about 3,000 victims were discovered by German soldiers when they overran the city of Smolensk, some eighteen kilometers from the site in Katyn Forest. This discovery was treated as a propaganda coup for the Germans, who were eager to point the finger at the genocide committed by their Soviet enemies. Subsequently it became known that Polish officers, soldiers and thousands of civilians had been shot in a number of locations in Smolensk and as far away as a village near Kharkov (now Kharkiv), the Ukrainian city more than 700 kilometers from Katyn.

It was outside Kharkov that Capt. Jakub Wajda, then age 39, was shot by NKVD assassins in April (or perhaps May) 1940. Among the thousands killed along with him was Maj. Maksimilian Krengel, born October 24, 1887, a Polish Army doctor and a cousin of my grandfather, Samuel Krengel. As with information about family that you glean from the internet much later, so it was with my discovery, after I had seen Andrzej's film *Katyn*, that a relative of mine had been with Andrzej's father in a Soviet prison camp near Kharkov. It is quite likely that they knew each other, seeing as my distant cousin was a doctor and the number of prisoners near Kharkov was far fewer than that in Katyn.

"Are you going to make a film about your father and the Katyn Massacre?" I asked Andrzej as the taxi was taking us up north in Kyoto toward my favorite temple, Entsuji.

"Well," he said, smiling at me as if to say that it would be very difficult to make such a film in Poland, "someday, yes."

Katyn was released thirty-seven years later, in 2007. When I visited Andrzej at his home in the lovely and green Warsaw suburb of Zoliborz on March 6, 2006, the day of his 80th birthday, I recalled our conversation in the Kyoto taxi in 1970.

"Did we talk about that? I don't remember," he said. "But anyway, I'm in pre-production now for my film about Katyn. Of course, my mother and I had no idea at the time what was happening to my father. But when the letters stopped coming in the spring of 1940, we had no doubt about what had occurred."

I was devastated by the death of Andrzej Wajda on October 9, 2016. His country went into mourning for the man who had maintained the integrity of its conscience for more than five decades.

5

Encountering My Great Grandfather

One cold winter's evening in 1985, I was walking through Shinjuku in Tokyo. I'd had a bit too much sake to drink and was talking to myself as I made my way through the nighttime crowds to the station. I was suddenly overcome with bitterness and anger that my grandfather, Samuel Krengel, had died in 1935, nine years before I was born.

"I had the right to meet you!" I said in a voice loud enough for others on the street to hear. "Why did Mother throw away your short stories?"

I felt a profound affinity with this man, my mother's father, who I could know only through a handful of photographs and the fleeting version of a few episodes that my mother recounted, usually with great reluctance, sighing, inhaling deeply and changing the subject. My maternal grandmother, Celia, had Parkinson's disease by the time I was old enough to approach her with sensible questions about her husband; that channel, too, was switched off forever.

* * *

After visiting Andrzej Wajda in Warsaw on that March day in 2006, I took the train down to Krakow, where I had moved as a post-graduate student on January 8, 1967. I will never forget that date because it was the day that the great actor Zbigniew Cybulski, star of *Ashes and Diamonds*, ran for a train in Wroclaw, slipped, fell under the train's wheels and was instantly killed.

When I had arrived in Krakow from Warsaw that day, my friends were virtually in mourning over Cybulski's tragic death. We all went to Feniks, one of the few Krakow night clubs open till all hours of the night, sat at the little private bar in the back and commiserated over shot glasses of vodka and braised mushrooms. (Club Feniks is located upstairs at 2 St. Jan Street and has occupied the premises since 1943.) Wojciech Has, director of *The Manuscript Found in Saragossa*, a brilliant film with Cybulski in the lead, was sitting on the bar's high stool beside me. (Beata Tyskiewicz, Andrzej Wajda's wife from 1967 to 1969, was in the film too. Their daughter, Karolina, is now a well-known actress.) Has got so drunk that, mumbling and shaking his head, he leaned back and fell over backwards, luckily striking the wall before landing on the floor.

But back to my visit to Poland in March 2006.

The second man from the right in the photograph of five generations of Krengel men is thickly bearded, sporting impressive sidelocks and a skull cap. He is Menachem Mendel Krengel, who, like his father seated next to him, was a Talmudic scholar and outdid the old man by making it into the *Encyclopedia Judaica*.

I have another photo of great-grandfather Menachem. It was taken in 1906 by a photographer named Sprung, whose studio was located at 18 St. Gertrude Street in Krakow.

I was walking along St. Gertrude Street a century later. I came to number eighteen and found a four-story building with the date 1888 engraved in stone above the old glass and wooden doors. I peered through the glass into the courtyard, which was overgrown with tall grass and weeds.

A middle-aged man leading a golden retriever on a leash came to the door with keys in hand.

"Excuse me," I said. "Do you by chance live here?"

"Yes, I do," he replied.

I showed him the photograph of Menachem Mendel Krengel.

"This is my great-grandfather," I said.

"Ah, it certainly must have been taken here. My mother was born in this building before the war and she might have known about a photographer having a studio here. But she is no longer with us, and I am afraid I cannot help you."

I thanked him and asked him if I could just go into the courtyard. "Of course," he said, smiling and opening the doors.

I stood in the tall grass and stared at the windows facing the courtyard on all sides . . . and, while wondering which window Mr. Sprung the photographer and my great-grandfather would have looked out of, I wept uncontrollably.

But why weep? What would I have to say to this Talmudic scholar, a rabbi who spent his entire adult life poring over old Hebrew texts, referencing and cross-checking religious "facts"—I, who am an atheist who has lived most of his adult life in Japan, "of all places!" (as Menachem Mendel would no doubt have said)?

All of the above, about ancestors and massacres and trains and film actors and a jumble of flashbacks and flash-forwards, prompts neurons to instantly connect. They comprise what we know as sense. The mechanisms of memory are not chronological. Our memory is our only time traveler. This is what allows me to reflect now on the taxi ride to Entsuji in Kyoto in March 1970 sitting beside Andrzej Wajda, and on his father and my cousin, who may very well have been together in the last days of their lives in 1940. Associations in the mind respect neither time nor place. In the end, it all comes to make perfect sense to me as a single bundle, an experience that is nothing less than a reassembling of fragments of memory.

I had met Andrzej at the film festival held at Osaka Banpaku, or Expo '70, as it was called in English. He had come to Osaka as the representative of Poland, though the Polish film showing was not one directed by him. It was *The Life of Matthew*, directed by Witold Leszczynski, a beautiful and lyrical film based on the novel *The Birds* by the Norwegian author Tarjei Vesaas. It so happened that I was an ardent fan of Vesaas's fiction and was struggling to read his works in the original with the generous help of my Norwegian wife.

I went up to Andrzej after the film showing and introduced myself, offering to take him around Kyoto and to see a production of the bunraku puppet theater that was playing at the time. He was overwhelmingly friendly from that first meeting. It wasn't thanks to anything I said that day. It was merely due to my speaking his native language. There were very few foreigners who had taken up the study of Polish. (On May 2, 1970, he wrote to me from Poland: "What staggered me was how magnificently you have understood our language and culture in a century when young people are normally not drawn to anything except records and sports.") He removed a small newspaper clipping from his jacket pocket. It was cut from a Polish newspaper and showed some men carrying a coffin up a barren hill.

"This is an article about Tarjei Vesaas's funeral," he said.

I'd had no idea that Vesaas had died. Though seventy-two, he had seemed indestructible to me. His face on the end papers of his novels had the chiseled appearance of permanence.

* * *

That summer of 1970, my Norwegian wife Solrun, who I had met the year before in Kyoto, and I left Kobe on the Soviet ship, the *Ordzhonokidze*. After landing in Nakhodka, we boarded the train to Khabarovsk, flew to Irkutsk, on to Moscow and Leningrad, and then to Oslo. Not long after arriving in Oslo, we drove to Telemark—Vesaas had lived in Vinje, a small town in that picturesque mountainous region—to get the feeling of the kind of countryside in which Vesaas's novels are set.

I went on to Poland. Andrzej met me at Warsaw Central Station and drove me to his country home in Gluchy, a village on the road east to Lublin. (Andrzej pointed out to me the superb condition of the road, saying, "They keep it this way for Russian tanks that may need to use it.") The home itself, furnished in the Napoleonic style that Andrzej loved, was the birthplace of one of the greatest poets of nineteenth-century Poland, Cyprian Norwid.

I spent three days with Andrzej that summer, talking about film, theater, Japan, Poland, the Soviet Union (he was an excellent speaker of Russian), the United States and a host of other subjects.

"You know what appeals to me as a story?" he said. "A film director is making a film, let's say in a country in South America or somewhere. He begins to feel that he's omnipotent, so he decides to give up filmmaking and become a politician, which he does, finding himself as dictator of the country and able to do whatever he likes."

"That's surely not the way you see yourself, is it?" I asked.

"Me? No. It's more a story about someone like Fellini. I'm happy just being a director."

Back in Warsaw, we came to the edge of the Stare Miasto (Old Town). The Polish government had painstakingly restored the old buildings, using, among other documentary materials, the detailed paintings of Canaletto as a guide.

"I stood here at the end of the war. I was only nineteen. This entire area that you see was flattened . . . rubble. The entire Stare Miasto was just one big gaping pit."

Even though he never became the president of a country, he maintained a core interest in politics. He shocked the Communist leadership of Poland—and that, I suspect, of other Soviet-controlled countries—when, in 1977, he released his deft attack on their ideology in his film *Man of Marble*. I spent a month in Poland in May to June 1977 and met with him a number of times then as well. He told me then that First Secretary of the Communist Party Edward Gierek had threatened to ban distribution of the film.

"What did you tell him?" I asked.

"I told him that if he blocked distribution I would leave Poland for good."

The first secretary backed off. The effect of Andrzej Wajda abandoning Poland would have been that consequential. He was not dictator of his nation, but something more precious: an artist with the distinction of being indispensible to his nation.

"I believe that cinema can be more than pleasure, entertainment and even art," he said. "It occurred to me that it could change the world and give a form to human knowledge."

I received letters from him over the years. The one that gave me the deepest pleasure was written on January 19, 2003, for it spoke of his love of Japanese culture, a love so ardent that it had led him to found the Manggha Museum of Japanese Art and Technology in 1994 in Krakow. On July 11, 2002, the museum was visited by Japan's Emperor Akihito and Empress Michiko.

"A few months ago," he wrote, "we were visited by the imperial couple, which is something we never would have been able to look forward to had I not been introduced to the secrets (of Japanese culture) thanks to you, dear Roger."

Why begin this book about the "unmaking" of an American with a narrative about Poland? After all, I never knew any of my Polish relatives except for my great-aunt Sylvia, my grandfather's younger sister, though we only spoke once, and very briefly, about topics related to Poland. I have spent a total of about four months in Poland—nothing compared to my time lived in Japan and Australia. My parents didn't speak Polish or any language other than English. I had learned Polish as an adult.

The answer is in the collective memory that I carry inside me. Not everyone is blessed—or burdened—with thoughts from a distant land and a remote time. Yet for me, Poland, with its profoundly rich culture, is inescapably embedded in my consciousness. The jumble of contradictions from the history of my family and encounters with remarkable Polish people somehow became ordered in my mind, allowing me to include part of the country's narrative in my own.

As far back as the reign of King Kazimierz III (1310–1370), Jews were welcome in Poland as in no other European state. Kazimierz III is the only Polish king still called "Great," and the Jewish district in Krakow is, to this day, named after him. My maternal ancestors, the Krengels arrived in Krakow from Spain at the end of the fifteenth century, becoming, over the centuries, pillars of the pious Jewish community. Fortunately, as far as I am aware, no Krengels were left in Poland when the country was overrun by the Nazis and the Soviets in September 1939. An old rabbi in Krakow, the only Polish one left in Krakow, told me in 1967 that the last

Krengel, a female lawyer, had emigrated in 1939.

I have little idea of what thoughts and aspirations were entertained in the minds of the five males in my old photograph. Yet I see myself as the sixth person in it—invisible, yet to be born, but nonetheless present in its contemporary reflection.

6

The Soviet Past and Two Books

I recall, when a student of Russian in the 1960s, reading Ilya Ehrenburg's memoir *People, Years, Life* not long after it was published in six volumes in the U.S.S.R. It contained revelations of details in the lives of many people whose stories had been suppressed for, in some cases, decades. Around the same time, I also read Yuri Olyesha's *Not a Day without a Line*, a compilation of the Soviet author's jottings published after his death in 1960. Both books contain philosophical insights into the tenor of their times, and, while fascinating in their episodic character, fell short of forming a coherent whole.

One inescapable feature of Soviet life was guarded circumspection. Despite their outgoing nature, both Ehrenburg and Olyesha only half express the truths of their time and the inner mechanisms of the national character of the Soviet people. Ehrenburg in particular was reluctant to question himself as to why he remained alive when so many of his close friends and colleagues disappeared in the gulag or were simply shot in the back of the head overnight in a Moscow dungeon.

How can you link the myriad episodes in your life and the lives of others with your real inner self; how can you be honest about yourself without succumbing to either a masked conceit or a mealy-mouthed and coy modesty (which is often yet another mask for conceit)? How to bring together your times with the times of others in a narrative that rings true? These are the questions, linked to the quasi-confessionals of Ehrenburg and Olyesha, that intrigue me now.

Perhaps the answer lies in the seemingly paradoxical Japanese proverb *isogaba maware*: if you are in a hurry, take the circuitous route. Whatever route we are on—and we are on several at the same time—we owe our direction to family, friends, strangers and teachers who pull us out on tangents from which we cannot return to our starting points.

7

Remarkable Teachers

I was blessed with remarkable teachers of Russian. Three in particular shaped my life. Had I not encountered them, I doubt that I would have become an author of fiction, a translator and a teacher myself. Yet I wonder if most of us realize at the time we are being taught by truly inspiring people that they are giving us the greatest good fortune of our youth.

My first such inspiration came from Vladimir Markov, my Russian professor at UCLA in the early 1960s. My understanding of his greatness came much later, yet his passion for the Russian language infected me from the beginning. I didn't realize until two decades later that I had been taught elementary Russian conversation in 1961 by the world's leading expert on Russian Futurism.

Prof. Markov was born in St. Petersburg in 1920. He lost his father and grandfather in Stalin's Great Purge of 1937, and his mother was sent to a Soviet camp, where she remained until after World War II. He himself joined the Red Army, was seriously wounded, and spent four years in German captivity. When the war ended, he made his way to the Bavarian city of Regensburg, where he worked for the United Nations Relief and Rehabilitation Administration. It was then that he began writing and translating poetry. He was the first Russian to translate and publish the poems of Emily Dickinson.

In 1949, Markov emigrated to the United States, landing eventually in southern California where he worked as a lemon picker in Ventura County. He told us this story in class, acting out lemon picking while speaking Russian to us. This was the first complicated spoken Russian I ever understood, and the image of him acting out the picking of lemons while explaining it in Russian has remained with me since, teaching me a lesson about the trials of the émigré—in his case, one who went from lemon groves to the groves of academe at the University of California Berkeley to gain a PhD before joining the faculty of Slavic languages at UCLA, where he taught for thirty-three years. Vladimir Markov's 1968 book, *Russian Futurism: A History*, had an enormous impact on Russian literary studies, though it did not appear in Russian until 2000.

In 1964, when I went from UCLA to do an MA at Harvard's Russian Research Center, I planned to specialize in political science. After all, the towering figures of two historians, Richard Pipes and Adam Ulam, were there. Yet I found their classes a bitter disappointment. Both scholars were virulently anticommunist, which was fine in itself, I suppose. But I had the distinct feeling that I was being taught modern Russian history in Washington D.C. and not Cambridge, Massachusetts. (Pipes, a stalwart opponent of detente with the Soviet Union, subsequently became a key adviser to U.S. President Ronald Reagan.) The two famous professors turned me off the dogmatic study of Soviet politics as it then existed in the United States.

By good fortune, however, I also enrolled in Prof. Kiril Taranovsky's seminar on Russian poetry, and I decided to audit Prof. Roman Jacobson's course on the history of Russian prosody. Those two teachers had an enormous influence on the course of my life.

Kiril Taranovsky was born in Estonia in 1911. His family left the Soviet Union in 1920, emigrating to Yugoslavia. After studies in Belgrade and Prague he went, in 1958, to the United States, eventually joining the Russian faculty at Harvard.

In class, Taranovsky sat behind a desk, lecturing in a dry calm drone, his eyes looking like little beads behind glass as thick as the bottoms of milk bottles. His course centered on nineteenth- and twentieth-century poets. He personally loved the poetry of Lermontov, Tyutchev and Mandelstam, but his greatest passion was reserved for Pushkin.

Roman Jacobson, on the other hand, was neither sedentary nor calm. He stood in front of the class moving around as if, at times, dancing. When he spoke in English it was with a drippy Russian accent. (We used to say about Professor Jacobson that "he spoke Russian in fifteen different languages.") Known now as the father of modern linguistics, particularly phonology, Jacobson was born in Moscow in 1896. He moved to Prague in 1920 as a Soviet diplomat, quickly turning to language study. He was a founder of the so-called Prague School of Linguistics that eventually wielded a stunning influence on studies in that field.

With the outbreak of war Jacobson shifted to Scandinavia, then to the U.S., where he joined Harvard's faculty in 1949. (Most of the great Russian intellectuals who left their country after the 1917 Soviet Revolution settled in Berlin, Paris and Prague—primarily Berlin, where the émigré literary community was most active. Unlike German refugee intellectuals, who for the most part landed in the U.S. before the war, the Russians generally tended to stay in Europe as long as possible. Nabokov, for instance, lived in Berlin, then Paris until it became dangerous for him to be there, and left for the U.S. at the last possible moment in May 1940, returning to Europe once he and his wife Vera were sufficiently stable financially to manage life there.)

I had gone to Harvard all fired up to study political science as it related to Soviet reality. But the intense devotion to Russian literature that I absorbed from my two wonderful professors led me down another path. Kiril Taranovsky's monotone recitations of Pushkin—to say they were understated would be an understatement—were thrilling. The crystal beauty of the language shone through in its full light thanks to his emotionless reading. Roman Jacobson's telling us about Mayakovsky, who he personally knew well, and his readings of Blok, Akhmatova and Mandelstam, took my breath away. After all, he was a living link with the giants of twentieth-century Russian poetry. (Nina Berberova, the remarkable Armenian-Russian émigré and author of the magnificent memoir *The Italics Are Mine*, told me about her meetings with Jacobson before the war when she was living with her husband, the poet Vladislav Khodaseivich. Jacobson was a great admirer of Khodaseivich's poetry and visited the couple often, though Berberova's recollections of him in her memoir are not particularly endearing. I came to know her through my friendship with her brilliant translator, my dear, now sadly departed, friend Philippe Radley, and visited her at her country home in Connecticut in the summer of 1967. "The Soviet Embassy in Washington D.C. won't leave me alone," she said to me. "It's because they think I'm an Armenian nationalist." She had had many devoted students of Russian while teaching at Yale and Princeton, and though she had become an American citizen in 1959, I had the distinct impression that she, like many other Russian émigrés of her generation, felt more at home in Europe than the U.S.)

I devoured the gifts of my two professors at Harvard. I memorized upwards of a hundred Russian poems and recited them to myself as I walked around Boston, and after leaving Boston in June 1965, around the streets of Copenhagen, Aarhus and throughout the pleasant countryside of Jutland, then in Helsinki and cities of the Soviet Union where I spent four weeks that summer.

8

The Double-edged Sword of Russian Poetry

Among countless poems there were two that seeped deeply into my consciousness and have remained there. One has the plaintive strain of pathos and longing; the other, the cut and thrust into the heart of the oppressor. These qualities form the double-edged sword of Russian poetry. I've translated these two poems that are on either side of the vast steppe that is Russian poetry. The first strain, the one of pathos and pain, is exquisitely expressed by Sergei Esenin in his "Poem about a Dog."

In the morning, in the barn for rye
Where rush mats stand in golden rows
She gave birth to a litter of seven
Seven newborn chestnut-color pups.

She fondled them until the evening came
Licking them all over
As the snow melted into streams
Under the warmth of her belly.

But in the evening, when the hens
Dirty their perches with droppings
The grim master appeared
Dropping all seven puppies into a sack.

The mother raced over the snowdrifts
Not letting the master get ahead.
And for ages the smooth surface of water
Still unfrozen, would not cease its trembling.

And when, in the end, she dragged herself back
Licking the wet off her flanks
She took the moon, shining over the shack
For one of her puppies.

She gazed up into the dark blue sky
Whining in a loud voice.
But the thin moon slipped behind a hill
Disappearing beyond the fields.

And just as when they mock her
By tossing a stone at her instead of food
Her eyes rolled silently
Like golden stars into the snow.

The second, with its cut and thrust that tragically worked both ways, is Osip Mandelstam's poem about Joseph Stalin. When Soviet authorities found out about "We Live Apart from Our Land," Mandelstam was doomed to transportation to the gulag.

We live apart from our land
Our words die at ten paces
And anything slipped in edgewise
Concerns the Kremlin backwoodsman
His coarse fingers are thick, like worms
His statements trusty, like weights on a scale
Cockroaches smile on his upper lip
The rims of his shoes blind

He is surrounded by a flock of pencil-neck hacks
He plays on the servility of half-men
Who whistle, who meow, who sob
But he alone roars and sticks it in
Forging his edicts like so many horseshoes

One in the groin, one on the brow, one in the eye
Execution is his relish, this southerner
With an open heart

9

("Stormy Applause!")

The trip in 1965 actually marked my second time in the Soviet Union. In the summer of 1964, having just turned 20, I went there—my first foreign country—in a group of American graduate students of Russian. We traveled around the country from Moscow to Kiev, Kharkov and Donetsk (the center of present-day hostilities between Russia and Ukraine, a conflict unthinkable at the time), from Yalta in the Crimea to the capital of the then Latvian Soviet Socialist Republic, Riga, and from there to Leningrad and Novgorod.

It was hard for an American or any other visitor from the West to grasp how shockingly ignorant of the outside world Soviet citizens were. The ability of the government to keep them closed off and focused on their glorious future depended upon a high degree of suppression of outside information. The Russia of today manages to accomplish a similar result, though now via the massive barrage of misinformation-as-entertainment that the state-controlled media inflicts on the people. But back in the U.S.S.R., the sole role of the press was to flood the nation with positive "news" of a domestic nature while providing negative dribs and drabs about the capitalist world to an isolated populace.

Many Soviets believed that serving a vision faithfully, blindly and relentlessly could somehow make that vision come true. During the Brezhnev years (1964–82)—the nearly two lost decades of economic stagnation, military overexpansion abroad and environmental degradation at home—the vision diverged too drastically from reality, and the nation's bulky ideology collapsed of its own weight, and with it the existence of the Union of Soviet Socialist Republics. The West didn't win the Cold War; the peoples of the U.S.S.R., disillusioned, simply lost the will to wage it any longer.

Soviet newspapers often carried the entire text of speeches of the nation's leaders. At the end of a paragraph you might find the word "Applause" in parentheses, indicating which section of the speech you should be paying the most attention to, much in the same way that Japanese magazines insert "(Laughter)" to show that the statement preceding the parentheses is meant to be amusing. Just as Soviet citizens would know when it was safe to sit up and take notice, Japanese readers would sense when it was safe to laugh. In the case of the Japanese, a witty remark may be lost if the readership is not advised that it has been made deliberately. In the case of the Soviets, the addition of "(Applause)" signaled that the comment preceding it was part of a polemic that the leader/speaker wished his enemies to note. And these signals, like missiles fired into the air, had their deadly measured escalations and droppings.

A particularly crucial point in a speech printed in a newspaper would be followed by "(Stormy applause)," and a truly vehement statement would have "(Stormy applause leading to an ovation)" after it. If we went all the way up the scale to a warhead capable of mass destruction, a point in a speech would be succeeded by "(Stormy applause leading to an ovation, everyone stands and sings 'The Internationale')." "The Internationale" served as the national anthem until Stalin replaced it with "The State Hymn of the Soviet Union" in January 1944 as a catalyst for Russian nationalism during the war. The new anthem's music was composed by one of Stalin's favorite musical talents, Alexander Alexandrov, with lyrics by Sergei Mikhalkov, the father of the two brilliant filmmakers, Nikita Mikhalkov and Andrei Konchalovsky. But "The Internationale" remained the official "anthem" of the Communist Party, and its singing continued to follow the storms of applause.

Alexandrov's and Mikhalkov's anthem began with words

glorious and, I always thought, unwittingly paradoxical: "The indestructible union of free republics. . . ." How, I wondered back then, can a union be indestructible and free for its members to, God forbid, choose secession, at the same time? When the entire state edifice crumbled down to its foundation, thanks to the absence of the rule of law and the diminished power of the state to intimidate and suppress dissent, the many republics did not hesitate to dislodge themselves from the union, proving it to be, in the end, far from indestructible.

One man I met in Leningrad in 1965, an engineer who showed me a set of the *Complete Works of V. I. Lenin*, all with blank pages, told me of an incident that occurred at a Komsomol meeting he had attended.

"The silence after the leader of the Komsomol made an important point was deafening," he said. "So a young ambitious fellow bolted up and shouted, 'Stormy applause!' Sure enough, the next day in Pravda '(Stormy applause!)' appeared just after the leader's statement."

The term "(Stormy applause leading to an ovation, everyone stands and moves to the buffet table)" is attributed to the marvelous satirist Mikhail Zoshchenko. Such quips were, however, highly underappreciated by the leaders of Stalin's Soviet Union; they also must have contributed to the denunciation of Zoshchenko, his virtual banishment from the printed page and his being kept in poverty until his death, five years after Stalin's, in 1958.

10

Enough Condoms for You?

The absurdity of many aspects of Soviet life in the 1960s was striking, and yet the majority of Soviet citizens were used to the situation. The daily routine became a predictable absurdity, and if you behaved yourself in public, you could lead a stable and predictable life. Today, it is for that kind of life that many older Russians long. People who yearn for an ordinary life—"the old normal"—with neither precipitous heights nor precarious troughs, are content with a lack of freedom if they get some security and social cohesion in the bargain.

Never having lived in the Soviet Union I could gloss over the absurdities of Soviet life, some of them exceedingly pernicious in nature. Laughing it off is the luxury of the outsider.

I stood in line at a large Moscow pharmacy in 1965 to place an order for condoms. In the old days, you had to wait in three lines to buy many things: the line for placing an order, the line for paying for the order, and the line for receiving the order in exchange for the receipt you were given in the second line. After about twenty minutes I reached the head of the first line.

"I would like to buy condoms please," I said to the pretty young woman in a white smock behind the counter.

"How much?" she snapped, glaring at me, obviously a foreigner up to no good in her visionary country.

"How much? Uh, I don't know. Ten rubles' worth, please."

She scribbled my order on a chit and handed it to me, glancing past my shoulder and shouting, "Next."

I waited in the second line for about half an hour, thrust my receipt into the arched hole at the bottom of the cashier's window with a ten-ruble note and, given my receipt, returned to the first line. Unfortunately, however, the clock struck twelve noon when I was the third person in the line, and all the young women behind the counter disappeared in a flash.

"What happened?" I asked the man in front of me.

"Lunch happened," he sighed.

I was happy to grab a bite myself and went into one of Moscow's many workers' cafés where you could have a decent meal for a few kopecks. At lunch Mayakovsky's advertisement for Soviet condoms kept turning over in my mind:

Yesli khochesh byt' sukhim
V samom mokrom meste
Pokupai prezervativ
V Rossrezinatreste

A loose, if you will, translation:

If you want to stay bone dry
In that wettest of all places
The condoms from the Russian Rubber Trust
Are a must!

I returned to the pharmacy precisely at one o'clock to find a long line leading up to the order counter. It took well over half an hour this time for me to get to the counter. I handed my receipt to the same young woman I had ordered my condoms from. She turned to the shelves behind her and brought down a huge cardboard box, holding it above her head, bringing it down on the counter and shoving it along to me with outstretched fingers.

"Is this . . . them?" I gulped.

"Yes, twelve dozen. *Vam khvataet?*"—Enough for you?

I was dumbstruck. All I could do was immediately take my flimsy cardboard box of 144 Soviet condoms back to my hotel room, thanking my lucky stars that the box carried no markings. How would it have looked? A young American carrying a box marked "Twelve Dozen Condoms" across Red Square . . . .

The condoms, by the way, were thick and rubber-pungent, not unlike the tubes in the tires of my old twenty-inch Schwinn bicycle.

11

With or Without God

While in Leningrad in August 1964 our group of American graduate students was taken to the Museum of the History of Religion and Atheism. This museum had been established as far back as 1932 inside the majestic Kazan Cathedral. Here were exhibits of posters blatantly attacking organized religion, exhibits that openly displayed rusty racks and large screws on torture tables (the real things!) and reproductions on the walls of scenes depicting the promulgation of intolerant ecumenical edicts, as well as portraits of sinister Orthodox priests glaring down with revulsion at downtrodden serfs.

My American fellow travelers balked openly at the highly charged propaganda on display, though I pointed out to a few of them my fascination with this museum and its largely realistic presentation of the history of religion, particularly as it related to Russia.

At the museum shop I bought a postcard showing a happy peasant woman skipping down a country path. The postcard carried the slogan "*Bez boga shire doroga*" ("Without God the road is wider"). Perhaps I shouldn't have, but I noted to the old woman selling me the postcard that the proverb had once been "With God the road is wider." She shrugged her shoulders, raised an eyebrow and smiled at me, saying, "It used to be wider with, now it's wider without."

Now that the Kazan Cathedral on the wide Nevsky Prospekt in the center of St. Petersburg has reverted to its former role, the old woman's remark resonates with a double irony.

The massive suppression of religious observance in the Soviet Union gave rise to a policy of, at best, the neglect of, or, at worst, the willful destruction of the rich heritage of church architecture in Russia. The exquisite and unadorned churches of Novgorod, one of them from the tenth century and said to be the oldest in Russia, were in hideous disrepair. Radical poet Mayakovsky had urged his compatriots after the revolution to "Burn down the museums/ Once burnt down we can sing again." Official Soviet policy in the 1960s was not to burn down these beautiful churches, which were museums in their own right, but to let them rot from the inside out.

While I was at Harvard in the autumn of 1964, First Secretary of the Communist Party Nikita Sergeievich Khrushchev was deposed in a Kremlin coup for the gross failure of his agricultural policies, the nepotism that symbolized his regime (he had appointed his son-in-law Aleksei Adzhubei as one of his closest advisers, and ironically it was Adzhubei who, among others, turned against him and helped bring about his ouster), and his ignorant outbursts, such as the one at the United Nations in New York in 1960 when he banged his shoe on the table in protest. (Though the veracity of the shoe-banging incident has been questioned, it appears to have been true. In any case, it was reported as such in the world press and was totally in character for the earthy anti-intellectual former metal worker and one-time obsequious Stalinist who led the U.S.S.R.)

I had left Harvard in June 1965 and lost track of my wonderful teachers. Kiril Taranovsky died in Boston in 1993; Roman Jacobson also in Boston, in 1982. Vladimir Markov, who had done pioneering work on the poems of Khlebnikov, Bal'mont and Kuzmin, passed away in Los Angeles on January 1, 2013. He was 92. Could he have ever known that a young student in his conversation class more than a half-century ago can still see him acting out lemon picking, and that the simple gesture of his arm reaching upward into the branches would pull me away on a wild tangent and hurl me into an unknown trajectory in life?

12

Traveling on the Rim of a Glass

It was thanks to being able to speak Russian and Polish that I was able to take up a job in Japan as a lecturer at Kyoto Sangyo University in the autumn of 1967.

What is travel through the time and space of your life if not sitting securely on the rim of a glass, with toddler's feet dangling freely over the inside edge, the glass itself whirling and moving swiftly, silently and with an uncanny smoothness without encountering fatal friction in the air, but only, if you're lucky, the occasional bump and jolt? The air itself—the time and space you move through when you are young—is exquisitely clear, radiant to the point of blinding you. And despite the swift motion of the glass itself and despite the fact that you do not know where you are headed on it, you feel and believe that you are safe, that nothing untoward will happen to you and that you will make it over the next horizon and deal with whatever is waiting for you there.

But then you notice something that did not seem to be there before you started moving. Around the glass, on the far side from where you are, there is a figure perched on the edge just like you, with feet dangling playfully just like yours. The figure is looking across the mouth of the glass directly at you with the very same facial expression that you have—a concentrated delight bordering on the ecstatic. You squint to get a better look at this person who is smiling directly at you, and it doesn't take long for you to realize that this person directly opposite you and now holding onto the slippery rounded edge of the glass just as you are is *you yourself.* But this is no mirror image! The person *is* you, and is moving through space together with you, but with one startling difference that causes you to suddenly grab onto the edge of the glass for dear life and hold fast until the tips of your knuckles turn bone white.

One of you is moving forward and the other backward, and

neither of you can tell which. You are too young, too enamored of your own zeal for life, too bound up in yourself and the intense pleasures of your daily discoveries to be able to know where this whirlwind of motion is transporting you. This journey is not so easy and smooth and full of pleasure alone as you thought. The world is most certainly not your oyster, as you expected it to be—always so clever, best in the class, student body president at high school, scholarship to Harvard—now there is suddenly only motion in the dark. And though you fervently believe this during the summer of 1965—traveling around northern and eastern Europe by yourself, meeting and being with beautiful girls, not knowing where the next night's bed would be—it dawns on you that you don't know who you really are and what kind of a person you wish to be. Your old friends don't recognize you ... or worse, they spread half-truths about you.

In some countries in the world the names of cities are about to change. How will you find a place for yourself in that not-so-brave new world? You will have to jump off the moving glass at some point in time. But when? And where? The other person who *was* you is, in a flash, gone. Will you land on your feet when you finally come down?

THE UNMAKING OF AN AMERICAN

13

Stars, Stripes and One Nation Under God

I had little to complain about. I was healthy and had never suffered a serious setback. I had had a middle-class upbringing and was not wanting for any of life's necessities. I was born and raised in a country that valued freedom of choice for many people, though a glaring racial and class inequality of opportunity was and still is America's most serious social problem. Being among "the haves," I had not so much as an inkling of how the other half—the "have nots"—lived.

Despite the advantages of birth, I had no vision of a future for myself. I envisioned a fortune-teller's crystal ball caught in a terrible fire and saw myself trying desperately to peer into it through the film of soot covering its surface. I was leaving Europe in May 1967 for "home" in just such a soot-like fog. The invasion of Vietnam was taking more and more young American men to the war zone. Gen. William Westmoreland addressed a joint session of Congress in the first week of May, the first general to do so while prosecuting a war. He assured the senators and congressmen of America's victory, if the military could count on domestic "resolve, confidence, patience, determination and continued support." General Westmoreland appeared on the cover of *Time* magazine on May 5, 1967, as the American of his day. The war would not end for nearly eight more years—without resolve, without confidence, without patience, determination or the support of the American people.

As for me, I arrived back in the thick of it. I could no longer rely on a student deferment to keep me out of the war. The empty space ahead of me looked pitch black.

I had thought that marrying my French girlfriend and remaining in Paris might have provided a refuge for my budding and disorderly talents. I could have added French to my other foreign languages, both of which were considerably harder to learn than French. But Anne-Marie broke off the relationship, and I was crushed. My life, I thought, was now aimless. She had another young man, a brilliant student of philosophy, to love.

"I can see the future ahead of me with him, but I cannot imagine what a future would be with you," she had told me when we sat in my little British racing-green Austin Sprite in front of the old church in the village where she lived, Villiers-sur-Morin.

She was dead right. I couldn't imagine a future for myself, so how could she? I had been obliged to leave Poland in a hurry in early February of that year, having been dropped right into the middle of a major international spy scandal involving the American National Students Association. The NSA, as it was known, was being substantially funded by the CIA. I was in Poland on an exchange program sponsored by them, neither knowing about nor suspecting such a connection. When this funding was made public in the press, the spotlight was turned on me. I was about to turn twenty-three and had no idea what profession I might pursue. The gate to the world of Slavic studies was now, it appeared, shut and locked, and a return to Eastern Europe, innocent of spying though I was, would entail a dangerous flirtation with imprisonment, becoming a sacrificial lamb in the midst of teams of sly CIA foxes and cunning Russian bears.

I flew twelve hours and five minutes nonstop from Paris to Los Angeles. There was no glass to cling to. I had been dropped in an ocean, a buoy amid powerful waves that I felt were coming toward me from all sides. If I had been giddy on the rim of my traveling glass up till then, I now felt as if the entire glass had dropped out from under me. I had hurtled in freefall into that raging ocean. My parents were indignant that I had "wasted all those years on studying Russian and such things" instead of doing what all smart Jewish boys did—become a doctor, a lawyer or a certified public accountant, the holy trinity of Jewish callings.

Growing up in the United States in the 1950s meant coming of age in the long shadow of World War II. The war's shadow loomed over my generation like another planet so near that it obliterated half the sky. Not that my father had offered stories of fierce battles or cruel camps; there was no shaking of the head and falling silent halfway through a discourse then mumbling, under the breath, "You'd probably rather not know." Dad, born in 1903, was lucky: he was too young for World War I and too old for World War II. In my family, I had no uncles who had been captured by the despicable thickly-accented Germans or cagey Japanese we saw in our Hollywood re-creations of the war. There was no escaping the triumphant sensation of righteousness—our own American variety of self-righteousness that has morphed into the blind exceptionalism of today. The victory in war had been in our eyes totally an American one, and it was brandished before us young people as the ultimate triumph of Good over Evil. God, it was good to be American in the golden age of the 1950s!

Only in the 1960s did some of us begin to question, however haphazardly at first, the absoluteness of our unique national virtue. Though I was a proper teenage goody-two-shoes, always striving to please and impress adults, there was the trace of another strain in me, a strain of undefined rebelliousness that runs through the personality of most young people. This rebelliousness was not directed at my parents, as it is with many others. It took another form, one that I had no way of comprehending at the time.

I was only fourteen early in 1959 when I was called into the office of the Boys' Vice-Principal at Louis Pasteur Junior High School in Los Angeles and severely reprimanded. I was lucky that it ended there, with a reprimand. The man was a well-known sadist at the school who had dealt violently with what he called "unruly elements" among the pupils. When I entered his office, he was removing a thick strap from around his waist and, clearly incensed, glaring at me. I was able, however, to cajole him with obsequious apologies for my awful transgression. Perhaps this willingness to apologize profusely even when I believe there have been no grounds for apology has stood me in good stead and helped me assimilate in my many years living in Japan, the Land of the Gratuitous Apology.

The transgression in question had occurred only moments before I was summoned to the Boys' Vice-Principal's office. One of my duties as a "school leader" was to haul down the Stars and Stripes together with another boy leader, fold it properly and bring it into the administration building for storage overnight. That particular afternoon a tip of the end of the flag slipped out of my hands and touched the concrete below the flagpole. The Boys' Vice-Principal had seen this from his office window and had apprehended me at the entrance to the building.

Though I apologized in order to escape the whip of his belt, I felt indignant that he was able to intimidate me through authority and the threat of violence for a slip of the hand, flag or no flag. Wasn't it enough that I had pledged allegiance to the flag in an oath recited every single day since elementary school?

"Do you realize what that flag stands for?!" he threatened, rubbing his thumb over the strap in his hand.

Though I had pledged allegiance to it with my hand over my heart, I obviously was unclear as to what it stood for, if letting an end of it touch the ground made me eligible for a beating.

It wasn't until three years later that I exhibited my true feelings in public. As student body president of Alexander Hamilton High School, my duty at the assembly held as part of the graduation ceremony was to lead the graduating class, family members and school staff in the Pledge of Allegiance. While doing this over a microphone, I left out two words that had been added to the then twenty-nine-word pledge in 1954 as a statement of affirmation of faith in divine sponsorship of American democracy under threat from what was always referred to in the press as "godless communism."

My omission of "under God" may have gone unnoticed at the ceremony, seeing as everyone else in the auditorium had been reciting those words in the pledge. But it couldn't have been missed by anyone that I alone among those present on stage and in the audience remained seated for the playing of The Star-Spangled

Banner. No one mentioned either the omission of God in the oath or the refusal to stand for the national anthem, and I was still given the American Legion School Award Medal—the American Legion being the nation's leading war veterans' organization—which, in any case, seems to have been given every year to the student body president. The back of the medal was adorned with the Marine Corps motto *semper fidelis* (always faithful).

These two awkward public gestures of rebellion had been totally unpremeditated by me, and I now cannot fathom why I acted in that way at the time. Much later, when I gave up my American citizenship, I recalled that graduation day assembly in June 1961 and wondered if my feelings of alienation from American life had already begun to take form then. I doubt it. I was in my own eyes and those of my peers an all-American sort of guy who cared much more for who was on Dick Clark's American Bandstand and what kind of cars people drove (this was Los Angeles after all, where a car was a *sine qua non* of teenage self-fulfillment) than for gestures of a political nature.

14

The Democratic National Party Convention, 1960

The year before I graduated high school I had the chance to attend the Democratic Party National Convention held at the Memorial Sports Arena in downtown Los Angeles. An older cousin of mine, a confidante of Sam Yorty, had asked me if I would like to be "Head of Youth for Yorty." Sam Yorty, who had served in the House of Representatives, was planning to run for mayor of Los Angeles in 1961. Though I knew nothing about Sam Yorty, I gladly accepted the position. This led to my being asked to become "Head of Youth" for Sen. Stuart Symington in his bid to gain the nomination for the presidency at the 1960 convention held in mid-July that year.

In 1954, I had watched the televised Army-McCarthy hearings

conducted by the U.S. Senate (it was the first political event that I had taken notice of) and recalled, when being reminded in 1960, that Senator Symington's attack on an increasingly desperate and degenerate Sen. Joseph McCarthy had been a highlight of the hearings and a stimulus to McCarthy's national humiliation. I was delighted to work for Senator Symington primarily because it meant that I could go to the convention every day.

It is the red, white and blue balloons that I remember most vividly, wondering even then who would have been lucky enough to have the balloon concession at American political party conventions. I was also struck by the many different kinds of hats, plastered with badges and stickers, that the delegates from the fifty states wore. Though all I was able to do was shake hands once with Senator Symington, I did witness at close range Lyndon Johnson, tall and impressive, talking in his shirtsleeves to several reporters on a staircase, and I saw Robert Kennedy going around the state delegations handing something to delegates. When I asked one of the party insiders at the convention what Robert Kennedy was handing delegates, he answered, "Why, hundred dollar bills."

As everyone knows, John F. Kennedy won the nomination that July in 1960, going on to become president. Sam Yorty also won his election for mayor of Los Angeles, with no help from his "Head of Youth," I might add. (Yorty, by the way, supported Richard Nixon in the campaign leading up to the presidential election.)

15

"My Son the Overachiever"?

I think at the time that I, too, wished to be a part of this great American celebration of freedom and democracy, and I told my parents when I returned home from the convention one day that I wanted to be a United States senator. This pleased them no end, though, on balance, they said, "We would prefer it if you became a doctor or a lawyer or at least a certified public accountant, but there's nothing wrong with being a senator, too." My mother then added what could be classified as a sacred motto of Jewish-American philosophy: "Remember, Roger, there's no such thing as an overachiever."

Was I an overachiever? Is this what was implied when I was voted "Most Likely to Succeed" by my graduating high school class? Could I take credit for things that just came my way without my having to overachieve, as when, in February 1958, I was acclaimed "Mr. Smile of the Year" for having the best teeth in the City and County of Los Angeles? Perhaps this is an "achievement" to be truly proud of. "After all," said Ryszard Taedling, a journalist with the daily *Echo Krakowa* in Krakow in 1967, "whatever you do in your life, no matter what you succeed at, it will say on your gravestone, 'He had the best teeth in Los Angeles.'"

Ryszard may have hit the nail on the head, for my teeth will surely outlast the brief collective memory of any other moderate successes I may have had in my life. Ryszard Taedling, by the way, left Poland the following year when a new wave of anti-Semitism was washing over the country. Born in 1938 in Lodz, where there had been a large Jewish population, he had spent the war years in hiding. Ryszard has lived since 1968 in Denmark, having enjoyed an illustrious career as a journalist. (It was Ryszard who taught me the Polish word *brukowiec*, which means "tabloid newspaper," or more closely, "rag." It apparently derives from *bruk*, or pavement, because the cobblestones that make up the pavement are essentially worthless. *Echo Krakowa*, the rag that Ryszard openly referred to with this word, folded in 1997.)

I was a model university student, finishing the units required for graduation from UCLA in three years. I was still more concerned with doing well in terms of what was expected of me than in formulating an idea of where my education was leading me. I had given up the idea of becoming a senator, and definitely did not want to be a doctor, lawyer or certified public accountant. So, what else was there? I couldn't deny a certain amount of envy for my friends who knew at an early age what they wanted to become. Ever since then, in bringing up my own children or speaking with hundreds of students from around the world, I have empathized with young people who cannot put their finger on their future and have advised them not to fret over an absence of decisiveness. Had someone told me when I was young that I would spend most of my life in Japan, speaking, translating and writing books in Japanese, I would have considered their prophecy patently absurd. The only thing I could genuinely claim for myself as an overachiever is that I had the best teeth in the City and County of Los Angeles in 1958.

16

Another America

By the time of my graduation from UCLA in June 1964 a change was beginning to take place in the appearance of the people around me. The protest sentiment against American participation in the civil war raging in Vietnam was in its formative stages, much too early to warrant the label of a "movement." After all, there were fewer than 25,000 American troops stationed in Vietnam at the time. (By the end of the next year the number had multiplied nearly eightfold.)

Yet spurred on by the shock of the assassination of President Kennedy in November of the previous year, and by the surges of dissidence sent across the country by the civil rights movement from the South, our consciousness of American wrongdoing at home and around the globe was being heightened. Until then, criticism of the chief aspects of American life had been considered a form of "anti-Americanism" due to obeisance to a foreign ideology or—in a succinct phrase coined many years later by George W. Bush—our enemies' "jealousy of our freedoms." (Why foreign people who are jealous of your freedoms will fight to destroy America is a conundrum whose logic still escapes me.)

The black population of America raised the social consciousness of us all, bringing us face to face with the deeply rooted injustices of American social intercourse, showing those of us who had had a privileged upbringing that our society could boast unprecedented wealth while concealing equally unprecedented misery without so much as a question mark at the end of a sentence. We privileged white people had not known a thing about any other America save our own.

How could a young white boy still in mourning over the deaths of his heroes, Buddy Holly, the Big Bopper and Richie Valens in a light plane crash on February 3, 1959, know what Bessie Smith was singing about in her 1929 hit, "I'm Wild About that Thing"?

If you want to satisfy my soul
Come on an' rock me with a steady roll

I had never heard of Bessie Smith then, was in the dark as to what "that thing" was, didn't know what "soul" meant, and hadn't a clue what she was inferring with her "rock" and her "roll." How could I have known? No one ever taught me or clued me in about sex. The closest I got to Bessie's sort of rocking and rolling was a hand-held copy of *Peyton Place*, dog-eared at the "good parts."

White America, of which I was inextricably a part, had expropriated the music of blacks for a century, going back to the minstrel shows and through to jazz and rock 'n' roll. But we young white middle-class kids were still unashamed prudes at heart and had not so much as an inkling that there was another cultural grammar in use in America, the grammar that expressed the needs and desires of the psyche in colorful argot.

By the mid-1960s, however, our burgeoning social consciousness was taking on a more freewheeling and richer mode of expression, and we were to have our first real brush with, and partial assimilation of, an alternative America. It wasn't the Beatniks and the Hippies who opened up that other country and that alternative consciousness to us; it was the American people of color.

Yet despite the changes gradually spreading into the consciousness of white middle-class America, many Americans still imagined an "ideal" America, something that would be akin to a colossal mural painted by Norman Rockwell called "The Triumph of Optimism over Reality." On its broad surface, little babies would stare in awe at kindly hometown doctors (I have watched four babies grow up, and the single thing I have seen them stare with awe at is a breast full of milk); even dogs would appear to be smiling; women would be flirting with shakes of their long curls or their cute little pageboys; cows would be strappingly healthy; farmers, honest as the day is long; prayers, faithfully answered. There is little or no room in this world for the sordid. Anything that offends the ideal sensibility must be kept out of sight and, hence, out of the public mind. This hypocrisy forms the basis of the two Americas: one of public prudery, the other of private vice.

This is the America that once again, with the election of President Donald Trump in November 2016, has come to represent the "values" of the nation.

17

From Walden Pond to the Meadows of Jutland

During the first twenty years of my life I was as innocent as the people in that idyllic, if imagined, mural. But by the middle of the sixties, like many of my generation, I began to wonder if it was all too good to be true. America, we were taught, had saved the world from tyranny. Our teachers did not tell us that, among others, the British, Canadians and Australians, let alone the Russians, had also made "our" victory possible.

While at Harvard, I had sat at the edge of Walden Pond, surrounded by a kaleidoscope of intense autumn colors, and in winter, I had driven around the old towns of Massachusetts with the bare branches and twigs of trees pressed against the gray sky like

scrawny birds' feet. In this cold and exquisite landscape, so different from the radiant seascapes of Santa Monica and Venice Beach that I had grown up with, I began to wonder what my identity was. The identity as a young white American, a bright Californian who once believed that his country was the single bastion of freedom of the whole world, the sole salvation for the oppressed peoples of all countries, was not sitting well with me. I was only twenty after all, and wanted to believe that what I had been taught about my country was true. But I was experiencing a restlessness that I, least of all, could understand. I suddenly wanted to leave. I felt alien. Were the justifications that I made—either of "seeing the world" or of protesting against an unjust and brutal war against the people of Vietnam—simply that, namely justifications for a run-of-the-mill adolescent restlessness? Or was I turning into a person with political and social convictions different from those inculcated in me during the years of my upbringing and education?

Luckily, due to my acquired command of Russian, I passed the master's qualifying language exam at Harvard's Russian Research Center. Then, when my thesis "The Development and Organization of Soviet Science in the 1930s" was accepted, I received an MA from Harvard in one year in what was normally a two-year program. Had I not, I probably would have dropped out and lost myself.

There was no need to think about identity or what might happen in the future when I left for Europe in June 1965. That summer, spent in Denmark, Sweden, Finland and the Soviet Union, would never end. I could not see past it. I hitchhiked around the Danish countryside insane on discovery, devouring the sights and smells of everything. In Jutland, I ran up hills like a child, arms flailing in the air, and raced across meadows. My only possession was a little suitcase. I never knew the name of the village in the distance. I craved adventure, yet something that would endure; pleasure, yet something that would leave a trace in the heart; the present, yes, always this very moment, but accompanied by a longing for a way to stretch it all out so that I would not have to think about its ending. I was determined that the summer of 1965 would last a lifetime. This was because I had no idea whatsoever as to what I would do once it came to an end.

18

In a Word: Vietnam

My passion was the Russian language, literature and culture. As I gained greater fluency, I read avidly and sought out Russians to meet wherever I went, particularly when I was living in Paris in the spring of 1967, for Paris was crawling with émigré Russians (many of the taxi drivers were White Russians).

Americans, however, associated such interest in things Russian with an unrelenting suspicion. The Soviet Union was the perfect postwar bogeyman to give focus to American nationalism, and Americans could not see past the barricades of their own highly held ideology any more than Soviets could see past theirs. Both views of their rivals' national character were based on entrenched ignorance fostered by misinformation and the secretive manoeuvres of political and military expediency. This remains the essence of the fundamental relationship to this day.

Americans have always needed to establish and prop up a suitable dark devil, often attributing to him a greater potency than he actually possessed, in order to view themselves as standing forever in the glow of a halo of light. After the Cold War ended there has been a Conga-line of such devils from Saddam Hussein to Colonel Gaddafy, from the leaders of the "Axis of Evil" to Bashar al-Assad, and now, I fear, to the new "sinister leader" of the line, the Chinese devil. China is fast becoming the primary threat to American power in our century as perceived by Americans, who are wont to interpret a challenge to American power anywhere in the world as a threat to their domestic liberties and lifestyle. Are Americans sacrificing those very liberties due to their self-styled perceptions of "threat"?

I shared these preconceptions of the world when I was growing up. I surely thanked my lucky stars that I was born and raised in what is now referred to by Americans as "the greatest country in the history of the world."

What changed me? What put me out of step with my country? Why did it not all end with a vague restlessness, so common in the psyche of the young people of any generation in any country, to be channeled back into something useful at home, where my parents constantly told me I "belonged"?

The one-word answer is "Vietnam." But even the war in Vietnam changed me gradually. The source of my unmaking as an American was the feeling that the war was *unfair*—this was simple and naive, I suppose; it certainly comes across in that way. Why should wars be fair? Are they ever fair to both sides? I could not bear to watch gigantic American bombers dropping their payloads, to use the insidious euphemism that equates the weight of a plane's load of bombs with monetary value, many of them filled with chemicals deadly to human life, on what was essentially a rural nation of people fighting for their independence from colonial rule, first French, then Japanese, and now American. I did not want to be the citizen of a country that could destroy the livelihood of an entire nation in the purported interests of their freedoms, something that was done later in Afghanistan, Iraq and Libya. I took the easiest way out: I left.

I left the United States for Japan in September 1967, never to return to live there, so I could hardly have taken part in the protest movement that was then only beginning to resound in voice and action across the country. Yet, I don't even know if I would have taken part had I stayed. My opposition to the war was still something felt in my bones, not evidenced in my actions. It was only some years later, while living in Australia, that I was able as a writer, journalist and radio broadcaster to voice my opposition to the war.

I do not, however, consider this as constituting major protest, and I do not think of myself as an activist like the many people I admire who put their careers and lives on the line in the cause of their beliefs. While I have written extensively of my convictions over the years, I view myself, alas, as timid and passive. My leaving the U.S. and abandoning my citizenship over the war in Vietnam comprised my only act of defiance, if the option of escape can even be justifiably called that.

What goes into making us the person we become? The twenty-first-century metaphor is DNA. Historians talk of the DNA of a country, a medical metaphor for collective national memory.

While it may be a useful handle for historians, to my mind it doesn't explain much about an individual's actions. My going on about ancestors is part of my story because I have chosen to make it so. To millions of people the distant family past is nothing but scrap in an old album. And as for the influence of parents, while it can be stunning, in both the positive and negative senses of that word, it can also be insignificant. We have all known the most awful parents who have had remarkable children, as well as horrid children coming out of the homes of angels.

I was so different in temperament, behavior and aspiration from my parents that my mother remarked to my wife Susan when she met her for the first time, "We thought, where did this boy come from?" DNA may matter when it comes to a propensity toward certain illnesses, but, even then, we know little about our ancestors' maladies and characteristics. You form your own character, and it's better looked upon in that way, for this puts the responsibility for your actions on your own shoulders and not on those of the people in the pale ephemera of the past.

It was after I left the United States in September 1967 that the issue of Vietnam began to tear the country in two. By the next year there were more than half a million American troops in Vietnam. When, that month, I flew to Tokyo's Haneda International Airport (Narita Airport wasn't to open for another eleven years), the prime minister of the Republic of Vietnam was the former chief of the country's air force, Nguyen Cao Ky.

"I liked LBJ," said Ky of President Lyndon Baines Johnson. "He is a Texan and maybe in a way I am a bit of a Texan myself."

Those were the days when the CIA was claiming that Ky was working for them and Ky was letting it be known that the CIA was working for him. They were both right.

The French president at the time treated him with typical Gallic scepticism.

"*Qui est Ky?*" (Who is Ky?) quipped Charles de Gaulle.

Ky was a warrior-politician who cared more for his reputation than the welfare of his people.

"Even if we had lost Saigon," he said after the defeat in the American-backed civil war, "we still had the Mekong Delta. My plan was really to make Saigon a Stalingrad. This is worth dying for. A battle the world will always remember."

This highlights the danger of putting your country in the hands of military figures, a danger from which the Japanese people of the second decade of the Showa era, 1935–1945, were to learn an exceedingly bitter lesson.

As for the Americans in Vietnam, it didn't matter to them that this was an ancient culture whose view of humanity was based on cultural and historical premises vastly different from those cherished by the self-styled Green Mountain Boys of the Johnson administration. In Japan, I often listened to American Forces Radio, and I jotted down the following from one of its broadcasts in 1970:

> For those of you staying on in 'Nam, here's a little advice regarding our Vietnamese friends. As you know, they're kind of jumpy now, so please remember the golden rule. Never pat a Vietnamese on the head. Stand on low ground when you talk to them. They kind of resent looking up to you. Okay?

Had Americans been aware that they were fighting their equals, who had themselves been waging a prolonged war against foreign domination, they might have understood why the Vietnamese people were "kind of jumpy" and resentful of outsiders lording over them. Had that awareness sunk in after America lost the war, it might have prevented similar invasions that took place much later in the Middle East. You can't tell your people to stand on low ground when they believe in their heart that they occupy the moral high ground in every corner of the globe.

The result of what the Vietnamese call "the American War" was a loss during the decade of active American engagement that far exceeded a million Vietnamese lives, with millions more wounded and injured. It has been estimated that upwards of three million Vietnamese children have been congenitally afflicted with disease or deformity as a result of the use of chemical weapons by the United States. Where were the so-called red lines then?

All of this began affecting me deeply as the media broadcast one atrocity in Vietnam after another. But I still considered myself an American and wanted to do something to redress the injustice perpetrated by my country on a much weaker enemy. I thought that perhaps Robert Kennedy might become president and acknowledge America's mistakes, if not admit its crimes. But when he was shot and killed on June 6, 1968, in my hometown of Los Angeles, all hope vanished. By then I was teaching at a university in Kyoto, Japan. I was so upset that I walked into my Russian class at Kyoto Sangyo University, stood before the blackboard for a moment and, with tears in my eyes, cancelled the class "in honor of Senator Robert Kennedy." (The students applauded, but apparently not in homage to the American politician. They were, it seems, simply happy to have no class.)

I stayed in Kyoto for five years, from 1967 to 1972, publishing my first collection of short stories, *On the Edge of Kyoto*; my first play, *The Perfect Crime of Mrs. Garigari*, translated into Japanese and carried in the leading drama magazine of the day, *Shingeki* (Modern Theater); and my first major essay, a winner in an international essay contest sponsored by the Mainichi Newspapers.

And then, one day in 1972, I found myself in Australia.

19

The Benefit of Chance

Chance is the novelist's hapless obsession. Hidden among the lines of chance's complex arabesques lies a question: What is it that decides the direction of a person, where they "end up," how long they remain where they are and who they live their life with? All angles of space and lines of time intertwine, until they converge on the point of this question.

To the writer, whether in fiction or real life, coincidence is fate, pure and simple, and that which chance determines takes on a peculiar magic with unpredictable results. "It was meant to be" may be one of any language's most banal little phrases. To the writer, all characters may seem to be moved by this phrase's opportunistic twisting logic. Yet nothing was meant to be; everything merely happens and becomes what *is* whether we like it or not.

Look at it this way. Novelists weave and patch together a piece of cloth out of threads. They happily include everything under the sun in its fabric, as their imagination directs their hand. Thousands of trees can be planted in magnificent columns along a road, or no trees at all adorning what is just a stretch of dirt, stones and blackened potholes. Good men and women disappear and are brought back to life in the memory of other characters dear to them. Even that ugly question one stitch off the frayed edge of all art may suddenly appear: Why are we here in the first place?

Is the only answer contained in the old World War I song, a kind of existential slap in fate's face, sung to the tune of "Auld Lang Syne": "We're here because we're here because we're here because we're here"? Or is there a reason for our little existence? And if there is a reason, who supplies it? You yourself? A superior being? Your superiors and leaders in life? Or is there no rhyme or reason, and life is only a random series of little fires that are extinguished all at once in the end? This is the question novelists ask themselves, consciously or subconsciously, and it is a question that relates equally to real life and fiction.

There is an essential difference between fiction and real life. All logic-defying coincidences are fair game as they are presented to us in prose or drama, because in fiction or in the theater there is a moral to every story, even if that moral is an existential one denying a moral. In the made-up world, coincidence is connection. But all of us in real life are compelled to accept the potholes that suddenly appear before us along our own road, coincidentally or not. We must make hasty, often arbitrarily derived decisions about which way to turn when several roads appear. We are left standing alone when a road abruptly ends and a friend or loved one who was standing there "only a moment ago" is gone. There are few if any warning signs in real life (fiction—at least good fiction—contains many such signs, if half-hidden amid any number of extraneous details). In real life, it is only after the fact that we come to see the signs and tell ourselves, "I didn't see it coming, but I should have." In fact, you cannot see them coming. If you could, you would avoid them at all costs. We are victims of hapless mundane circumstance, and there is no moral to our little story. Being here is all there is.

Perhaps this is why I haven't minded being manipulated by the most ludicrous quirks of fate, being hurtled across a hemisphere for what appears to be no more than an indifferent whim of circumstance decided upon by someone I didn't know. The spy scandal that I was dropped into was a good lesson to me. It doesn't matter if you were a spy or not, and, needless to say, I wasn't. It's how you deal with the aftermath of those quirks of fate that determine what kind of a life you are going to lead. Had I been born tens of thousands of years ago I would definitely have been one of those people who made a small contribution to humankind's movement across the face of the Earth. The moment things began to look desolate, I would have started searching for another pasture in the hope—because it is hope that drives us—that it might be greener than the last one.

20

Australia for the Tourist

Australia turned out to be that greener pasture, despite the fact that more than two-thirds of the continent's land is semi-arid or desert.

On the very day in early 1972 that I decided to move to Australia to teach at a university in Canberra, I found myself walking around Hyakumanben, the area in Kyoto where Kyoto University is located. Along Imadegawa Boulevard across from the university, there were a number of second-hand bookstores. I had never stepped into one.

One day I suddenly stopped in front of just such a bookstore, perhaps to stare at my reflection for a moment in its sliding glass door: white T-shirt sticking out at the neck of my button-down checked shirt; high bush of curly hair—the pride of my mother but of no young person in an era that worshipped Elvis's smooth shiny straight hair—and pseudo-Scandinavian-trim beard; black and white sneakers; white cotton socks below pants that were much too short for my toothpick legs. In that old wavy Japanese glass door, with my image broken into little boxes by the thin wooden latticing that formed its panes, I looked, to be succinct, like a typical Southern California teenager stretched into his late twenties, an upstart fellow-traveler of the beatniks or *haimisher* (Yiddish—nice and innocent) hippie well past fashion's use-by date. The trouble was that this was not the 1950s or even the 1960s, but 1972, and here I still looked like a California teenager at twenty-eight on an exotic excursion to god-knows-where.

I slid the door aside and entered the old bookshop. A repository of dust and mold from its toppling shelves assaulted my nostrils. Even the lightest earthquake would have brought hundreds of books down on one's head. I pulled the door closed and glanced down at a stack of magazines by the entrance. On top of the stack of old editions of *Life* and *McCall's* was a paperback book of some

150 pages in length picturing on its cover a woman of Gibson-girl proportions dressed in a long white flowing skirt, lace-up black boots and the jaunt of a cute red cap. She was pointing into the background where a green valley wound its way back to a tall mountain and, above it, a track of white puffy clouds.

The book's title: *Australia for the Tourist.*

I asked the old woman behind the cash register the price and she answered, "Fifty yen." This was the equivalent in those days of less than fifteen American cents. I bought the book, leaving the shop, in which I had spent no more than two minutes, and stood once again in front of the mirror-like door.

I have *Australia for the Tourist* on the desk in front of me now. It was the first book that I was to read about what was to become my new country. In fact, I was even more ignorant when it came to Australia than I had been about Japan before going to that country.

Australia for the Tourist was published by the government of the Commonwealth of Australia in July 1914 and is authenticated by the signature of Patrick McMahon Glynn, Minister of State for External Affairs. It is illustrated in both black-and-white and color, with fancy curly-Q lines forming the borders of its photographs. There is a chapter devoted to each state as well as to Australian history, topography, climate, fauna, flora and "Advance Australia, a Striking Story."

It was not until a few years later that I was able to put the wicked misconceptions and peculiar Australian biases of *Australia for the Tourist* into some perspective. I did wonder, however, even on my first reading, why the population of Papua was given as a mere 1,219 people. (They were counting only whites, of course. It wasn't until 1971 that indigenous Australians were counted in the census of what had been a blatantly racist nation.)

I knew virtually nothing about Australia's history, yet somehow the following description from my precious fifteen-cent guide seemed too *amai*, to use the Japanese word which means both "sweet" and "glossed over," to be true.

This is from page twenty-three:

Here is a vast Territory rich in soils and minerals, which has been added to the British Empire without war or violence, a Commonwealth not won by the sword or sprung from lust of territory; in whose bloodless records there is no stain of external or internal strife. The conquerors have been the hardy explorers and pioneers, whose sole battles have been waged in subduing nature. There is no ancient civilisation to hurl back reproaches for its extinction, no people worthy to live who have been forced out of existence. The process by which Australia has risen has resembled a natural growth rather than a deliberate creation. It has been won, not by clash of arms, but by the triumphs of brain and muscle, and the highest human virtues.

In quoting this heady passage I was tempted, as is an author's cynical wont, to put some words in italics with the proviso that "the italics are mine" to stress points of hypocrisy and unashamed racism. Had I done so, however, I would have had to italicise the entire paragraph, which in spirit could easily have been used as a "rationale" for the Final Solution of the Nazis.

Among the flowery phrases in it, however, I cannot help but draw attention to three words: *worthy to live*. These give Minister Glynn's opinions the extra cutting edge that allows one ethnicity— in this case the white Anglo-Australian ethnicity that ruled Australia and controlled its justice system at the time—to commit genocide against a people, the indigenous Australians, without so much as an afterthought.

While living in Kyoto, I had been offered a lectureship in Japanese at the Australian National University and, without the least foreknowledge, entertained the notion that I might be able to settle in Australia and become a practicing playwright and published author. I could, I reckoned, always return to the haven of Japan, if things didn't work out.

Was the country described in *Australia for the Tourist* the one to which I was migrating with my permanent resident's visa? Had Australia fundamentally changed between 1914 and 1972, only one year after the census that gave nominal equality to the indigenous peoples of the country? If I had left my home country because of my convictions, how could those convictions justify the move to a country that was not only at least on a par in its racist biases but had also been equally gung-ho in supporting and participating in the invasion of Vietnam?

What did Americans know then about Australia? They knew that some of our white people had emigrated there for the sick and inglorious reason that "our coloreds got guns and yours don't." We knew that a prime minister, Harold Holt, had fallen helplessly into our president's arms, going all the way with him, an obsequious and odious remark inadvertently equating the action of a state with a sexual one. (For years, similarly, and with undisguised sexism, Japan was referred to by some as America's "mistress.") It was Prime Minister Holt who had allegedly coined the phrase "All the way with LBJ."

Now I was learning from my official guide to Australia that the country had a heroic past of its own, made up of "hardy pioneers and explorers" who "conquered" the vast continent as nonchalantly as if going through the rounds on a vast golf course.

Yet much of what I subsequently learned about the birth of the nation appeared not at all "natural and virtuous" but rather artificial and sinister. Had European Australians, in subduing the people who were here before them, displayed the "highest human virtues"? In my years in Australia I found few virtues and even fewer ideals in the story of its founding, either as a colony in the late eighteenth century, or as an independent nation state at the beginning of the twentieth.

When I arrived in Australia in August 1972 with my American passport wedged inside my precious copy of *Australia for the Tourist* I encountered a country as essentially ignorant of its beginnings as it was when my guidebook was issued in July 1914. It was not to be until a decade later that most Australians truly began to turn over the falsity in their minds, to acknowledge the cruelty of their ancestors toward the people who were here before them and, conversely, to feel a bit of pride in their convict past.

The sentiments expressed in *Australia for the Tourist* are not all that far removed from those cherished by many Australians today, though we would wildly insist that they are. The book refers to Australia before the coming of the Europeans as a "distant unknown region." Distant from where, one might ask. It is still a question that we, uncomfortable and fidgety in our Asian-Pacific location, have trouble answering. We Australians still see ourselves geographically moored somewhere off the west coast of Cornwall and culturally located within sight of California's Catalina Island.

I was puzzled, sitting on the tatami mat of my little rented house on the northern edge of Kyoto and poring over the guidebook to a country so remote and unknown to me, why Canberra, the nation's capital, a city where I was destined to live for nearly eight years, did not appear on the book's official map of Australia. The capital, as I discovered, had been founded as such only one year before the guidebook's publication, and its authors obviously had not bothered to include it.

I suppose that a Japanese person had bought *Australia for the Tourist* on a trip to the country around the time of World War I, when the Japanese were on "our" side. In what frame of mind, I wondered, would the tourist from Japan have read the descriptions of Australia's past and national character? I have no idea. But what I do know—as unpleasant as the knowledge may be—is that by becoming an Australian myself, I, too, claimed that warped history as my own. You cannot migrate to a country and cherry-pick its history for the purposes of your self-identification. You become lumbered with it all, the whole kit and caboodle of your new country's sordid past.

Why does a person change citizenship in the first place? There are any number of answers for every individual. I certainly know why my four grandparents chose to be Americans. They fled countries and regions where they were not felt welcome despite centuries of their ancestors living in relative peace there. War and peace played a part in my choosing not to remain an American.

But why embrace another country that also rushed into a poor Asian country and strove to pacify it—another wicked little wartime euphemism—exercising the same old "highest human virtues" as it had once when "pacifying" its own land?

What did I gain from jumping from one warhorse in the middle of a raging current to a similar warhorse right beside it?

21

The New Nationalism

Australia in 1972 was just beginning to enjoy a rapid movement toward what was then called "the new nationalism."

This new nationalism in cultural and social terms stressed an unambiguous confidence in the ability of Australians to entertain themselves in their own accents and to initiate a progressive package of social policies for all citizens. Until then what had represented Australia was an imitation-Brit elite priding itself on outdoing the mother country in adoration for everything that was royal puckery, and a rural squattocracy that entertained sawed-off genteel ways and a sweaty-upper-lip smugness that Australia was, is and would always remain "Godzone on Earth."

Now young progressive urban Australians were to have their say in the cultural bargain. And migrants, who until a few years previous to that had been derided and patronized as *reffos* (from "refugee") or *dagoes* (from the Spanish-Mexican name Diego; this was originally an Americanism), were being reclassified up the social scale as "new Australians."

You couldn't go to a restaurant without being forced by eager young Australian waiters and waitresses to order garlic prawns and garlic bread, and takeaway menus featured not only your run-of-the-mill Australian chop suey but pizza, falafel and stuffed capsicums. A bloke could now take his girl out to Mario's and impress her by nodding his head in a sophisticated continental manner as the waiter held a chilled bottle of Quelltaler Hock in front of his chest waiting for permission to pour. This European-style sophistication, I might add, was superimposed upon the home-grown Aussie suavity as celebrated in the then popular "Newcastle Song," according to which all you had to do was wink and say "G'day" to a sheila, and Bob, as well as Hugh Heffner, was your uncle. Now the Australian male had everything, not only his profound grasp of the grape and the prawn but also his artless diffident machismo to boot. Crocodile Dundee, here I come.

I envisioned an ethnographic film to be shown at the Congress of Papua New Guinea Anthropologists. A young white Australian male rolls up to the curb beside a female of similar ethnic origins, rolls down the window of his General Motors Holden, rolls a timid smile off his lips, pauses and, with a studied nonchalance, says, "G'day." When that doesn't "do the trick," he goes straight to the pub, works his way through half a dozen schooners and punches the bloke beside him in the face. Such an ethnographic film would not have been unusual, for in fact this was much like the scenes and themes in some Australian plays of the period of our newly-found "nationalism."

On August 11, 1972, I arrived for the first time in Australia, about to scratch lines on what, at the very least, was to be my third clean slate.

What would it be like to stay in your own country for most of a life, never to speak a foreign language, never to try your luck all over again among perfect strangers? I cannot conceive of such a life though many people, needless to say, live it and would find one such as mine mildly inconceivable.

On the first night, with the cold of the Canberra winter enveloping me, I stood in the long grass by Lake Burley Griffin near University House and looked up at the sky, unable to recognize constellations. The stars, my hobby since childhood, had always allowed me to gain a footing wherever I found myself, to feel as if I knew my way around above my head if not below my feet. Should I make a U-turn then and there, hightail it, as we Americans said, back home to Japan? I had heard Prime Minister William McMahon say on the radio that too many Asians could not be let into Australia because they "breed more prolifically than we do" and before you know it the white face of Australia would be changed forever. If the stars and politicians were that foreign to me, perhaps Australia was no place for a wandering Jewish-American-Japanese budding novelist/playwright.

Dinner at University House was high tea, and it was at high tea, seated at a long French-polished oak table that I found myself the next evening across from a distinguished-looking portly gentleman in his mid-fifties.

"You're American," he said in a tone of voice that was half question half statement.

"Yes, I am. I've just come from Japan. Yesterday."

He looked up at me, about to put a mushy wedge of carrot into his mouth (Australian food at those high teas was largely overcooked and indistinguishable in its lack of taste from British).

"Japan, eh? They still eating each other up there?"

He was referring to incidents of cannibalism among Japanese troops that had occurred in the South Pacific. Prejudice against Japan and the Japanese after the war was rife in Australia. This was long before the Japan culture boom of the 1980s had started to affect the country. In 1972, Sydney had only a few Japanese restaurants and one small Japanese grocery. You would be hard put to find a Toyota in an RSL (Returned and Services League) parking lot. The returned service men and women, referred to as "veterans" in the U.S., would not permit it. The word "Jap" was used frequently and without a trace of distaste in the mouth of the speaker, and it was quite normal to speak of Japanese people in a kindly manner as "our new little friends to the north." The memory of some starving Japanese soldiers during the war cannibalizing dead bodies had apparently stuck in the craw of my fellow diner.

"Oh yes," I replied, trying to saw my way, with a blunt table knife, through an enormous slab of charred sirloin. "They particularly seem to prefer plump white people these days, you know." I flashed him the big toothy smile that had won "The Smile of the Year Contest" for the City and County of Los Angeles in 1958.

Australians could not be blamed for having only a vague notion of what were then the esoteric trappings of Japanese culture. The Japanese at the time were not keen on promoting their own culture overseas. It was more valuable to them as a misunderstood item. They brandished the mystery of it all in the air and gloried in their culture's alleged impenetrable riddles, believing that this smokescreen strategy gave them power in a Western world dominated by articulate lawyers and moralizing politicians.

Yet what shocked me more than anything I had seen in Eastern Europe, Western Europe, the United States or Japan was that Australians seemed to have an even vaguer notion of their own cultural past than people in the other countries I had been in. What could they possibly be basing the "new" nationalism on?

22

"We Don't Have a Culture"

In the mid-1970s, I was called upon to interpret for the first officially government-sponsored cultural delegation sent from Japan to Australia. I stood, cocktail in hand, between two senior officials, one from Japan the other from Australia, eager to bring the two sides together, the gap between my two adopted countries bridged at last in this little encounter. After outlining some proposals for the future course of cultural exchange from the Japanese end of the gap, the Japanese representative asked, "And what aspects of Australian culture would you be prepared to introduce and promote in Japan?"

"Oh," said the Australian representative, looking his counterpart straight in the eye, "we don't have a culture in Australia."

That's all he said . . . and I was mortified. Was this some kind of Aussie joke—not a lobbing off of the head of the tall poppy, but a total uprooting of it and a trampling down of the soil to ensure that nothing of the kind ever flowered in that spot again? How could I translate this into Japanese? I knew that the Australian representative was dead serious.

"Oh," I said in Japanese, "we are still undecided on this."

The Japanese representative said, "I see," in English, turned away and joined his fellow delegates at the buffet table. It goes without saying that he had understood the Australian's English perfectly. I could write a book about "The Diplomacy of Deliberate Mistranslation."

In fact, it was generally believed by the aging elites of Australia that they did not possess a high culture of their own, that culture filtered down to Australia from outside sources, overwhelmingly Anglophone, far away. Oh yes, there was the local ballet, and it was often world-class. But what value could it really have when compared to the "real thing," a night at the ballet in exciting London or marvellous New York? The only way we could compete, according to the ingrown-toenail logic of the times, was to imitate, and we had to admit that, on the odd occasion, one of our talented imitators did manage to leave and find a way into an artistic profession overseas where it really counted.

Theater, opera, museums and the like certainly did exist. But the England-adoring ladies and gentlemen of the cultural establishment saw them somehow not as a part of a genuinely Australian scene but rather as a transplanted artefact. I knew people who would go to the theater every night while visiting London but never bothered to see a single play at home. I heard critics, who, in the main, exhibited the worst features of the cultural cringe and thereby prolonged its influence, boasting about great Australian actors who had fled Australia to enrich the cultural life of foreign countries and saying in the very next breath, "There are no world-class actors in this country."

This was not, mind you, hypocrisy. These Australians were

simply unable to view their own country as anything but an appendage of another body, in some cases the British body, in others the American. They were fiercely proud of being Australian yet did not know how to encourage and support an Australian culture.

Now, long after the new nationalism has become old and Australia boasts a vibrant homegrown culture viewed in terms of its own derivation, it seems like this could hardly have been true. But this was the Australia that I saw for the first time more than four decades ago, the Australia that I decided to become a part of.

When it came to Australia's place in the world, Australians were naturally adamant, particularly when the subject turned to Asia and Japan, about their allegiance to the Anglo-American axis (as indeed they still are today, as fiercely and unapologetically as ever). Australians spoke often of the war, of the uncle who was imprisoned in Changi or the mate who died constructing the Thai-Burma Railway. They spoke of it in a different way from Americans. There was more bitterness in their voice, more rancor, less forgiveness, as if the Japanese race rather than the Japanese state had done this to them. Americans of the older generation had largely come to terms with Japan earlier and more thoroughly. We Australians are still claiming the Thai-Burma Railway as an essential part of our national heritage, as we do for Gallipoli and Vietnam, without making much effort to understand why we were in Singapore to be captured or in Turkey defending Britain or in Vietnam demonstrating undying loyalty to the United States of America. Being the eternal victim has become a core theme of our national narrative. And yet ensconced in that self-styled victimhood is a race-oriented combativeness that prevents us from coming to terms with our independent place in the world.

As for the young Australians of the times, they were celebrating the new nationalism with a new nationalistic art.

Theaters, such as the Nimrod in Sydney, and Melbourne's Australian Performing Group, also known as the APG at the Pram Factory, put the Australian accent on stage. Until then many Australian actors actually had trouble speaking Australian in front of an audience, another puzzling feature of the culture for the outsider, but, given the nature and depth of the cultural cringe, perfectly understandable at the time. Sydney theater made up in mild bourgeois self-criticism of society what it lacked in rich theatricality. Melbourne theater substituted a roughly hewn plank for polished boards and belted it all out, the radical new Aussie message: unabashed iconoclasm, political sideswiping and a gutsy feminism.

The latter style was bound to fade out, unfortunately, when Australia turned away from its brash new cultural iconoclasm, leaving the mainstream largely intact with its considered middle-class watered-down faux-soul-searching and its portrait of the downtrodden sulky Aussie male feeling sorry for himself in the sundrenched batter of suburbia.

As for me, an outsider if there ever was one, with my theatrical roots wrung from the plaintive and biting humor of Jewish family life through to Russian satire, Polish dream plays and Japanese schematic imagery, the Australian mainstream brand of naturalistic theater made little sense in my mind and less impact on my heart. Yet it was no accident that when, in January 1980, I was to abandon stability in favor of insecurity—that is, leave the university life for the theater life—I drifted to Melbourne and not to Sydney. Melbourne had the contradictions, the polemics and the theatrical confrontations that I naively thought I could enhance in my plays and meld into a life in the theater.

23

The Dialect Barrier

It was the early seventies when I had arrived in Canberra and had just begun to familiarize myself with the fundamentals of Australian culture. All of the literature that I had come to love until then seemed unknown to Australians, and I was unfamiliar with the works that Australians kept, like bibles, on their bedside tables. I wanted to talk with friends about authors Hamsun, Celine and Gombrowicz, and they thought I was referring to a law firm for assisted migrants. I brought up Sakaguchi Ango and Dazai Osamu, two iconoclastic Japanese writers, not Subaru and Toyota, not even sushi and teriyaki. I had never read a line by D. H. Lawrence, an author who spent some weeks in Australia and thanks to them inspired dozens of doctoral theses that took considerably longer to compose. The ignorance was mutual: I lacked a British education or, at the time, the fervor for British culture necessary to be a literate Australian.

So I delved into volume after volume of Australian literature, Australian history, Australian geography, Australian biography, Australian botany and Australian zoology. One day a friend visiting my flat in Canberra took a book from the shelf and said, "Who wrote a play called Australian Frogs?" He was shocked to see that it really was a book about *Australian frogs*. I quickly went into my study and, out of intense embarrassment, clapped an article that I was reading into my top drawer, a study on "The Cloacal Temperature of the Western Australian Bobtailed Skink."

But it was the infernal Australian language, not that country's culture, that was continually defeating me. I was finding the dialect barrier harder to breach than the language barrier, even when such difficult languages as Japanese, Polish and Russian had presented that barrier. To this day, I think that there can be almost as much misunderstanding and discord occurring between speakers of different dialects of the same language as there is between those of different languages.

One day a telephone call came in to the office of the Department of Japanese at the Australian National University.

"Hello, this is Merise Cochis," said a pleasant female voice. "We are looking for someone, perhaps a student, to do a tour guide job for some Japanese tourists. Is there anyone there who might be interested?"

I asked Ms. Cochis to hold the line and went to the students' common room.

"Hey," I said to a group of some ten students, "there's a lady called Merise Cochis on the phone and she wants to know if any of you wants to do a job guiding some Japanese around town."

"What was her name?" asked one of the students.

"Cochis, I think. Merise Cochis."

One of our better students stood up and took the call that, to my intense embarrassment, had been from the bus company, "Murray's Coaches."

If the reader finds this amusing, I defy them, whether native Australian, new Australian or not even remotely Australian, to produce a sonogram or other some such phonological representation of the two words in question and prove to me—who after all was a student of the father of modern phonetics, the great Roman Jacobson—that there is any difference whatsoever in the Australian pronunciation of the sound of "Merise Cochis" and "Murray's Coaches."

You see, I even learned to be hurtfully defensive—one of our quainter Australian national characteristics.

24

The Reappearance of Rose and the Emu that Flew

Family often follows in the migrant's footsteps. At least it seemed to in my family. Everywhere I moved on this planet, my parents followed . . . and within weeks! Oh, not to live. They would not ever contemplate life outside the world's greatest democracy.

They visited the Soviet Union not long after I did; they were in London and Paris soon after I arrived in 1967; they saw me in Norway when I went there with my first wife in 1970; and they came all the way from Los Angeles to Canberra in 1972, bringing with them my suddenly wonderful Aunt Rose.

Jewish relatives are truly special: they move from being ostracized on grounds of purported insult to being re-embraced as if nothing had ever happened, which it probably didn't anyway. It's no wonder that the first person to think up the theory of relativity was a Jew.

Aunt Rose greeted me in the lobby of the Kythera Motel on Northbourne Avenue in Canberra with that gaping kiss, her mouth open like that of the huge face at the entrance of Sydney's Luna Park. (I had made the mistake of ordering a "cot" for her, which is an American English word for a bed but, of course, is a crib in British and Australian English. At 72, she had good reason to complain, on the first night, about Australian bedding.)

Not knowing where to take them in Canberra, which at the time was a sleepy capital of about 170,000 people, I drove to the nature reserve at Tidbinbilla where they could see, in one natural setting, some of the famous native Australian animals. Aunt Rose, sadly, was not interested in famous native Australian animals. In fact, she wasn't interested in animals at all.

But my Aunt Rose, bless her dear swollen heart, had been impressed upon entering, despite my pleading to stay out, the emu enclosure at Tidbinbilla, even though the sign on the wire fence explicitly read, "Closed. Emus breeding."

"Leave me alone, will ya? Would I harm an emu?" she said. "Don't answer, it's not a question."

Of course, she wouldn't harm an emu. She had never even seen an emu. She didn't even know what an emu was. And she pronounced it "eh-moo" to boot. To be fair to Aunt Rose, however, it was not her boisterous personality or her painfully, if barely subdued chutzpah that made history that hot November 1972 day inside the confines of the emu enclosure at the Tidbinbilla Nature Reserve in the environs of Canberra. It was more, I should say, her startling presence itself as she opened the gate and stepped into the enclosure with two large slices of rye bread in her manicured hand to feed the emus. The emus, about eight of them, no doubt exhausted from breeding, gingerly approached this exotic mammal from another land and, I dare say to all appearances, another planet. Aunt Rose was dressed in a knee-length pink skirt, red and blue rayon blouse, sporting, under her wide-brim sunhat, the most gaudy pair of rhinestone-studded sunglasses ever sold by J.C. Penney. She looked like a Miami Beach version of Edna Everage sans gladiolus, armed with a temperament so brazen that it would have sent that brash gentile Australian Dame rushing back home to London for cover.

And this is what those jaded emus did when Aunt Rose outstretched her puffy fingers, blood pooled in them for years by rings that would not come off till the day she died, to offer them perfectly good rye bread, probably kosher, and brought all the way from Los Angeles. (Dear Reader, I swear to you that this is not fiction. I wish you had been there.) The head emu raised its head, took a good hard stare at Aunt Rose, then promptly pirouetted on the scrub and headed for the hills as fast as its legs would take it. The other emus followed, and I swear, at least one of them had, for a moment or two, both of its legs entirely off the ground. For the first time in the history of the black or white settlement of Australia, the flightless emu flew; and it was all thanks to my Aunt Rose, who passed away in late 1990 with my dad commenting, "And it didn't happen a moment too soon."

What is family, if not an inseparable fusing of the farcical and the tragic? I can hear my dear departed aunt say, "Don't answer. It's not a question."

25

Swimming with Judith Wright and Platypuses in the Poetry Capital of Australia

The Japanese word *soboku* seems to define at least one overriding characteristic of life in Canberra in those days. *Soboku* means "unspoiled simplicity."

People from the larger Australian cities who were posted to

jobs in the public service or found themselves at the university in the nation's capital generally complained about this "artificial" city. If they were from Sydney they would waste no time shooting up Northbourne Avenue on a late Friday afternoon for what was then a four-and-a-half-hour to five-hour drive home (now, all highway, it takes three). Those unfortunate temporary residents who hailed from Melbourne or points more distant had to content themselves with what they universally considered "the dreaded Canberra weekend." Nothing to do, hence artificial. No billboards, little or no neon, no signs on restaurants or shops larger than the size permitted by the National Capital Development Commission (NCDC), the suppressor, in their eyes, of spontaneous fun.

It did not matter that Canberra is the most beautifully and meticulously planned city in Australia and that its closeness to the bush alone negates the artificial label, as if foul air, clogged streets, and the need to be streetwise in order to avoid crime somehow makes a place "natural." For me Canberra provided the best possible introduction to the culture of the Australian landscape, since Australia's culture, like Japan's, is intimately bound up with the lay and look and feel of the land.

In the early 1970s, Canberra was, for one thing, the poetry capital of Australia. Poet Judith Wright moved to the Limestone Plains from Queensland where she had been fighting the reactionary premier, Joh Bjelke-Petersen, and his oil drillers on the Great Barrier Reef. Her homebred radicalism and her commitment to the Aboriginal cause when it was still not a popular one, particularly in Queensland, made me feel like I was back living in Eastern Europe, where writers felt compelled by their calling to have their say in the polemic against crass bureaucracy, invidious government policy and biased folkways.

"Would you ever leave Australia if things went from bad to worse?" I asked her on one of several trips to her property at Edge, some ten kilometers outside Braidwood, where she had built a house and settled.

"I often feel like I should leave Australia," she replied. "I've thought of going to New Zealand."

Though she despaired of the political reaction against Prime Minister Gough Whitlam's far-reaching reforms that had set in during the second half of the seventies, you could hardly believe that she would abandon Australia, for she was as intimately attached to her burnt Australian soil and translucent sky as Anna Akhmatova was to the river winding through her beloved northern Russian city of St. Petersburg and the fairy white light of its summer nights.

After the sudden dismissal of Prime Minister Whitlam by the Governor General in November 1975, Judith seemed alternately despondent and fighting mad over the political and social situation in Australia. She had values concerning the environment that long preceded movements to achieve them in the country. She taught me the names of native plants that I saw for the first time while staying overnight at Edge. She became livid when we came upon a carcass of a kangaroo, evidently shot by a trespassing hunter. She chided me for picking through the mud of an uprooted gum—was I looking for gold? There were fragments of pottery and bottles from the nineteenth century strewn about the bush on her property.

We all stripped down to our happy birthday suits and swam beside two platypuses in the river that traversed Edge, "we" all being my ex-wife Solrun, Judith, Judith's daughter Meredith, who was a student of mine (and is now a prize-winning translator), and Meredith's partner at the time. The platypuses swiftly disappeared at the sight of stark white intruders.

The days spent at Edge were marvelous ones, the hospitality was warm and the conversations enlightening, just as days had been for me in Russia, Poland and Japan.

The same delight and enlightenment came from occasions in the company of another Canberra poet, David Campbell. David was a big man with wide bony features. In photographs, he looks like a stone-faced Boris Pasternak: indestructible. He was a superb reader of his own poetry. I shut my eyes and envisioned Mayakovsky. No, not only Mayakovsky. He could be the Edward Lear of the Limestone Plains. I will never forget his reading of his long poem about an unexpected visit to his home in Australia by the Queen of England and the Queen Mother and how he bedded down between them. Titled "The Australian Dream" it ends like this:

A hand touched mine and the Queen said, "I am
Most grateful to you, Jock. Please call me Ma'am."

David Campbell lived not far outside Canberra on a hilly family property adjacent to the old road to Captain's Flat. Though he was born on a station outside Adelong in the beautiful rocky country of the Monaro District, his family, he told me, had been associated with Canberra for many decades, and the inner-city suburb of Campbell had been named after one of his relatives.

To my taste, he may be the greatest Australian poet, though I doubt that many would go that far in their appraisal, perhaps choosing Judith Wright instead. He could instantaneously switch from a one-line quip to an expansive lyric. His metaphors are startling: a forest grows from a single tree "with orchids at its heels." What could be said more simply and be more revealing about Australian nature than his description of Eleven Mile Creek in Victoria's Kelly country?

Four eagle-nests in one tree:
A country rich in poverty.

I stayed out at his farm off the road to Captain's Flat, and he visited me at my home in the Canberra suburb of Aranda. He was always spontaneously warm. He was fascinated by the poetry of Russia's Silver Age, particularly Mandelstam's. (When I gave a talk at ANU on that subject, he came to it with another wonderful Canberra poet, Rosemary Dobson.) In 2007, a park was opened in Gungahlin in the Australian Capital Territory dedicated to the memory of David, known as "the poet of the Monaro." Mullion Park is named after a beautiful long poem he wrote in 1956, "The Miracle of Mullion Park."

With Judith, David, Rosemary and the celebrated poet A.D. Hope living in or near Canberra, we had going a regular Moscow on the Mononglo. At least that is the way I saw it (surely no one else shared this particular vision). I wallowed in the intoxicating atmosphere and wanted to be a small part of this scene from the beginning.

I marveled at every leaf-curling spider I saw, and, as I lay down on the dampening grass of my house in Aranda at night, counted meteors as they traversed constellations I had not seen as a child. I could believe that the spider webs floating in the air over my backyard grass were truly a part of the Veil Nebula, even as I reached up to the sky to grab them.

Australia stirred my imagination in the same way that Japan had—in the *sensations* that they conjured in me. I was discovering elemental things around me for the first time. That is one of the reasons why I started to think of myself as an Australian, as its secrets sunk into me. Such a thing is what poet Miyazawa Kenji called "the landscape of the heart." (There is a wonderful Japanese word—*jokei*—made up of the characters *nasake*, meaning compassion, kindness, sympathy, and *kei*, meaning view or scene. Combined they indicate a scene or a sight, but the connotation is that your inner sentiment and the external scene fuse inside you.)

There was another reason, one more clearly and painfully felt, why I began to consider myself an Australian. It had to do with politics.

26

The Dismissal of a Prime Minister

One of the first decisions of the new Prime Minister Whitlam in December 1972 was to free from incarceration the young conscripted men who had refused to fight in Vietnam. After America's brutal Christmas bombings of Hanoi and Haiphong that year, Deputy Prime Minister Jim Cairns denounced, in the strongest terms, the "maniac" moves of Richard Nixon who, Cairns said, acted "with the mentality of thuggery."

My country, the United States of America, had deployed 100 B-52s, equal in sorties to 4,000 bombers in World War II, in raids that would, in Secretary of State Henry Kissinger's words, "break every window in Hanoi." They may have broken the windows, but they did not break the will of the people of North Vietnam. I listened to the report of Jim Cairns's message on my kitchen radio with tears streaming down my face. Could this be the same country I had landed in a mere four and a half months earlier? This was a demonstration of how very quickly the esprit of a nation can change.

When, in 1972, the Labor Party won power after twenty-three years in the wilderness of opposition, victory picnics were held in Canberra's many parks. I watched these committed picnickers while living on the edge of a park, the Pine Break, near the center of the city.

Academics and public servants, ordinarily the cadres of social lethargy in the Canberra community, came together under the tall pines that were planted some sixty years earlier, when the city was established, to soften the force of the gales that sweep through Canberra. The picnickers stood in tight packs drinking rough red wine from flagons and casks in plastic cups, brushing away the flies with the hand that held the quiche, dancing on one leg then the other as they spoke, ecstatically, of a new beginning for their country. I watched close-by from my window. I walked out and stood near them, unable to understand many of the references but sharing in their excitement.

When, three years later, on November 11, 1975, the prime minister was dealt an uppercut by Governor General John Kerr, who was to suffer for his arrogance in dismissing a democratically elected government before becoming himself a broken and forgotten man, I was incensed. In fact, I was shocked to see how incensed I was. Had Australia's fate come to matter to me that deeply in three years' time?

In the ensuing weeks, I demonstrated in front of Parliament House, holding up placards made at home. Was this the kind of personal participation in politics that I had been too young or too timid to throw myself into a decade earlier in my own country? Was I making up for lost time and suppressed inaction?

The news of the dismissal of Gough Whitlam's government came as I was lying in bed recovering from a reaction to a cholera shot in preparation for a trip to Indonesia and Japan. I started talking to myself, cursing the bastards who had attacked Australia's most progressive prime minister, sitting up in bed banging my fist on the mattress while grasping my swollen arm in pain. I decided then and there to become an Australian citizen.

On December 13, 1975, when the forced election was held and Gough Whitlam was voted out of power, I was sitting in the Ichikawa home of my dear friend, playwright Inoue Hisashi. Around the table were a few actors, including Ozawa Shoichi, showman, vaudevillian and brilliant character actor in the cinema. The television in the corner of the room was on, as all televisions in corners of Japanese rooms were at the time. The nighttime variety program was interrupted for a newsflash, and Gough Whitlam's face appeared on the screen.

"Isn't that Australia or something?" said one of the actors.

"Wait!" I exclaimed.

They all stared at me as the news bulletin was read out. Whitlam had been roundly defeated and the "conservative Liberal Party," as the announcer said, was to form the new government.

I must have been sitting at that table for some moments, face down and chin in palm. When I looked up everyone was still staring at me.

"It's hard to believe," said Ozawa, "that someone can get so upset by a thing as trivial as an election result."

In Japan people in the arts back then would not have wasted their time discussing something as "banal" as politics. The politicians have their world and we have ours. To deign to talk about theirs would be tantamount to celebrating the importance of naturally corrupt men.

How could I convey to them my admiration for a prime minister who in a span of only three years had managed to introduce affordable state-subsidized health care for all people living in Australia, tuition-free tertiary education, legal aid for those who could not afford to hire a lawyer, and the orienting of Australian foreign policy toward Asia? When in 1973 the Australian government had purchased Jackson Pollack's "Blue Poles" for the new National Gallery in Canberra, the predictable outrage by the philistines in the media came down hard on the prime minister for allegedly wasting the taxpayers' money on "such elitist rubbish." (I never really understood this Australian usage of the word "elitist," which reflects an ingrained suspicion of anything intellectual or arty by an uneducated punditry pandering to what they take to be mass taste. They make the mistake of equating their own tabloid tastes with those of the public.)

Whitlam responded to the flak by choosing the painting to adorn the front of the prime minister's official Christmas card. Incidentally, the taxpayer has not done too badly for the purchase price of $1.3 million. The painting is now estimated to be worth more than $200 million.

For my first four years in Australia, I was an American, chided by bus drivers for my accent, serenaded by butchers who had been in the war (one butcher sang me Judy Garland's 1946 hit song "On the Atchison, Topeka and the Santa Fe"; I can still hear him crooning "Do you hear that whistle down the line?" as he trimmed the rind off my pork chops). But I was mentally fleeing the country of my birth and wanted to be considered an Australian playwright.

I supported new trends in theater and literature, and soon found myself writing theater reviews for the national daily *The Australian* and book reviews for *The Canberra Times*. Later I was to write for the *The Sydney Morning Herald*, *The National Times*, *The Age*, *Vogue Australia*, *Theatre Australia* and any number of other publications. I urged Australians not to be satisfied that "we can do American and English plays as good as they can in New York and London." This was the ultimate aspiration of most Australian creative people at the time: not to be distinctive or better than, but simply to be "as good as."

When I mentioned the name George Wallace in my ANU seminar discussion of Japanese comedy in order to compare it with Australian comedy, my students, without exception, knew the name of the governor of Georgia but not one had heard of the great Australian film comedian of the same name. I had been unused to a country so lacking in self-knowledge, one that related exquisitely to the outside while remaining ignorant of what it possessed at home.

I was once introduced as the "Polish-Jewish-American" playwright, another time as the "Polish-Jewish-Hawaiian" playwright. A leading director said in a public meeting, after I suggested that we should be presenting more plays from countries other than the U.S. and Britain, "But you know, Roger, that your tastes are very esoteric."

That's it, I thought: I am an esoteric Polish-Jewish-Hawaiian—what could be worse than that? I suppose they saw me driving home in my Subaru—"the Jap with Zap" as the Australian ad went—and reaching into my Westinghouse fridge for a kosher pickle-and-pineapple sandwich on Langendorf bread. These images were being saddled on me by a country that I was desperately trying to slip into, not exactly unnoticed, and these became my disqualifiers as a true-blue Aussie as he was circa 1975.

You had only one choice at the time. Either you supported your new nationalism in the arts completely, which meant opposing outside influences even from unintroduced places like Japan and Eastern Europe, or you ran the risk of being looked upon as a meddling Colonel Blimp if you were a Pom or an obnoxious Yank if you were an American, someone who had come to Australia fully expecting gratitude for simply being there and an everlasting reputation for staying on. As it was, I wasn't expecting either. I just wanted to be counted among the people who were to become my fellow countrymen and women.

27

The Two-headed Calf Comes to Alice Springs

In August 1973, my translation of Stanislaw Ignacy Witkiewicz's play, which he wrote as a result of the trip to Australia in 1914, *The Metaphysics of the Two-Headed Calf*, was produced by the Totem Theatre of Alice Springs and, thanks to a grant from the then Australia Council, I traveled to Australia's Red Centre to see it.

I found in The Alice, as the locals called it, a town that, in more ways than one, was probably not unchanged since the time of the Polish playwright's visit to Australia and the publication of my precious official guidebook.

Alice Springs, August 1973. Heavy rains that winter had brought flowers and frogs out of the ground that seemed to have been waiting years to greet the light of day. The light in the outback there was more intense than anywhere I had been, the clearest air a lens that allowed you to see perfectly all the way to the desert's red horizon.

But the atmosphere in this closed-off little town was less than transparent. I took a Pioneer Bus tour of the local sights. Pioneer was part of the then Ansett transportation empire. As we drove around the town, the bus driver, in company uniform—short pants, high white socks, black leather shoes, a singlet and tight cap—added his personal insights through his pin mic, pointing out as we passed a group of Aboriginal men standing beside a car that "they probably stole it" and that the new hospital "admitted Aboriginal children first . . . your sons and daughters couldn't get in there even though it's you and me bloody paying for it in the end."

Indigenous Australians were suffering from the highest incidence of infant mortality in the world. Many of them lived in and around the dry Todd River bed, the local lockup was full of them, and some of them painted pictures given by jailers to white agents who sold them in the well-patronized little galleries of Alice Springs. I was interviewed on the main Alice Springs radio station about the play and my visit, telling the young female interviewer, who hailed from Sydney, about the comments of the bus driver.

"If you mention that on air," she said, putting on the earphones before we began, "I lose my job."

Of course, under those circumstances, I couldn't mention it.

There were centenary celebrations at Uluru over the "discovery," in August 1873, of Ayers Rock. In those days the present name, Uluru, was unknown to white Australians, who actually believed that they were the first real people to happen upon this magnificent monolith, one of the most awesome objects I have seen in my life, described by its nineteenth-century white "discoverers" with the trite throwaway epithet, "a giant pebble growing out of the ground."

Jet-black cockatoos with bright red patches under their wings circled a cloudless sky, then perched on the branches of the bleached-white ghost gums; blankets of brown, sienna and what looked like burnt gray soil covered the mountains; and the most wonderful insects and tiny plants were at your feet if you crouched down low enough to see them. Biblical Adam, I thought, would have had a field day crawling on his belly in this desert garden!

The Totem Theatre production of *The Metaphysics of the Two-Headed Calf*, a fine re-creation of the bizarre encounters that take place in that 1914 Polish drama, was written up in *The Centralian Advocate* with an accompanying article about Witkiewicz, the first about him to appear in Australia. The article's headline called him "The Father of Modern Theatre." (The most respected Polish newspaper, the independent Krakow-based *Tygodnik Powszechny*, later featured a full-page piece about the production and me with the headline "The Return of Witkiewicz to Australia." The article was written by Jerzy Turowicz, the editor of *Tygodnik Powszechny*. Jerzy's family had known Witkiewicz personally, and I saw two portraits of his mother painted by the playwright/artist when I visited his Krakow flat in 1977.)

When I returned from The Alice to Canberra the canvas of my

sandshoes was permeated with red dust, dyed the bright color of the outback that, no matter how many times the shoes went through the washing machine, refused to wash out. It was as if the color had burnt my own skin and seeped into the marrow of my bones. That, only a year after arriving in the country, started to make me feel indelibly Australian.

28

I Become a BIG BLACK MARK Playwright

My plays started to have productions, two of them, *Bones* and *Ice* at La Mama in Melbourne, and several in Canberra, including *The Covenant of the Rainbow* and *Joe's Encyclopedia*, which has been produced in a number of Australian cities, as well as Singapore and Tokyo. Not that these brought either recognition or great financial reward. The reviews in Melbourne were positive, but those in Canberra damning, true to the form of the Great Aussie Rule of Reverse Perspective for Artists: the closer you are to home the smaller you must be made to appear. The Japanese proverb "It's dark under the lighthouse" applies to Australia with a greater aptness than to Japan.

In those early productions in Canberra I marvelled if there was anybody in the audience I didn't know. The first production of *Joe's Encyclopedia*, for instance, ran for seventeen performances with total audience attendance over the run a mere 311.

"Well, at least you broke 300," consoled a friend.

"Seventeen of those people were me!" I said.

On a trip back to Los Angeles in 1978, for which I required a tourist visa, to attend my father's seventy-fifth birthday, Sid Brown, one of dad's closest friends, asked me how much money I was making on my plays "over there."

"Well, Sid, twenty, sometimes, um, thirty."

He whistled through his teeth and shook his head.

"Well, mazeltov, boychik. Twenty thou, thirty thou ... it's a lot of *gelt* (Yiddish—money) under the belt."

"No, Sid. Twenty dollars. Thirty dollars. But an Australian dollar is worth more than an American one."

"An Australian dollar is worth more than an American one? How can that be?"

My parents were proud Jewish parents. They had put together an album of the clippings and reviews I had sent them over the past five-odd years. There was one strange thing about this album, however. Big black marks appeared on the articles to make some words unreadable.

I was Roger Pulvers, experimental BIG BLACK MARK playwright, or the BIG BLACK MARK playwright and translator Pulvers.

Had they taken the liberty of softening the critical damnation of my plays by marking out words and phrases like "second-rate" and "inaccessible to most audiences"? It was simpler than that. I realized that my parents had, in every case, crossed out the word "Australian."

"So what's all these big marks?" asked Doris, Sid's wife.

"Oh well," said my mother, "it's nothing. How about some more chopped liver, Doris?"

"It says Australian," I blurted out. "I've become an Australian citizen."

What followed was, I believe, the biggest pregnant pause in the long and often tense span of the history of Jewish-American conversation. In a single slip of the tongue, I had turned the mood of my parents' home from a Neil Simon comedy to an all-Jewish version of *Waiting for Godot* in which, in this case, Godot had appeared as the prodigal son who had committed the ultimate crime of changing the color of his passport from olive green to navy blue.

The pause continued. Even Samuel Beckett would have hollered, "Come on, so what's next?"

My mother took us out of our excruciating labor.

"Roger's bought a house down there."

"Oh," said Sid Brown, nodding, "if he bought a house down there then that's a different story, why didn't you say so? Of course, he's become an Australian if he's bought a house."

A few years later Sid Brown, who was in the barrel business, died of a heart attack on a trip to Salt Lake City.

"If only he had known," Doris said to my mother, "that he was going to die in a place like Salt Lake City, he would have thought it the funniest thing in the world."

29

Personal Happiness

When my study leave came up in 1977, the Nigerian author Wole Soyinka had been kind enough to invite me to spend it in Nigeria, basing myself at The University of Ife (now Obafemi Awolowo University) where he taught. I was to work with him in the theater. But the invitation from the university could not be arranged on time, and I left Canberra for Stockholm in May, then Oslo, Warsaw, Tokyo and southern Okinawa, not returning to Australia until January of the next year.

In the autumn of 1977, I wrote my first novel, *The Death of Urashima Taro*, which was published first in Japanese translation then in the English original, a pattern that I have repeated with virtually all of my novels. I lived through a period of mild neurosis, putting a strain on Inoue Hisashi and his wife, in whose house I was staying, though, ever kind, Hisashi later told me he was totally unaware of any difference in my behavior. (The Inoues were going through a trying period of their own and were subsequently, as was I, to divorce.)

Toward the end of 1977, a man phoned me at the Inoues'. He was editor-in-chief of *Newsweek*'s international edition.

"Listen, I just happened to be in Tokyo and I read one of your articles, a review of the Tokyo production of *Equus*, and could we meet to discuss the possibility of your writing for *Newsweek*?"

I had seen four productions of *Equus*, in Tokyo, Sydney, Warsaw and Oslo, and had compared them in the article (they were virtually all alike) in the *Mainichi Daily News*.

We met for lunch at the old Foreign Correspondents' Club at Yurakucho in Tokyo, down the street from the American Pharmacy.

"How would you like to write up Japanese plays and films for Newsweek?" he said, waving to a waiter for attention.

The Japanese cultural presence was beginning to be felt around the world as it had been in the Meiji era (1868–1912).

"I'd love to. Thank you very much. But I don't live permanently in Japan."

"You don't live in Japan?"

"I live in Australia. I'm an Australian, actually, even though I sound like an American."

The waiter was now standing beside our table, impatient to take our order.

The instant I pronounced the word "Australian," though we were most certainly indoors, a cumulus cloud of a foreboding grayish color passed over the face of the international editor and he joined the waiter in looking impatiently around the room. I knew precisely what was on his mind: Why do I waste my time with people like this? "Japan" was becoming the magic word in copy coming from American journalists' typewriters; "Australia" rarely made it as far as the ribbon.

"But nothing happens in Australia to write about," he said, as if he knew all about it.

"But it does! There's great culture happening all the time now. There have been at least two film renaissances in the last five years, not to mention a few reformations in literature and enlightenments in the theater. Really, I could write up some great stories for you."

"Yeah? Like what?"

By now the waiter was gone and my chances for lunch were rapidly fading away.

"Well, the Adelaide Festival is coming up next March."

"What's Adelaide? What do you mean, Adelaide?"

I remember being struck by the absurdity of a world in which the names Cincinnati, Milwaukee and Little Rock were known to most people but few had heard of that most lovely of cities of culture, gardens and excellent wine, Adelaide. (Since then both Australian culture and the city of Adelaide have become much more well-known around the world.)

"The arts festival is enormous, like the ones in Edinburgh and Europe."

He stood up. I must have been convincing on one point at least.

"Okay, I'll pay you fifty dollars for an article on that."

When sums from the past are brought up in books, the author often reminds the reader that they represented much more in those days than in these, as I did with the value of the jewels my great-uncle Sidney lost. Not so in this case. Fifty dollars for a long article in a magazine like *Newsweek* was a paltry fee in the late 1970s in anybody's bankbook.

"Is that fifty dollars American or fifty dollars Australian?" I asked.

"Oh, American of course."

Should I inform him, as I had informed Sid Brown, that fifty dollars Australian was more than fifty dollars American? I didn't want to hurt his feelings. I stood up, shook his hand and said, "A hundred American." It was equivalent to the fee that I was getting for an article at the time in the *Mainichi Daily News*.

He nodded okay, caught the eye of a foreign correspondent, smiled and left me at the table with my glass of ice water on it.

I wrote up the Adelaide Festival in March 1978, sending the article to New York through the "Keeper of the Public Telex" at Adelaide's central post office (no personal faxes in those days), receiving my copy of the magazine (with a photo of Patty Hearst on the cover) and my one hundred American dollars, but never so much as another word from the international editor.

I returned to Australia from Okinawa in mid-January 1978 after nine months "OS," as we used to call "overseas," determined to quit my tenured academic job and become a fulltime BIG BLACK MARK playwright, to do something, however modest, to get the message out that Australia was not a secret well kept by an Anglo-Celtic group of writers, critics and cringing pundits but a country with a burgeoning multiethnic character.

I had taken to the Australian way of life and fiercely considered myself a native son. I bristled when anybody from the outside knocked my country and I derided Britons and Americans with a woodchip on my shoulder as big as a plank. I pretended to mourn the deaths of Les Darcy, Aussie boxer from Maitland, and Phar Lap, Aussie horse (who was really from New Zealand) when the conversation turned to those icons of our cultural past. I didn't ask myself why I was caring about these two unfortunate creatures when I didn't give a fig for either boxing or horseracing. Because I was defending Australian culture! I was doing, in short, what many migrants do. I was over-identifying. I wrote a play about the American control of our defenses, setting it at a secret base in the desert. *Cedoona* was produced in Adelaide with the then unknown actors Colin Friels, Judy Davis and Mel Gibson in it. I created a clash between Australians and Americans in my play *Australia Majestic*, set in the spectacular Blue Mountains Art Deco Hydro Majestic Hotel, which during the war had been converted into a U.S. Army hospital. And after my musical, *Bertolt Brecht Leaves Los Angeles* and my translation/adaptation of August Strindberg's *Miss Julie* went on at the Playbox Theatre, I left academia for good to move down south, to that city that some lovingly called the Budapest of the Southern Hemisphere, namely Melbourne.

It frequently happens in the lives of artists, performers and writers that professional fulfillment increases as personal happiness declines. Mine was one such case. My personal life was in disarray, each day providing a new unplanned shock. I had fallen in love with Susan, and this was to cause much pain to three people. The bitterness between me and my former wife remained until her death from a heart attack in 2009, and I have only myself to blame for the awful rift. No matter how difficult it is for the person who leaves, the one who feels rejected is always the victim deserving of sympathy. It was, I would like to think, the only time in my life that I have ever done something knowing that it would cause suffering to a person. But perhaps I am closing my eyes to other transgressions that I am unaware of.

So, as my career flourished, my private life deteriorated, leaving Susan, my wife-to-be, and my soon to be ex-wife Solrun in a state of painful uncertainty, an awful state for them both brought about solely by me. I made two trips to Japan, saw old friends like Inoue Hisashi and radical playwright Kara Juro, with whom a relationship of great warmth had developed. This was just before Kara was to go off to Paris in search of material for his filmscript about the murderer Sagawa Issei. The script turned into a novel that won him the prestigious Akutagawa Prize. (I had read it in manuscript form and published a review of it the morning of the day it won the prize.)

Was I testing my feelings for Japan again as a place to live? I had been an expatriate American and perhaps it was now time to be an expatriate Australian. If so, I would be doing something very typical for an Australian artist or writer, taking the best inspiration from my country then dumping it for more artistically welcoming shores.

My career had its successes—such as the productions of plays by Sam Shepard that I directed at the Adelaide Festival in March 1982 and my musical for large puppets, *General MacArthur in Australia*, which toured from Melbourne and Canberra to the Drama Theatre at the Sydney Opera House—and those peculiar defeats in the arts where home-grown power brokers of the opinion circuit stop you in your tracks by deeming you "outside the mainstream of *our* culture" (the italics here *are* mine).

I had applied four times for a writer's grant of aid from what was by then called the Australia Council for the Arts, and four times was turned down. One board member told a mutual friend that I was "too radical" to get a grant. This was when my lush academic salary had become a dream of days long gone by and I was living off restaurant reviews written for *The Age* and Susan's student nurse's salary in a flat provided by Royal Melbourne Hospital.

Then, a letter arrived from film director Oshima Nagisa. He was planning to make a film called *Merry Christmas, Mr. Lawrence* and would I be his assistant?

I stood in the middle of our little flat holding the letter like a person trapped in a Vermeer painting. The letter was written, of course, in Japanese, but for some reason, as it is when a piece of personal news is either too good to trust or too unthinkably bad to accept, I was motionless for minutes, rereading the letter, perhaps afraid to understand it. What if it actually said that Oshima wanted me to introduce him to someone who could be his assistant? Susan came to my side and jolted me back into real time.

There would be no need to become an Australian exile in the way that I had been an American one. I had a country "to go back to," that is, Japan. I had come to see that I was not going to fit into the mold in Australia had I stayed there. It wasn't only a matter of not feeling moved when reading the stories of Henry Lawson or not racing the pulse for a Norman Lindsay nude or a Melbourne Cup heat. Every culture has its mainstream and its popular culture, and much within that can be genuinely dramatic and of lasting value.

But the Australian mainstream, especially in theater, was and still is a naturalistic one, marking a culture founded on matter, a dearth of spirituality (which we could have derived from the culture of our indigenous people), and an absence of wonder for the immense chaotic world inside us. Had we Australians incorporated the indigenous culture into our own "national" one, we might have had the best of both worlds. At best, our down-to-earth culture gave us freedom from the numbing post-modern rhetoric that characterizes much conceptual art in Europe and the United States. At worst, it denied the human need for illusion. Such is one legacy of colonialism, which lets go of culture last.

What was drawing me back to Japan in 1982 was not just work on a film and surely not the promise of a shining career. I knew that

with the slate wiped clean again I would soon turn forty, no time
to start over for the umpteenth time. But I wanted to test myself in
a culture where the aesthetic mainstream was not naturalism and
male-value oriented, where the logic of design that gained ground
in the mind was that of a pure and exquisite beauty. That beauty in
Japan is both eternal and temporal at the same time. I thought of
Ishikawa Takuboku's tanka about a train:

> *I hear a distant whistle.*
> *It lingers in the air before vanishing*
> *Into woods.*

I could "see" the whistle of that Japanese train lingering in my
mind's eye as I looked up at the sky in Australia on my last night
there in 1982. The sky was covered in a thin white film of cloud,
and I pictured myself wetting my finger, reaching up to the sky
and making a mark from one horizon to the other. I felt that in ten
years living and writing in Australia, I had made a mark, but only
one that I alone could see.

THE JAPANESE IN ME

30

England's Friend in the Far East

People from the West had been coming to Japan in droves for a century after the forced opening that brought the country out of its long period of national isolation. The year after my arrival, 1968, saw celebrations of the Meiji Centenary, the milestone anniversary of the founding of Japan as a modern nation state. This was after I had lived in Europe and left the United States, and before I ever thought of moving to Australia. I was twenty-three.

Westerners had brought with them myriad contradictory sentiments and eerie biases about Japan. These sentiments and biases found their way into hundreds of books in Western languages about Japan, forming what can only be called an encyclopedia of prejudice and exotica. What emerged from how "different" or "quaint" or "proudly belligerent" the Japanese purportedly were can be seen as a fascinating study not of Japan but of the West.

Up to the outbreak of World War II, many people from the West were desperately searching in Japan for spiritual things they felt lacking in their own countries, so it is no wonder that they found them there. The Japanese aspiration to become a powerful identity in Asia, just like the European nations they looked up to, was never understood by the West because its representatives would never permanently allow a non-white non-Christian nation to stand on footing equal to them in Asia or, for that matter, any part of the world.

As the Japanese transformed themselves from a poor and closed-off nation on the farthest edge of the Far East to a major industrial and military power, the people of the West, even those well disposed to the Japanese, were flummoxed. Why did this marvellous nation of basket weavers and exquisite craftsmen of lacquer and porcelain, this nation of the world's most gentle and demure ladies, this nation of the most polite and self-effacing gentlemen want to be a world power like us? The answer was simply the same answer it was for us: to ensure their long-term security through the acquisition of the natural resources they needed to sustain growth, increase wealth and expand empire. No, this was not the Japan that "we know and love."

However, as we look far back, we see that in Western eyes it was fine when the expansion of the Japanese state was accomplished at the expense of what was seen as the decadent and dying monarchy in Russia. And it was applauded when Japan gained hegemony over Formosa, today's Taiwan, and Korea between the years 1895 and 1910.

I have a lithograph from 1904 that portrays Mutsuhito, known posthumously as Emperor Meiji, in full military uniform astride a majestic horse whose front hooves are coming down hard on Korea and Formosa. At the top of the lithograph is the bold title: "England's Friend in the Far East."

Yet it wasn't to last long, this "friendship," when the hooves of the Japanese steed started trampling territory that was a part of Britain's empire. When Japan won victory in the Russo-Japanese War in 1905, the country was praised openly by people as diverse as lawyer Mohandas Karamchand Gandhi in South Africa, poet Rabindranath Tagore in India, soldier Mustafa Kemal Ataturk in Turkey, politician Sun Yat-sen in China and black activist W.E.B. DuBois in the United States. They had one thing in common: they were non-whites and they were or aspired to be leaders of non-European nations or ethnicities of people.

There is no doubt in my mind that historians of a future era will look back at the history of the world and credit the Japanese for being the first nation of people to demonstrate and prove that modernization was not a monopoly of the white Christian world. In that sense, the Japanese have been a beacon of progress for the entire developing world.

Tens of thousands of Chinese students came to study in Japan in the late Meiji and Taisho eras—roughly from 1890 until 1925—and the modernization of China today would have been unthinkable without the beacon of the Japanese as a shining example of progress. It is not surprising that today's Chinese leadership has adopted a road to development very similar to that taken by Meiji Japan: state-sponsored economic development and planning combined with military operations to secure the acquisition of natural resources and their safe transportation to the homeland. I hope their roadmap leads them to a different place from the one Japan ended up in the 1930s.

31

Quaint Japan, Belligerent Japan, Vanishing Japan, Regimented Japan

Back in the Meiji era, Japan appeared in Western eyes as if perennially lurking behind a mask or a fan or a beautifully decorated folding screen. Westerners believed that there existed something called "the real Japan," and that it was only just hiding out of sight. All you needed to do was to be lucky enough to steal some peeks behind the mask or fan or screen and you would be "one of the few fortunate foreigners privy to the secrets of the Japanese." Then you could easily find a publisher, introduce the "real" Japan to the West "for the very first time" and gain for yourself the right to interpret absolutely everything that transpired within those fog-bound shores.

For well over a century we had book after book "introducing the real Japan" to the outside world. Every Western novel set in Japan became a study of "the Japanese mind"; every glorified diary of a foreigner's years in the company of Japanese people chronicled encounters that were "typical of the nation." The hashed and rehashed exotica that inundated the West for decades created a gap in the perceived nature of the Japanese people in the West and their natural selves at home, a gap that turned into a dangerous and unbridgeable chasm as the Japanese military transformed itself into an imperial force that could rival the forces of the imperial nations of the West.

This gave rise to the concept of "the vanishing Japan." Japan "as we know it" was vanishing at a startling clip. Everything wonderful and praiseworthy about the country and its quaint ways was seen as being discarded in the name of a crude and out-of-character industrialization that was "bound to fail." Well into the 1980s, the notion that Japanese culture and the beauty of Japanese life were somehow "vanishing" was popular in the West. If all of this had truly been vanishing over the past century, it was nothing short of a miracle that there was anything left of the culture at all.

There was no need for me to think of Japan as having vanished. I knew absolutely nothing about the country and its people when I arrived in 1967. Yet, as I have written in my memoir of life in Japan, *If There Were No Japan*, I felt at home from the first moments I set foot in the country. It stood to reason that the Japanese were seen as "different" only if you were using your own customs, mores and lifestyle as the measure of what was standard. This was something that, thankfully, I had never done, despite being taught at home and in school that my country had created the world standard of democracy, the true model of freedom and the sole roadmap to the destination toward a good life. Perhaps it is this characteristic of my worldview—the complete absence of a cultural agenda—that has allowed me, on occasion, to enter the hearts of people in other countries.

After quaint Japan, vanishing Japan and belligerent Japan, once the Japanese had definitively lost the war to the U.S. and its allies in 1945 there appeared a number of other Japans. The old notion of the Japanese as a nation of imitators and the manufacturers of shoddy goods that had been first introduced to the world in the Meiji era was briefly revived. It comes as a startling revelation to young people around the world today that when I was a child in the 1950s "Made in Japan" was a symbol of cheap and untrustworthy materials and B-grade goods.

Then came "the Regimented Japan." We in the West all knew

that the Japanese were conformists, that they didn't possess the individualism that is in all of "us," and that they identified with their company more closely than they did with their families.

That the Japanese didn't display their individualism to the same open-ended extent that many people, but certainly not all, in the West do was true. (They keep it to themselves and their intimate circles.) That they expressed loyalty to their companies in ways that few in the West might do was also true. But did this mean that they were not as unique as each of "us" and that they personally loved their companies more than they did their spouse, children and parents? Of course, it didn't then, and it doesn't today. If American marines pledge their undying loyalty to the American armed forces, does that indicate that they love their job and their country more than they do their spouse and family? The two are not mutually exclusive in the United States and nor are they in Japan. The Japanese are not regimented in their life's choice: their private selves and public demonstrations of them differ from many people in the West. That's all it is: what you intend to show to others and what you decide to keep to yourself.

I was unaware of all these purported Japans as I was ignorant of what the people there were like. I identified with Lafcadio Hearn, the Greek-Irish journalist, translator and author who had come to Japan in April 1890 equally ignorant of the life of its people. But Hearn, at thirty-nine, was much older than I was when I first arrived, had never thoroughly learned to speak or read Japanese, and was one of the main perpetrators of the notion of the exotic Japan that was dazzling the world in his time.

I subsequently wrote a novel about his life in Japan, *The Dream of Lafcadio Hearn*. What fascinated me was his ability to absorb Japanese culture as if through the pores of his skin from the very first day of his arrival. I felt an affinity with this outsider who carried no Western or religious baggage with him, only his little suitcase, his wide-brim hat and his insatiable curiosity about anything growing deep in the subsoil of a culture.

32

Kyoto in the 1960s

In November of 1967, I moved from Tokyo to Kyoto to take up the lectureship at Kyoto Sangyo University, remaining there for five years.

What was Kyoto like in 1967?

In Tokyo, I had seen ex-soldiers dressed entirely in white hospital-like attire, some without an arm or a leg, standing or sitting in the precincts of a temple or shrine. Some played plaintive tunes on concertinas; others had a little dog beside them to garner the sympathy of passersby. Often the dog wore a little beanie or sported cheap plastic sunglasses to catch people's eyes. Those disabled veterans of World War II were begging for money from their compatriots—compatriots who wanted more than anything to forget they existed lest the guilt for sending them into battle remained with them.

These scenes were absent in Kyoto, and indeed disappeared shortly after that in Tokyo or any other Japanese city. (I had spent the spring of that year in France as an impoverished post-graduate student searching Paris for the cheapest place to have a hearty meal. I found it in the Club of the Association of Old Polish War Veterans. Being able to speak Polish, I felt right at home, though I was the only young person there, a lanky and cheery American among severely traumatized ex-servicemen. After all, the war had ended less than twenty-two years before then. You could get a great Polish meal at the club for five francs, the equivalent at the time of about one dollar. I can still see the poor war veterans, many of them in their forties but looking decades older, slouching over their meals. The hands of some of them shook so badly that all the soup in their spoons spilled before reaching their lips.)

Everyone in Kyoto, particularly outsiders both Japanese and foreign, would tell you that the city was only a shadow of its former magnificent self. In fact, this would continue to be said about Kyoto every decade right up to the present. It is a feature of the old "Vanishing Japan" concept, only here it is the ever-vanishing city of Kyoto. In actuality, the temples and gardens are still there, unchanged for centuries. The lovely dialect of its residents has not been swamped by *hyojungo*, the standard Japanese imposed on the nation by Tokyo and the Tokyocentric media. And the people of Kyoto are just as *haitateki,* or exclusionist, when it comes to accepting outsiders into their inner circle as they ever were. For better and worse, the spirit of Kyoto is pretty much the same today as it was in 1967, and I slip right back into the rhythms and social norms of the city when I am there.

33

I Am Mr. Higgins

The presence of America loomed large in Kyoto as it did all over Japan. This was an invisible presence permeating the entire non-traditional culture. Whenever comparisons were made with countries outside Japan, whether casual or studied, they were made primarily with the United States and its norms. It was common for little Kyoto children to scream out, *"Amerikajin da!"* ("It's an American!") when passing me on a street. All foreigners were assumed to be Americans.

Though I was still a citizen of the United States, I had ceased in my mind to be an American. I did not, however, have a clue as to what I was or was going to be instead. As with not knowing what I was going to "become" in terms of a calling in life, this mental statelessness did not bother me. I have always relished feeling at sea (so long as it didn't leave me in the doldrums for too long).

Yet by the spring of 1972, I was getting restless. I had published a book of short stories and a play, but my ambition to become an author of fiction and playwright could hardly be fulfilled if I stayed in Kyoto. The offices of all of the major publishers were located in Tokyo. There was no professional theater in Kyoto.

It was then that the invitation to teach Japanese language and literature at the Australian National University in Canberra appeared out of the blue. Perhaps, I thought, Australia had theaters. They were bound to have publishers. I would leave my beloved Kyoto and try to acquire a profession in writing for the page and stage. If it didn't work out, I could always come straight back "home" to Kyoto to teach and write.

Then a letter arrived from a director at NHK, the national broadcaster. They were going to produce a radio drama version of Nosaka Akiyuki's short story, "*Amerika hijiki*," and would I play the lead American role in it.

The *hijiki* in the title is a kind of edible seaweed that looks like black tea leaves when dried and shredded. The story is set in the immediate postwar years of the Allied Occupation. When some Japanese people open up a box of foodstuffs originating in the U.S., they mistake tea leaves for *hijiki*, hence the title.

Nosaka's short story dates from 1967 and accurately characterizes a certain Japanese servility that was manifest at the time of the Occupation toward the chief nation that defeated Japan in World War II. That mental servility continues in a more subdued form today. Until the 1980s, most Japanese had never met a foreigner. The word *gaijin*, or foreigner, then referred at that time solely to people of European origin. Asians and other non-whites were termed *gaikokujin*, a more formal form of *gaijin*. *Gaijin* effectively meant "Caucasian." (Now it is used to refer to non-Japanese of every nationality.)

I played Mr. Higgins, the stuck-up and bombastic American officer who is befriended by a young Japanese man named Toshio. Toshio spends his time trying to please Mr. Higgins with obsequious service and servile fawning to the American's every wish. Toshio remarks to himself that there is an American inside him. This made sense to me, for it was what I had seen in many Japanese people over the five years that I had lived in Kyoto. That

notion also corresponded to a similar complex in me: I had come
to feel that there was a Japanese living inside me.

34

I Face the Mountains—Speechless

It may have been strangely fortunate that I had not studied the
history or culture of Japan before living in the country, though this
is perhaps an incongruous thing to say for a person who has taught
the culture and literature of several countries for many years to
others. When I arrived, I had no preconceived notions of what
the people of Japan were like and entertained no misconceptions.
I had not bought into the interpretation of the Japanese national
ethos that I saw as a child in Hollywood war movies. Such
preconceived notions might have included the highly negative
ones that characterized the Japanese as dour, obsequious, lacking
in individuality and members of "a cruel race" to positive ones that
visualized them as genteel, demure and charmingly reserved. I was
obliged to form my own opinions as to what they were "really" like
and what aspects of their culture were admirable.

As I immersed myself first in the language and later in a great
many aspects of culture from the arch-traditional to the wildly
experimental, I naturally drifted toward those features that I
found most attuned to my cultural temperament and aesthetic
predilections. These ranged from *matsuri* (festivals) where folk
performances that had been presented to the people of remote
villages for hundreds of years—such as Kurokawa Noh in Yamagata
Prefecture and Nogo Sarugaku (a form of dance that predates Noh)
in Gifu Prefecture—to the rough tent theater of Kara Juro and the
dry witty plays of Betsuyaku Minoru. I read voluminously once I
became fluent in the language, from the grotesque lyrical stories of
Meiji author Izumi Kyoka to the black-humor postwar novellas of
Sakaguchi Ango and the contemporary novels of Inoue Hisashi.

I attached myself as a *deshi* (disciple) to the *naniwabushi* master Tsukuba Musashi. *Naniwabushi* is a performance art where one person, accompanied by a shamisen player, sings out a kind of high-pitched ballad and plays all the parts of a play. This art form first appeared in Meiji, became exceedingly popular up to the end of World War II and since then has been in gradual demise. I was "Roger Musashi," the first foreign *naniwabushi* balladeer.

I fell in love with Japanese art and craft, particularly pottery, traveling around the country to visit out-of-the-way kilns and buying pieces at the *kamamoto*, a word that indicates both the place that the potter works in and the potter himself or herself (though traditionally there were very few female potters in Japan). I saw every Japanese movie, old and new, that was possible to see. In other words, I was immersing myself in every detail of Japanese life and culture and absorbing it all with the unstained passion of a child.

The Meiji tanka poet Ishikawa Takuboku, whose work I translated and published in 2015 as a book titled *Jiko no genso* (The illusions of self), wrote of the majestic mountains that tower over the landscape at his home village of Shibutami in Iwate Prefecture:

I face the mountains
Speechless.
I owe those mountains everything.

That is how I came to feel about the country of Japan and its profound culture: I came to owe it everything. I doubt that I would have become an author of fiction and plays if I hadn't come to live in Japan. In that sense, the most upsetting setback of my life—having been tossed out of East European studies as a result of the NSA spy scandal and propelled out of my country of birth so as not to be a part of the killing in Vietnam—had provided me with the chance of a lifetime. Many famous scientists have said that their failures, accidental or otherwise, have made their successes possible. Well, this is true, at least to an equal extent, for people in the arts.

35

What is National Character?

What did it mean, I wondered, to be Japanese or, as was said of foreigners who were hopelessly enamored of Japan, to "act" Japanese?

I saw through my reading, traveling and associating with Japanese people from all walks of life that whatever constituted Japanese behavior and made up the Japanese national character was highly fluid—that the Japanese character in pre-Meiji Japan was made up of very different elements from those in the character of Meiji Japanese . . . and so on through the Taisho (1912–1926), Showa (1926–1989) and Heisei (1989–2019) eras.

This is, of course, a truism. No country of Japan's dynamism runs in place. Yet scores of authors in the West have, over the decades, perceived immutable characteristics in virtually all Japanese of any era, as if the entire nation were now and forever peopled by look-alikes and act-alikes. People are still reading the works of Lafcadio Hearn and finding insights into the nature of the Japanese mindset that have long ago morphed into something unrecognizable, though the ardent Greek-Irishman is now perhaps where he was most happy, in the isolated space of a nostalgic past darkened by shadow and hidden beneath a mountain of dust.

A close friend of mine, the brilliant publisher and editor Miyawaki Osamu at Shinchosha, and I spent several days together going over the Japanese translation of my first novel, *The Death of Urashima Taro*. It was the stifling Tokyo summer of 1980 and I was staying at the Shincho Club, a guesthouse that this major publisher maintains a stone's throw from their offices at Yaraicho in the fashionable suburb of Kagurazaka. We were mulling over and discussing how Japan might change in the coming two decades and into the twenty-first century.

"Some things may change for sure," said Miyawaki, "but one

thing will always be 'Japanese' no matter what."

"Are there really things so immutable?"

"I don't know how many, but I know for sure that this one thing won't change."

Now, over the decades since then I have often mentioned this conversation in speeches to Japanese audiences, asking them to name one thing that they think will never change. Certainly, some of them have come up with good answers, such as taking shoes off before going into a house (which is done in other countries and is not particularly "Japanese" to my mind), bowing and using formal polite language (these two practices have not changed, though they are less apparent than in earlier times), and so forth. No one ever guessed Miyawaki Osamu's "forever unchangeable" feature of the Japanese national character.

"Whatever happens," he said way back in 1980, "our resistance to tactile intimacy in public won't change. You will never ever see Japanese people hugging or kissing each other in public like at airports or in parks, or showing affection like they do in France and other places like that."

Well, it appears that this feature of physical reticence, while generally still applying to most Japanese people, has been dropped by many young people in the time since our discussion in Tokyo. Japanese people hold hands frequently, even old people, and do hug in public. I have frequently seen young people kissing, and in the summer of 2000 witnessed a young woman masturbating her male partner on the grass in a fairly crowded park, though admittedly from outside his trousers. The wall surrounding my editor's immutable feature of the Japanese *kokuminsei* (national character) has been chipped away by the young generation. (My dear, now deceased, friend Miyawaki Osamu would be hard put to communicate freely with Japanese millennials, who are much more like their counterparts in China, Korea, Vietnam and Australia than their elders.)

Major social changes began to be seen in the 1980s in the generation that knew neither war nor deprivation. It was the first time that many young people had money burning little holes in their pockets, and they transformed the mainstream of Japanese taste from the minimal and super-serious into the garish, light and frivolous. Their fathers and mothers had sacrificed everything to create the prosperous postwar economy whose benefits they were reaping. But why should they do the same . . . and for what purpose? The *shinjinrui*, or new breed as they were called, reminded me of my own generation when we were young. To us everything serious was "heavy" or "dullsville," and all we cared about was our clothes, our music and our cars. We, too, had only heard about world wars and great depressions.

If Japan was prospering and presumably on its way to becoming Number 1, as some were predicting, the United States was bogged down in a massive savings-and-loan scandal; the USSR was stagnating in corruption and ecological disaster, of which the catastrophic nuclear accident at Chernobyl in 1986 was only the most dramatic of countless, dire environmental and health crises, most of them kept hush-hush at home; and China was still a sleeping, if rousing, dragon, unaware until the Tiananmen Square Massacre of June 4, 1989, of how to deal with growing political dissent and opposition, much as it still is today.

The death of Hirohito, known posthumously as Emperor Showa for the name of his dynastic rule, on January 7, 1989, definitively marked the end of a historical era, and the shriveling of the asset bubble that began a year later signaled the demise of Japan as an economic rival to the United States. If that wasn't enough, the Great Hanshin Earthquake of January 17, 1995, and the sarin nerve gas attack on the Tokyo subway system by a homegrown quasi-religious terrorist organization called Aum Shinrikyo not long after took the last wind out of Japan's sails. What, people were asking in the media, did we struggle for during the five decades after the war if it was only for a society unprepared for natural or manmade disaster and an economy not resilient enough to bounce back and take on the challenges of the twenty-first century?

I published a collection of essays with Iwanami Shoten in

January 1997 titled *Nihon hitomebore* (Japan—love at first sight), a book that took up Japanese racism, sexism, the lack of multiculturalism and, among other things, "the myth of Japanese quality." It certainly looked as if Japan was on the skids, and in some ways, it still does. Will Japan be able to reinvent and redefine itself according to a new model that resembles neither the Meiji one of state planning with imperial expansion nor the postwar Showa one of loyalty to company, excess of diligence and the expansion of exports? That remains the essential question for the young generation of Japanese women and men to address in the coming years. And in order for them to address this, they will have to devise their own social model apart from merely assembling technological tools of social media. Tools won't build a society without a vision, blueprint and something to behold.

36

An Earthquake and a Nerve Agent Attack

Speaking of the earthquake that caused significant damage in the port city of Kobe, Susan, our four children and I had moved back to Japan from Sydney less than a month before it struck in mid-January 1995, telling our friends that "Japan was the safest place to bring up small children."

The earthquake was a mild one in Tokyo, given the distance of some 425 kilometers between the two cities, but the shaking of the bed at 5:47 a.m. was a reminder that Tokyo too would be struck one day by a massive earthquake, as it had once or twice each century in the past. The "big one," a so-called direct hit, is long overdue in this conurbation that is the home of some thirty-six million people.

The real shock of the earthquake that shook Kobe and its environs that morning came when the Japanese people realized that, for all the ballyhoo about Japanese ingenuity and spiritual readiness in coping with natural disasters, they had been unprepared for this disaster and did not know how best to handle issues relating to its aftermath. Was Japan "the safest place" for children? We began to wonder.

Then on the morning of Monday, March 20, 1995, Tokyo was struck by terrorism. Followers of Aum Shinrikyo, a self-styled religious organization run by highly educated and ruthless young fanatics, punctured plastic bags containing the chemical agent sarin, releasing its deadly gas on three subway lines. The incident occurred just after 8:00 a.m., when Tokyo's subway cars are crammed with commuters.

One of those commuters was my wife Susan. We had left Japan to live in Sydney in 1992 in order to give the children some English-language training and grounding in Australian education, settling in the beautiful bayside suburb of Mosman. While living there, Susan established a business to export Australian medical technology and knowhow to Japan. She traveled back and forth between Sydney and Tokyo while I looked after the children—who were then between the ages of about three and ten—and wrote the short stories that were later collected into a volume titled *Raisu* (Rice), published by Kodansha. After we moved back to Japan in late December 1994, Susan set up an office near Yoyogi-Hachiman Station. Yoyogi-Hachiman Station is located a short walk from Yoyogi-Koen Station on the Chiyoda Line, and the Chiyoda Line was one of the three subway lines in which the sarin gas attacks took place.

Susan left our home at Seijo Gakuenmae around seven thirty. I knew that she had a meeting that morning in the city and would, after stopping off at the office, be taking a Chiyoda Line train.

The children were packed off to school, and I rode our youngest, Lucy, by bicycle to Wakaba Kindergarten near Soshigaya Okura Station, a trip of some fifteen minutes one way. I always lingered on the main shopping street at Soshigaya, for we had moved to a little attached house there in November 1982 and had been living there when our two eldest children were born. (I set the final scene of my 2017 film *Star Sand* near that place of intense nostalgia.)

But this time I was anxious to get back home and change clothes. The Australian television station SBS was to arrive at nine to film an interview with me about my life in Japan.

The team arrived on time and we spent the morning taping the interview. Needless to say, in that era before widespread use of mobile phones and internet, we were totally unaware of what had transpired in the city thirty minutes away by train from Seijo Gakuenmae. We broke for lunch at about eleven thirty, and I took the team to a soba restaurant near the station. As we sat down at a long table, the cameraman pointed to a television on a shelf in the corner of the restaurant.

"What's that? It looks like there's been some big accident or something."

The television was showing the scene on a street by the entrance to a subway station. Many people, prostrate on the ground, were being attended to by ambulance workers and medics.

"I can't hear the sound," I said, standing up. "But it can't be anything really serious. I mean, guys, hey, this is the safest city in the world!"

I stood below the television and heard that there had been some sort of attack on commuters. I also heard the word "sarin," but assumed it was a Japanese word that I didn't know. Who had heard of sarin before then? Probably only chemical weapons' experts and historians of the Third Reich. (Sarin had been invented in 1938 by scientists at IG Farben, at the time the largest chemical company in the world. Its name was an acronym taken from the name of its inventors, Schrader, Ambros, Ritter and Van der Linde, the last two letters of the acronym being formed by the "in" in Linde.)

"It's okay," I assured the team, returning to the table. "It's just some sort of accident like you said."

When I look back at my gross misreading of the terror attack I shiver with dread. Had I paid more attention to the television report and not tried so nonchalantly to impress the SBS team with my knowledge of things Japanese, I would probably have panicked and called off the rest of the interview, which was filmed on the streets and in the shops at Seijo. Had I heard that the Chiyoda Line was one of the three lines attacked, I would have rushed to the phone and tried to contact Susan. As it turned out Susan had gone to Yoyogi-Koen Station, which was several stations before the ones at which the sarin was released, to catch a train into the city. But by then the operation of all subway lines had ceased.

After the filming ended and the team piled into their rented van, I switched on the television and got the shock of my life. I had no idea whether this was a one-off attack or if it was the beginning of some kind of terror campaign. The three older children were home safe by then. I rode to the kindergarten and picked up Lucy. Susan arrived home in the early evening on the above-ground train of the Odakyu Line. We watched the television with horror at what was the first violent mass attack on the city of Tokyo since the end of the war.

So much for being an "expert" on Japan.

37

Beside Ozu's Grave

When I went back to Los Angeles in December of 1978 to attend my father's seventy-fifth birthday celebration, he told me that he had not actually been born on December 25 as his birth certificate recorded.

"In the New York slums of those days a woman who had just had a baby couldn't get out to register the birth," Dad had said. "So, every once in a while, an official would come around and ask if any children had been born. People didn't take much notice of dates, and a lot of poor Jewish children have birthdays of Christmas Day and May first because they were just lumped into those dates."

My father told me that he was really born two weeks earlier. Two weeks earlier falls on December 11, 1903. December 12, 1903, (December 11 in the U.S.) happens to be the date of birth of one of the greatest film directors of Japan, Ozu Yasujiro, and I have wondered for years if my father and my cinematic hero were born at the same time. Dad died on April 25, 1993, eight months short of his official ninetieth birthday. Ozu died on the day of his sixtieth birthday, December 12, 1963. It is said that Ozu, ever the director with perfect timing, had actually predicted to friends he would die when reaching the age of sixty.

On the occasion of the 110th anniversary of Ozu's birth and the fiftieth anniversary of his death, an event was held at Engakuji, the temple where Ozu is buried. I was fortunate to be one of the three speakers at the event in the company of Yamanouchi Shizuo and Tsukasa Yoko. Yamanouchi, then eighty-eight, produced several of Ozu's films, including two of my favorites, *Sanma no aji* (*An Autumn Afternoon*) and *Ohayo* (*Good Morning*). Tsukasa, known for being one of the great beauties of the Japanese silver screen, had worked not only with Ozu but with Toyoda Shiro, Okamoto Kihachi, Naruse Mikio, Ichikawa Kon and other directors in some seventy-five films. The event at Engakuji was covered by a television crew and the print media.

It was a cold clear morning in Kita-Kamakura. Tsukasa Yoko and I first walked up to Ozu's gravestone, held our hands together and bowed our heads. A crowd of about a hundred people had gathered as a television crew filmed us praying before the large gravestone that has only a single character carved into its face: *mu*, or oblivion. We then returned to a large tatami-mat room in one of the temple buildings for the symposium.

Yamanouchi Shizuo and Tsukasa Yoko recalled many stories and anecdotes about the demanding director, both remarking on his insistence for precision. By precision, Ozu meant that the actor would perform a gesture or speak a line of dialogue precisely as he demanded. A glass had to be held up in a particular manner to a particular height; a line had to be delivered in what can come across as a totally deadpan voice. This has given the impression, particularly to non-Japanese audiences, that Ozu's films are somehow "zen-like," that they are dry and deal in subdued, if bitter and suppressed, nostalgia.

Actually, I have always seen Ozu as a creator of comedies-of-manners. Like the dialogue in the plays of Betsuyaku Minoru, the surface dryness and superficial absence of expression are a cover for a subtly wry and wicked sense of humor. Had Chekhov been a Japanese and a director in the cinema, he might have made films like Ozu's. In fact, many of Ozu's postwar films are wistful Chekhovian comedies about a privileged class that has seen better times.

Yamanouchi and Tsukasa complemented each other beautifully with their reminiscences, he from the producer's standpoint and she from the actor's. But they disagreed on one point. That point concerned Ozu's famous ubiquitous white hat. Tsukasa insisted that he had a large number of these hats to wear on the set.

"No," said the veteran producer, "he had only one. His mother was always on location, and she washed his hat every night."

Ozu's films are more often than not mundane in the meaning of that word as "of this world," from the Latin word for "world." They turn *nandemonasa* (the trivial and arch-ordinary) into art, a stunning achievement in a genre that is often dripping in melodrama and emotional overplay. Their themes are very "Japanese" in that they deal with the everyday dramas of family life, sometimes with three generations of a family living together or getting into each other's hair, and the little happinesses that come from old friendship and new love.

Ozu, who was brought up as one of five children by a single mother, was sent to boarding school at age thirteen and was a confirmed bachelor his entire life. He had reason to long for something lasting in a relationship. Though he never made films about his war experiences, they must have taken a toll on his view of human cruelty and human kindness. He was sent to Singapore as a soldier and was eventually taken prisoner by the British, returning to Japan in February 1946. Over half of his fifty-four films are silent. This stubborn genius and old-fashioned martinet of the cinema was late coming to sound (1936) and to color (1958).

The old drunk teacher in *Sanma no aji*, played by Tono Eijiro, speaks for the director when he tells his pupils who are now adults, "I'm lonely, you know. Life is after all very lonely." But then the bespectacled Nakamura Nobuo, playing one of the pupils, lifts up a jug of sake and immediately comes back with, "Well, what's the big deal? Let's have another drink." Ozu was a prodigious drinker who was not averse to phoning his staff at all hours of the night, dragging them out to a bar to, ostensibly, discuss the next day's shoot. If there is a deep-seated wet solitude in his films, there is always a dry witty remark to hold it in check.

One theme that runs from his early silent films right through to the end is the freewheeling innocence of children. Children are often dropped into a whirlpool of adult problems and forced to fend for themselves as they get tossed about. Most people consider *Tokyo monogatari* (*Tokyo Story*) to be Ozu's masterpiece, and this film was voted by directors in the 2012 Sight and Sound poll to be the greatest film ever made.

I vote for *Ohayo* (*Good Morning*), in which the mundane details of family life in a Tokyo suburb take on a wrenching pathos and biting humor. The two little naughty brothers who say, "Good morning," and "I love you," in English are a hilarious reminder that Ozu understands and yearns for the guilelessness that he perhaps was never able to have as a child himself.

38

The Japanese Anne Frank

Besides the experience of being Oshima Nagisa's assistant on *Merry Christmas, Mr. Lawrence* I have had other encounters with the Japanese film industry.

In the mid-1990s, when the economy was still stagnating and the Japanese were looking for a light at the end of a tunnel of unknowable length, veteran film producer Araki Seiya, who I had known then for over a decade, approached me with a proposal. He was preparing to produce a full-length animated film version of *The Diary of Anne Frank* and would I write the script together with him. I was of course thrilled. Being the only Jewish playwright who wrote in Japanese I guess I had the market cornered on scriptwriters for a Japanese film version of *The Diary of Anne Frank*.

The producer and I set out on a location scouting trip to Amsterdam in 1994. I had been to Holland in March 1967 but had not visited the secret annex where Anne Frank had taken refuge during the war with her sister, parents, the Van Pels family and a dentist named Pfeffer.

The people who managed the Anne Frank Museum where the secret annex is located were very courteous and helpful, though apparently nonplussed as to why "the Japanese" would be making this film. I told them that *The Diary of Anne Frank* was arguably the most popular book among young Japanese girls and that, in all probability, a greater percentage of people in Japan had read it than people in the West. To the managers of the museum it seemed that Japan was seen only as an ally of Germany in the war. While it is true that many Japanese readers of the book might not grasp the significance of historical elements of anti-Semitism in Europe of the time, they could identify with the story of Anne as one of an isolated girl in puberty coming to terms with the agonies of familial pressure and first love.

Once the film was finished and ready for release, Araki Seiya hired out the Budokan, the indoor arena in Tokyo's Kitanomaru Park near Kudanshita Station, for a preview. Upwards of ten thousand people, most of them young women and girls, filled the hall for the screening. British composer Michael Nyman, who wrote the film's score, came for the screening and played the two theme songs on a grand piano. I had written the lyrics for these two songs, "If" and "Why." It was a thrill to listen to Michael play them, as it was to hear the amazing Welsh contralto Hilary Summers sing them at the Edinburgh Festival in August 1997 when Susan, the children and I fortunately happened to be driving around Scotland on a holiday.

The film, however, was not a commercial success, though it was beautifully animated and voice-acted. I had not seen eye-to-eye with the producer, my co-scriptwriter, who had insisted on following the book scene by scene. I had begged him to emphasize the budding love between Anne and Peter van Pels. Anne was thirteen and feeling the pangs of puberty, which she discusses with amazing candidness in the diary. Peter was sixteen. The kiss in the attic of the secret annex was fleeting in the film, and Anne's intense longing for a relationship was played down. I could not get my co-scriptwriter to go along with giving the kiss scene and Anne's feelings for Peter more screen time, for one thing. He was, after all, also the producer, and a most insistent, to put it mildly, partner in the creation of the script. But even if that young love had been developed in the script, the film itself might not have become a hit. While Japanese audiences of all ages do love animated feature films, most of the ones that strike a chord with them are fantastical and full of bizarre happenings, or based on strictly Japanese themes. I suppose the young women and girls of Japan that we considered our potential core audience had derived everything they desired from the story out of reading the diary itself and felt there was nothing to add to their experience of it in a full-length animated feature film.

39

Finally in the Company of a Real-life Spy

In March 2002, a letter came to me from an old agent friend in Tokyo, Takahashi Junichi. Shinoda Masahiro, film director of the same generation as Oshima Nagisa and Yamada Yoji, had contacted Takahashi to get in touch with me about a role in his upcoming film, *Spy Sorge*.

Susan and I had taken the children to Sydney in early 2001. It was heartrending to leave Kyoto. We had felt utterly at home there. The house we'd rented in Kyoto's north, built in the 1920s, was admittedly old-fashioned (which is why Japanese people did not want to rent it), with a sprawling floor plan of tatami-mat and polished wooden floorboard rooms surrounding a *nakaniwa*, or inner quadrangle garden, with a Japanese maple tree and a large stone lantern in it. It was wonderful for the children to be able to experience life in such a traditional Kyoto home. Our son, the eldest of our children, was about to enter university, and the three girls were in need of English-language education. The four children were speaking Japanese—and Kyoto dialect, at that— among themselves.

The letter from Tokyo had come at a good time. I was about to return to my teaching job at Tokyo Institute of Technology, Japan's leading science university and, founded in 1881, the second oldest national university, after the University of Tokyo, in Japan. (I commuted between home in Sydney and work in Tokyo about ten times a year from 2002 until 2012.)

I arrived in Tokyo on April 1, 2002, and moved into the old home of my dear friend, the brilliant translator and author Shibata Motoyuki, in Nakarokugo, not far from Kamata Station in the southwest of the city. The Shibatas had moved out and were drawing up plans to demolish the old house and put up a new one. They were kind enough to let me stay at that home while it still stood. Three days later I flew to the port town of Moji in northern Kyushu for the *Spy Sorge* shoot. Moji, now a district in the large city of Kitakyushu, boasts beautiful stone and brick buildings erected in the Meiji era suitable for film locations.

Born in Baku in 1895 to a German father and Russian mother, Richard Sorge had spent his early years in Berlin. He fought on the German side in World War I, was wounded and awarded an Iron Cross. His subsequent studies of political science—he received a PhD in the subject in 1920 from the University of Hamburg—and a growing despair over the inability of capitalism to alleviate postwar Europe's gaping inequities led him to embrace communism. He joined the Communist Party and, in 1924, made his first trip to Moscow, where he was promptly recruited and trained to be an agent for the Comintern. In 1930, he was put directly under Red Army intelligence supervision and ordered to base himself in Shanghai. It was in Shanghai that he first met Agnes Smedley, the famous American journalist sympathetic to the Marxist cause, and Smedley, in turn, introduced him to Asahi Shimbun reporter Ozaki Hotsumi.

Ozaki proved to be an invaluable source of information for Sorge, providing him with a slew of contacts in Shanghai's radical underground. When the Japanese invaded Shanghai in January 1932, Sorge's meticulous accounts of the battles were the most accurate information that Moscow was to get on the events.

Sorge returned briefly to Berlin in 1933, bolstering his cover by joining the Nazi Party. Shortly after that he made his way to Japan, again to act as a Comintern agent. An excellent journalist armed with impeccable credentials and devastatingly handsome, he soon earned the confidence of Germany's ambassador, Eugen Ott, as well as the favors of the ambassador's love-stricken wife, Helma. The doubly unsuspecting Ott went so far as to elicit Sorge's help in composing his reports to Berlin, reports that Sorge also secretly sent to Moscow.

Sorge and Ozaki were arrested in Tokyo in October 1941 and held in Sugamo Prison, where they were tortured, interrogated and, in November 1944, hanged. His Japanese executioners chose November 7 for Richard Sorge's hanging because it marked the anniversary of the Russian revolution.

Spy Sorge charts the flamboyant and clandestine movements of the man that Ian Fleming called "the most formidable spy in history" right up to his end on the prison gallows. As for me, I played the American journalist who introduced Sorge to Ozaki, a part so vital to the story that, I knew, no matter how bad my acting, would not be cut. I was thrilled. Back in the late 1960s, when I had been framed by the CIA and the reporters who were in their sway (if not their pay), I had missed the chance to knowingly have an encounter with a real spy. Now in *Spy Sorge* I had one.

I had another brush with Ozaki in 2008 when the New National Theater staged Kinoshita Junji's play about him: *Otto to yobareru nihonjin* (A Japanese named Otto). Otto was Ozaki's code name during the years of his espionage activities. I was asked by my good friend, director Uyama Hitoshi, who had also directed many of Inoue Hisashi's plays, to provide English-language dialogue for the play, as a good portion of it is purportedly spoken in English by Ozaki and the various foreign spies, though written by Kinoshita in Japanese.

A Japanese named Otto was first performed in 1962, and this is critical to understanding its context. Kinoshita had been a sympathizer with leftist causes ever since his prewar days at the University of Tokyo (then called Tokyo Imperial University). But it was the anti-American riots of 1960, motivated by popular opposition to the Treaty of Mutual Cooperation and Security between Japan and the U.S., that catalyzed Kinoshita's ire toward Japanese official acquiescence over the gradual remilitarization of his country at the behest of the United States, a pattern that has continued since the 1960s and was accelerated by Abe Shinzo, prime minister of Japan in the second decade of this century. Kinoshita shows deep sympathy for Ozaki, a man who allegedly betrayed his country in the belief that true patriotism may require one to do just that.

It was a shame that Shinoda's film about Richard Sorge failed miserably at the box office. After all, James Bond has nothing on Sorge—consummate spy, dyed-in-the-wool womanizer, gambler, drunkard, motorcycle geek. When I was first shown the script at the beginning of April 2002, however, I was worried. Written by the director, it strove to be a document of Japan's historical lead-up to war rather than an intimate portrait of this amazing man, his exploits and inner torments. Sorge resisted returning to Moscow in the late 1930s. He knew that he would come under the suspicion of a paranoid Stalin and be liquidated, yet he unfailingly and tirelessly dedicated himself to his ideal of a communist revolution. This conflict of the heart and the intellect alone makes him a superb character for a drama in such brutal times. The themes for both the real Richard Sorge and the real Ozaki Hotsumi revolve around national guilt and personal betrayal. How the two men maintained their faith in their beliefs and in each other is a heroic saga of tragic proportions.

The 200-odd letters that Ozaki wrote to his wife and daughter from prison were collected and published posthumously under the title *Aijo wa furu hoshi no gotoku* (Devotion is like a shower of stars). These moving letters comprise, to my mind, the most remarkable personal documents to emerge from the war years in Japan. By all rights, Ozaki Hotsumi should be considered a hero to present-day Japanese as a man who loved his country too deeply to permit it to victimize millions of people in Asia and the Pacific.

40

Best Wishes for Tomorrow

The war continued to provide the vehicle that took me, after working with Oshima and Shinoda, to yet another Japanese film.

Ashita e no yuigon (*Best Wishes for Tomorrow*) was directed in the late spring and early summer of 2007 by Koizumi Takashi, a man who had been Kurosawa Akira's first assistant director on some of his later films and who had become, after the great master's death, a director in his own right. *Best Wishes for Tomorrow* was Koizumi's fourth film. This time I was asked to co-script the film with the director himself. But this also gave me the opportunity to be on the set and on location every day for nearly a month. Since the set was at the Toho Studios near Seijo Gakuenmae Station, the daily trip there on the Odakyu Line was like going home. (We had lived at two different homes in Seijo, one of Tokyo's most beautiful suburbs, once in the mid-eighties and again in the mid-nineties.)

Best Wishes for Tomorrow takes up the real-life story of Maj.

Gen. Okada Tasuku of the Tokai Army that was given the task of defending central Honshu. Several weeks before World War II ended on August 15, 1945, Okada ordered the execution of captured American fliers without giving them the benefit of a proper military hearing. He and his men considered the Americans to be war criminals for the indiscriminate bombing of Japan that was killing hundreds of thousands of innocent civilians.

After the war, Okada and nineteen of his subordinates were brought before an American military tribunal. He was convicted of war crimes and sentenced to death. Those tribunal proceedings were part of the Yokohama War Crimes Trials that ended in 1948.

Okada was one of the very few Japanese military leaders who took full responsibility for his actions—and perhaps even welcomed the verdict as one that allowed him to assuage his guilt. There is sufficient evidence in the historical record to believe that Okada saw his own death as the beginning of a new era of friendship between Japan and the United States. (I had pored over more than 1,000 pages of trial transcripts in preparation for working on the script.) He hoped there would someday be a world in which the mentality that led to his extreme actions and those of the American bomber crews would cease to exist. Hence, best wishes for tomorrow.

Much of our film was taken up by the trial of Okada, played brilliantly by veteran actor Fujita Makoto, known in Japan primarily for his detective roles. (Sadly Fujita Makoto passed away from esophageal cancer not long after the release of the film.) His wife, Haruko, played by Fuji Sumiko, sits in the courtroom during the trial. The two are not allowed to speak to each other. The silent bond between them, as Okada faces a sentence of death by hanging, is strong and poignantly expressed in looks, smiles and nods. (By coincidence, I directed Fuji Sumiko's daughter, Terajima Shinobu, in my own film, *Star Sand*, ten years later.)

The real hero of *Best Wishes for Tomorrow* is the trial itself. That judges on an American military tribunal could be utterly fair, even going to the extent of trying to get the general to give his testimony in a way that would exonerate him from the death

penalty, symbolizes a milestone of American military justice. I was
confident when we were shooting the film that American audiences
would respond to its messages. In the end, however, we could not
get an American distributor to take it up.

The Okada trial marked, to my knowledge, the only occasion
when testimony stating clearly that the dropping of the atom
bombs on Hiroshima and Nagasaki constituted a war crime was
admitted as evidence in an American court. Perhaps this evidence
remaining in the dialogue, however faithful to the trial's transcript,
proved to be an obstacle to an American distributor accepting the
film for distribution in the United States.

Any film of a trial can get bogged down in tedium. The tension
in the drama must be maintained through the onscreen expression
of the characters' inner motivations. Why did Okada execute the
Americans? What were his feelings when assuming responsibility
for his actions? What was going on inside the mind of the American
defense attorney, wonderfully portrayed by actor Robert Lesser, as
he accused his own people of having been war criminals?

This is where the use of three cameras came in to good effect. A
luxury in filmmaking, it meant that all the actors in the courtroom
had to be present at all times, since virtually all angles were visibly
covered during a take. Hence, when Camera A was filming the
prosecutor grilling Okada, what were the fears and hopes of his
wife and son, who are sitting in the courtroom? Camera B picked
this up. Meanwhile, Camera C might be focused on the nineteen
subordinates on trial with Okada. Are they going to be given the
death sentence for following orders? These portraits can be intercut
in the editing of the scenes of questioning, giving insight into the
torments Okada's loved ones and his former subordinates are
experiencing.

One of my roles during the shoot was to make sure the English
dialogue was spoken properly and to liaise between the non-
Japanese actors and the director. The other role was as an actor
playing the head of Sugamo Prison, which, during the Allied
Occupation, housed suspected and convicted war criminals.

As prison head I wore, for the first time in my life, a U.S. Army uniform, just a costume of course, and stood beside the Stars and Stripes in front of photographs of Pres. Harry S. Truman and Gen. Douglas MacArthur. Were my parents still alive they would finally have been able to say, "My son, the captain!"

Best Wishes for Tomorrow, which was based on the book *Nagai tabi* (The long journey) by Ooka Shohei, one of the postwar era's greatest literary figures, presents the life of a man who believed that those at the top of the chain of command must take responsibility for their decisions. If this theme had resonated with people around the world and we could have recalled it subsequently in bringing leaders on all sides who commit war crimes to trial, then Okada's wish for a better future might not have been made in vain.

In the film, as in the real trial, Okada praised the fairness of the proceedings, telling the military commission that tried him between March 8 and May 19, 1948, "This trial has been very generous in its proceedings. I firmly believe that my feelings of gratitude will be the basis of a spiritual bond between the elder brother, America, and the younger brother, Japan, uniting our two countries in the future."

41

The Yamashita Precedent

The theme of war crimes was not a new one to me. In 1970, I had written a play titled *Yamashita* while living in my tiny rented house by Midorogaike, the Deep Muddy Pond, in the north of Kyoto. The title referred to Gen. Yamashita Tomoyuki (who was also called Tomobumi). Called the "Tiger of Malaya," Yamashita was the general who led troops down the Malay Peninsula, some of them on bicycle, to capture Singapore on February 15, 1942. Later in the war the general was in Manila when that city fell to the Allied Forces.

After the war, General Yamashita was arraigned for failing "to control the operations of the members of his command," tried before an American military tribunal in Manila, found guilty of war crimes and hanged a few minutes after 3:00 a.m. on February 23, 1946, despite the fact that he had specifically issued orders to his troops not to exceed the bounds of accepted engagement and was unable, given the desperation of the Japanese situation and the breakdown of communications, to prevent the committing of atrocities by his men. Gen. Douglas MacArthur, Supreme Commander for the Allied Powers, refused to commute General Yamashita's death sentence, issuing a short statement in which he condemned the convicted general for, among other things, "transgressions (that are) a stain upon civilization and constitute a memory of shame and dishonor that can never be forgotten."

The Yamashita case surfaced in the U.S. media many years later in the context of alleged crimes committed by American troops in Vietnam. The case had created a precedent: that a general in charge of soldiers may be held accountable for the actions of those soldiers even if he had issued orders to prevent them. U.S. prosecutor at the Nuremberg Trials, Telford Taylor, writing in late 1970, made the stark comparison: "If you were to apply to (General Westmoreland and other U.S. generals) the same standards that were applied to General Yamashita, there would be a very strong possibility that they would come to the same end as he did."

I wrote *Yamashita* in 1970 before becoming aware of the case's relevance to American war crimes in Vietnam. A trip to Nagasaki in December 1968 had started me thinking about the theme of war crimes; I visited the Peace Museum that month. Among the awful remnants of destruction caused by the dropping of the atom bomb on August 9, 1945, was a single photograph that had transfixed me. It pictured a small group of America fliers standing beside a Boeing B-29 Superfortress. They had their arms over each other's shoulders and were grinning. Behind them, painted on the side of the bomber, was the image of a cute little choo-choo train car with the wings of an angel attached. On one side of the train was the word "Nagasaki," painted in the bamboo-like letters that you often see in Western depictions of "Oriental" writing; on the other side was "Salt Lake." Below this logo symbolizing nuclear catastrophe was one word in rounded bold lettering: "Bockscar," named after the plane's usual pilot Frederick C. Bock.

All of this must have been painted on the plane after its return from its mission, for the original target was the city of Kokura in northern Kyushu. An overcast sky saved that city and doomed Nagasaki some 150 kilometers away. A little sign by the photograph in the Nagasaki Peace Museum stated that this airplane that had dropped a bomb causing up to 80,000 deaths by the end of 1945 was on display at the U.S. Air Force Museum in Dayton, Ohio. It is still on display to this day beside a replica of "Fat Man," the bomb itself.

That photograph was the most horrible and upsetting thing I saw that day in Nagasaki in 1968. It spoke of my country's arrogance of triumph and giddy delight, punning crudely on the word "scar," over what comprised, together with the dropping of the bomb on Hiroshima, the greatest single acts of mass murder in the history of the world. Hiroshima and Nagasaki are Japan's Holocaust, though the world, Japan included, seems reluctant to accept that fact. That photograph became the initial impulse behind the writing of *Yamashita*.

The play is only laterally concerned with the Japanese general's trial. In fact, it takes place not in Manila in 1946, but in Hawaii in 1959, when a teacher of Japanese, a Chinese-American named Chow, finds himself alone in a classroom with a student named Yamashita. The name triggers memories of his being tortured by Japanese during the war. An old janitor comes into the room thinking that the lesson is over. In a transformation of place and time, the classroom turns into a courtroom, and the janitor—with the black curtains over the window serving as judicial robes—a judge. The re-enacted "trial" ends with a recreation on stage of the dropping of the atom bombs. The judge reverts to his former role of janitor and walks out, leaving the student named Yamashita in the hands of the former POW teacher.

Yamashita, published in Australia in 1981 by Currency Press, has had a number of productions, including one that I directed myself in Canberra as my farewell production before leaving for Melbourne in January 1980. But the play brought about an encounter with a remarkable man in the United States as well.

42

Mako and his Father

I was contacted by the Japanese American actor Mako in the autumn of 1978. He had heard about a production of *Yamashita* in Australia, somehow had gotten hold of the play and wrote that he would like to meet to discuss a possible production in Los Angeles at a theater he had co-founded in 1965. Fortunately, I was making a trip to my old homeland—the first as an Australian with a tourist visa for the U.S.—for my father's birthday.

I invited Mako to my parents' apartment on Sepulveda Boulevard in Culver City. My mother, who had never heard of him, took his leather jacket from him, but before hanging it up stole a peek at its label, raising her eyebrows and nodding in approval. Alas, I never did find out the brand of Mako's leather jacket, but it must have been a classy one. If Mako's career in Hollywood had not made an impression on her, at least his jacket had.

Mako was very committed to the production of plays with Asian themes. I told him that I was delighted for *Yamashita* to go on at the East West Players. After about an hour he left my parents' apartment, but not before my mother insisted on helping him on with his jacket and stealing another peek at its eyebrow-raising label.

It wasn't until January 1983 that the East West Players mounted a production of the play that I, unfortunately, being in Tokyo, was unable to see. (The play had another production in Hawaii that I also missed.) But the play had given me the opportunity to meet the soft-spoken actor Mako who, after Hayakawa Sesshu (known as Sessue Hayakawa in the West) was the greatest Japanese male actor to be active on the American stage and screen. Mako spent his entire adult life fighting the racial stereotypes of Hollywood.

When *The Green Hornet*, the old radio and comic book series about the masked white vigilante, was turned into a television series in 1966–67, it was Mako who played the Chinese Low Sing, while Chinese Bruce Lee played the Japanese Kato. You gotta love Hollywood! It has never mattered very much to the moguls of schlock "what part Asia you from." (Hayakawa Sesshu was noted for playing a number of various Asians in the silent era. It was only after the war, when a real Japanese tough guy or military officer was called for, that he moved over exclusively to Japanese roles.)

The race barrier for blacks in film has been broken for decades, thanks to the pioneering work of such brilliant actors as Dorothy Dandridge, Sidney Poitier and others. Roles for blacks are no longer necessarily race specific. Black actors have played top spies and presidents. Morgan Freeman has even played God. But the last and most stubborn racial barrier in Hollywood has been the Asian one.

Mako's full name was Iwamatsu Makoto. He was born on December 10, 1933 in Kobe, the son of Iwamatsu Atsushi and Sasako Tomoe. Mako's parents left Japan in 1939 for New York and were not able to bring their son to the United States until after the war, by which time they had changed their names to Taro and Mitsu Yashima.

Shortly after arriving in the United States, Mako enlisted. Though special naturalization provisions for non-Americans serving in the U.S. armed forces had been in place since the Civil War, Mako didn't naturalize until 1956. It was in the army, while performing for his buddies, that Mako became aware he had acting talent.

After leaving the service, with his family now living in Los Angeles, he took up study at the Pasadena Playhouse, a school of the theater arts that has produced major talents over many decades. While actors such as Ernest Borgnine, Charles Bronson, Gene Hackman and Dustin Hoffman left the Pasadena Playhouse to shoot to the top of their profession, Mako was offered roles "befitting his background." He became determined to break through the bamboo curtain and be seen as an actor, first and last.

Between 1962 and 1964, he played various types of Japanese soldiers opposite his Pasadena Playhouse friend Ernest Borgnine in the popular TV series about a U.S. PT boat in World War II, *McHale's Navy*. But his big break came in 1966 when he acted with Steve McQueen, Richard Attenborough and Candice Bergen in *The Sand Pebbles*.

The Sand Pebbles is a film about an American gunboat on the Yangtze River in the mid-1920s in China. Mako played Po-han, a tough Chinese working in the engine room. This role brought him a nomination for an Academy Award as Best Supporting Actor. A number of parts came his way on television, where, as in *M*A*S*H* in the 1970s, he portrayed Koreans from both sides of the Demilitarized Zone, as well as a Chinese.

But perhaps Mako was most at home on a stage. He fought hard to get the part of the reciter in Steven Sondheim's 1976 Broadway musical, *Pacific Overtures*, which told the story of Commodore Matthew Perry's 1853 expedition to Japan. ("We couldn't let people say Asian American actors can't act," he said.)

Mako had a career in Japan as well. He first appeared in Japan in 1967 in the TBS TV drama *Naite tamaru ka* (Who cry, me?) together with the brilliant actor Atsumi Kiyoshi, star of Yamada Yoji's *Tora-san* series. Other roles followed, such as that of pre-Meiji era interpreter John Manjiro (whose real name was Nakahama Manjiro) in *Tenno no seiki* (The emperor's century) in 1971. Film director Miike Takashi used Mako to play a Chinese named Shen in a remote Chinese village in his 1998 film *Chugoku no chojin* (The bird people in China), and Shinoda Masahiro directed him as the daimyo warrior Hideyoshi in his 1999 movie *Fukuro no shiro* (Owl's castle), based on the Naoki Prize–winning novel by Shiba Ryotaro.

But in many senses Mako was just as much an exotic figure to the Japanese as he was to the Americans. That was the irony encapsulating the careers of Japanese who left Japan to act elsewhere, including such stars as Hayakawa Sesshu. This bias has thankfully died out, and now many Japanese actors who appear in foreign films are lauded. (There was even once a genre of film in which such actors appeared called *kokujoku eiga*, or films that "insult the nation." Happily, this term is now obsolete.) Mako appeared as Admiral Yamamoto Isoroku in the 2001 war blockbuster *Pearl Harbor*. "*Tatakau shika nai!*" ("We have no choice but to fight!") he says to his cohorts in that film, informing them that Japan was on course to attack the U.S. But despite all this, the leading role freed of ethnicity that he craved as an actor never came his way in the United States.

One of my favorite performances of Mako's is as Tan the grandfather in the 2007 film made in Singapore, *Cages*. This is a film about a little blind boy who always smiles. Mako overwhelms us with his tenderness and grace. He was, plain and simple, a world-class actor.

"I've always been interested in character development, more than plot or action or special effects," he said of the role in *Cages* and, by extension, all his roles.

Mako passed away in the small town of Somis, California on July 21, 2006, leaving his wife, two daughters, three grandchildren and his sister, actress Momo Yashima Brannen.

Once, when he was nominated for a Tony Award for Best Actor in a Musical (for *Pacific Overtures*), he had an unpleasant experience on the way home from the ceremony. He was still wearing his kabuki-style costume when someone on the street hollered, "Hey, why don't you go back to China!" He said later he would have refused the Tony had he won it: "Asian American actors have never been treated as full-time actors. We're always hired as part-timers . . . for race-specific roles. . . . I didn't feel I could accept the award as long as Asian Americans were not treated (as equals) in our profession."

Mako goes down in history not only as a world-class actor and theater producer, but also as a warrior for the civil rights of all minorities faced with the ingrained racist stereotypes of a majority.

And his father Taro Yashima was just as remarkable. But first, a story.

A little boy cannot be found at his village school. He is hiding under its floorboards. His name is Chibi, which means "little tyke" in Japanese. He cannot make friends, and other children will not play with him. In class, Chibi stares at the ceiling for hours. He loves all kinds of yucky insects. No one can read his handwriting. Everyone calls him "stupid" and "slowpoke." But when Chibi is in the sixth grade, a new teacher, Mr. Isobe, recognizes his rare talent. Chibi is so intimately in touch with nature that he can commune with it. One day he performs for Mr. Isobe and all his classmates, revealing his hidden gift. Chibi can imitate the voices of crows, from the calls of hatchlings to those of the mother and father crow.

This is the story of *Crow Boy*, a picture book written and illustrated by Taro Yashima, whose own story is not unlike that of his creation, Chibi.

Taro Yashima was born Iwamatsu Atsushi on September 21, 1908, in Nejime, a small village on the coast near Cape Sata, where Kagoshima Bay in southern Kyushu flows into the ocean. (Nejime has now merged into the larger entity of Minami Osumi-cho.) His father was the village doctor and an ardent collector of Asian art. Mr. Isobe in the story is modeled on two of the author's teachers at Kamiyama Elementary School—Isonaga Takeo and Ueda Miyoshi.

As a young boy, he exhibited significant talent as an artist. At age thirteen his satirical manga were being published in the *Kagoshima Shimbun* daily newspaper, today's *Minami Nippon Shimbun*. At nineteen he gained entrance to Tokyo Bijutsu Gakko, the Tokyo School of Fine Arts, in Ueno. (That school merged in 1949 with Tokyo Ongaku Gakko, Tokyo Music School, becoming today's Tokyo Geijutsu Daigaku, Tokyo University of the Arts.)

Yashima, then Iwamatsu, refused to participate in military exercises at the school and in 1929 was expelled for insubordination.

He became an active participant in anti-fascist political causes and sketched the death mask of Kobayashi Takiji when the prominent proletarian writer's corpse was released by his jailers with visible signs of torture on it. Yashima himself was also repeatedly jailed and beaten in prison for his political activism, as was his wife Tomoe, who he had married in 1930. In 1939 both managed to leave Japan for New York, having left their six-year-old son, Makoto (Mako), with his grandparents in Japan. Yashima wasn't to see Mako until after the war when he returned in 1945 as a member of a U.S. strategic bombing survey team.

In New York, both the Yashimas continued their art studies at the prestigious Art Students League on West 57th Street. But when war broke out between the United States and Japan following the Pearl Harbor attack on December 7, 1941, Yashima enlisted in the U.S. Army and was posted first to the Office of War Information and then to the Office of Strategic Services (OSS), the predecessor of the CIA. It was then that the Yashimas abandoned the birth-name Iwamatsu for fear of repercussions against their son and parents in Japan. Being fearful of retribution back home, Tomoe—whose prewar pen name was Arai Mitsuko—took to using the name Mitsu.

Yashima published two illustrated autobiographical books in the 1940s, *The New Sun* in 1943 and *Horizon is Calling* in 1947, detailing his and his wife's maltreatment by the Japanese secret police. Yet he also conveyed what he considered his message to Americans at the time: that all Japanese are not "wild monkeys." Several picture books followed in the succeeding decades, including *The Village Tree* in 1953, *Crow Boy* in 1955 and *Seashore Story* in 1967. The tree in *The Village Tree* is the home of "all sorts of bugs on the leaves, and places to play in the branches." That book—and all the others by Yashima—harks back to a Japan in which nature was cherished and children felt it to be their constant friend.

In 1948, Makoto joined his parents in the United States, and Mitsu gave birth to a daughter, Momo. As Momo grew up her parents created exquisite picture books for her, such as *Momo's*

Kitten and *Umbrella*. I love *Umbrella*. It captures the simple thrill of a little girl who gets an umbrella for the first time. When she grabs hold of it she lets go of her parent's hand, the first sign of self-reliance.

By 1954, the Yashimas were living in Los Angeles, having settled in the city's Boyle Heights district, where many poor Jews lived as well. They established the Yashima Art Institute and taught there. But the couple separated. Mitsu moved to San Francisco, where she lectured at the University of California, Berkeley, on "People's Art in Japan." She also taught art in the 1970s at Kimochi, a community center in the city that continues today to bring together younger and older Japanese Americans. At that time Mitsu—having never forsaken her activism—took part in the Women Strike for Peace movement against nuclear weapons and the Vietnam War.

Taro Yashima suffered a stroke in 1977, and passed away in hospital in Los Angeles in 1994. His motto for his books should inspire young people around the world today: "Let children enjoy living on this Earth, let children be strong enough not to be beaten or twisted by evil on this Earth." As for Mitsu, she returned to Los Angeles in 1983 to live with Momo, who had become an actress. Mitsu's death in 1988 preceded her husband's by six years.

Taro Yashima had spent some months of the war years in India on intelligence missions. Upon his return to the United States he wrote and illustrated handbills in Japanese that were dropped by U.S. forces over battlefields bearing the phrases "Don't Die!" and "Papa, Stay Alive." To charges in Japan that he was a traitor, he remarked that his sole aim was to save Japanese lives.

"At the time, it was easy to say I was one who was against his own country," he explained. "That's the most terrible thing, because my feeling was, I'm doing it because I love my country."

It is that genuine love of country—so powerful that it urges you to act against its evil excesses—that is rarely celebrated in Japan, or anywhere for that matter. It did exist in Japan. The life of journalist Ozaki Hotsumi attests to the existence of that form of true patriotism. The lives of Taro and Mitsu Yashima are part of the same exemplary narrative.

And that is why I have dwelt on the story of their lives. We Westerners are always being told that we will never be truly accepted by the Japanese, something that I most definitely do not agree with. You can be accepted. It just may take a good deal of time and effort to learn to adapt to Japanese codes of behavior, which are generally more formal than those many of us are used to in our native lands. But equally it has not been easy for Asians to be accepted in Western countries unless they prove that they are fully assimilated into the mores and conventions of those countries. A former Japanese student of mine who went to live in Poland and stayed there for several decades told me how exotic he appeared to the Poles. Though he became fluent in Polish and brought up his Japanese family there, he was often treated with a polite standoffishness and underlying disbelief that he could be "like us."

Japanese artists who forged careers in the West have put up with much prejudice and stereotyping. With the intervention of the hostilities between Japan and the United States, some of them, like the Yashimas, were forced to choose one country over the other and declare their allegiance through action and word. It is by becoming familiar with lives of these artists torn between two countries they love that we Westerners who have chosen to live in Japan can come to better understand how to spend our life there.

43

Harry and Nancy

Two other Japanese people in the arts who became successes in the United States are Harry Mimura and Umeki Miyoshi. I felt the need to know about these artists because I immodestly felt that I was trying to do the same thing in reverse.

Harry Mimura—or, to use his Japanese name, Mimura Akira—went on a journey from Tokyo to Nagasaki and Hiroshima and some twenty other devastated Japanese cities in March and April 1946 to record, as cameraman, the lives of innocent civilians who were "forced to go through such suffering." The result was a record of moving pictures in color that provide an invaluable look into the ways that the Japanese people coped with survival in the first year after the war. Mimura, who had worked in Hollywood for years, was the ideal choice in all ways except one. He had never before shot using color film.

A specially equipped train, on which the film crew carried all of its camera and other equipment left Tokyo for its first destination, Nagasaki. Mimura used the time on the journey to bone up on color filming from an American manual he had brought with him.

His footage is not the sort that we are used to seeing of the decimated cities. It is full of people going about their lives as best as they can. Women in colorful kimonos are out and about on errands. Children smile. Panoramic shots from high vantage points lend a sense of scale to the destruction and the perspective of life among the ruins. (Mimura would sometimes borrow fire-truck ladders from the authorities to get those shots.) Who was this man, successful as a cinematographer in both the American and Japanese film worlds?

Mimura Akira was born on January 6, 1901, in what is today Etajima City, an island town in Hiroshima Bay and home, from its founding in 1888, of one of Japan's most prestigious military educational institutions, the Imperial Japanese Naval Academy (now the Maritime Self-Defense Force Naval Academy). It was this academy that produced many illustrious military figures, the most notable being Yamamoto Isoroku, commander in chief of Japanese forces in the early years of World War II. The place of Mimura's birth was no happenstance. His father Kinsaburo was a colonel in the navy and subsequently, for eleven months from December 1, 1917, captain of the battleship *Kirishima*.

After finishing middle school in Zushi near Yokohama, Mimura was sent to the United States. There he entered the Nicholson School for Science and Math, then, as now, located on Peoria Street by Lake

Michigan in downtown Chicago. His ears were no doubt ringing with his father's wishes for him to pursue what was then the most reputable of professions in Japan, namely that of the soldier. But Mimura, already generally known as Harry, the name he picked up in the United States, entertained quite different aspirations. He left for New York where he studied filmmaking, then set out for the film capital of the United States, Los Angeles, where, in 1929, he landed work as an assistant cameraman on *The Trespasser*, Gloria Swanson's first talkie. Later that year he numbered among the crew of *Condemned*, a film in which the star, Ronald Coleman, was nominated for an Academy Award.

In 1930, Mimura worked on the Howard Hughes-directed film *Hell's Angels*, which starred Jean Harlow in a tale about two brothers in the British Royal Flying Corps. From then on, he was the only Japanese behind the camera in Hollywood, shooting some five dozen films before returning home to Japan in 1934.

Back in Japan he began working as director of photography the very next year, collaborating on such major films as *Tokyo Rhapsody*—directed by Fushimizu Osamu and starring crooner Fujiyama Ichiro, who gave Japan one of its greatest prewar hits with his song of the same name, "Tokyo Rhapsody"—and a tragedy set in the middle of the feudal Edo period (1603-1868), *Ninjo kami fusen* (*Humanity and Paper Balloons*), directed by Yamanaka Sadao. Mimura collaborated again with Fushimizu as director of photography on the iconic wartime propaganda movie *Shina no yoru* (China nights) and with Kurosawa Akira in the making of *Sugata sanshiro* (*Sanshiro Sugata*) in 1942.

After being conscripted in 1944, Mimura spent the rest of the war translating U.S. radio broadcasts. So, at war's end, the seasoned Japanese cinematographer with an American first name was the perfect choice of the Allied occupiers to enlist into recording the toll that their indiscriminate bombing campaign had taken on the people of Japan.

In 1946, the year he shot his color footage of Japan's razed cities, Mimura also made his postwar debut behind a movie camera with

Toho Show Boat, a musical once again starring Fujiyama, who had recently been repatriated from a POW camp in Indonesia. In that sense, the film marks the comeback of two celebrated Japanese film artists. In 1947, Mimura joined the production company Shintoho (New Toho) that had been founded in March of that year, and this led to him being offered a great deal of work. (Ironically it had been the defection of many Toho actors to the new company that created an opening at Toho for a "new face" named Mifune Toshiro, who was to become Japan's most famous postwar screen actor.)

From that time on Mimura shot twenty-eight features in Japan. He was also cameraman on the foreign locations of the American blockbuster, *Around the World in Eighty Days*. In 1955, he directed, co-wrote and photographed his own film, *Kieta chutai* (The vanished company), about a group of Japanese soldiers in Soviet-occupied territory in 1941.

All in all, the career of Harry Mimura is unique, not only in the immense contribution he made to film culture in Japan and the United States, but also in the fact that he was accepted as a master of his art in both countries despite the enmity engendered by the war and the lingering bitterness that remained in many circles in the postwar years.

He died on December 23, 1985, and is buried in the cemetery that is the final resting place of scores of people who were active in the film industry: Forest Lawn Memorial Park in Los Angeles's Hollywood Hills.

I particularly like something of his that was published in the launch issue of the magazine *Eiga Satsuei* (Cinema photography) on January 20, 1962. He offers what may quite possibly be the most concise and profound description of the cinematographic art:

> Whatever changes may come, the basis of it all will always be light and shadow. . . . Cinema photography differs from still photography in that the person being filmed is in motion. . . . The cinema photographer matches the story by factoring in what is being shot, its continuity, the mood, etc., constantly

bearing in mind the primary condition: that the images must appeal to the viewer. What's required is the technique to express the narrative on film without calling attention to the camera.

* * *

And there is the female actor, singer and amazing comedienne, Umeki Miyoshi. Of all the Japanese actors from the past she is the one I most wish I had met.

Umeki Miyoshi became a cinema and television icon in the United States. Yet her death in 2007 was barely noted in Japan despite her meteoric rise to stardom in America and the fact that she remains the only East Asian to have received an Academy Award for acting.

Did she not, then, achieve "acceptance"? Isn't this what all migrants crave? But nearly all migrants *are* accepted. The question is: Is it on their own terms or those of the mainstream majority? Umeki Miyoshi achieved stardom, but not acceptance by her own definition of the word.

Umeki Miyoshi—appearing "petite, adorable, demure and graceful"—pressed all the right buttons. Yet throughout her life in the United States, she was to be suitably stereotyped and encaged in an image created in the highly race-conscious Hollywood of those days: the impeccable and ideal Japanese female type as seen in the eyes of people in the West.

Born in Otaru, Hokkaido on May 8, 1929, Umeki Miyoshi was the last of nine children, all born two years apart from their closest sibling. Her father was a wealthy industrialist who owned an iron foundry. Frequently left to her own devices as a child, she immersed herself in music, studying various instruments including harmonica, mandolin and piano. After the war, one of her brothers, who was working as an interpreter for the Allied Occupation, brought home some G.I. musicians. They immediately recognized his young sister's talent as a singer. Soon she was singing with those G.I.s in their band under the name Nancy Umeki. Nancy was a lot easier to pronounce than Miyoshi, an unusual given name even in Japan (she insisted, however, despite the difficulty of pronunciation, on being called Miyoshi throughout her career).

In 1953 and 1954 she appeared in the Japanese musical films *Seishun Jazz Musume* (Young jazz girl) and *Jazz on Parade 1954, Tokyo Cinderella Musume* (musume here, too, means "girl"). Her rendition of the 1949 American hit song "*Orokanari waga kokoro*" ("My Foolish Heart") was gorgeous. She had her sights set on America, and in 1955 moved there determined to make a name for herself.

After the war, Americans were smitten by what they saw as poised, dainty and doll-like Japanese females. They embraced her as their ideal of that type: unassuming and gracious in kimono with a shiny little bauble in her hair, dimpled cheeks, coy smile and a voice like pure honey. To be fair, Umeki Miyoshi could play it that way. She had no choice. In that manner, the person acts out the roles of the set image, merging seamlessly with the stereotype and, in doing so, plays a part in their own confinement within it.

The prime venue for amateur talent in 1950s America was *Arthur Godfrey and His Friends*, a TV variety show instrumental in the discovery of entertainers as varied as singer Pat Boone, and comedians Wally Cox and Lenny Bruce. From her debut in 1956, Miyoshi was an immediate and wild favorite on the show. It was her performances there that led to her being cast as Katsumi, the wife of airman Joe Kelly, played by Red Buttons, in the 1957 film *Sayonara*.

Sayonara opens with your proverbial shots of temples and shrines, with kimono-clad women scurrying along in a most "Oriental" fashion. Starring Marlon Brando and James Garner, it is the story of American-Japanese love that defies prejudice on both sides. For Katsumi and Joe, however, the prejudice triumphs, and although Katsumi is pregnant, they commit double suicide and are discovered together in bed by a bereft Brando. The lyrics of Irving Berlin's ballad "Sayonara" set the tone for this plaintive love story: "*Sayonara, Japanese goodbye/ Whisper sayonara but you mustn't cry."*

The film catapulted Umeki Miyoshi to stardom. She received her Oscar in 1958 when, ironically, the British film depicting unmitigated Japanese brutality, David Lean's *The Bridge on the River Kwai*, took the award for best picture. Receiving the Oscar from presenter Anthony Quinn, she was the picture of bashfulness. She bowed to Quinn, saying in a soft voice, "I wish somebody would help me right now." Then she thanked "all American people."

On December 22, 1958, Miyoshi graced the cover of *Time* magazine. She was appearing on virtually every major TV variety program, including *The Merv Griffin Show*, *The Andy Williams Show* and *The Dinah Shore Chevy Show*. She was also a guest on the hugely popular *What's My Line?* I especially admire her appearance on *The Gisele MacKenzie Show*, where she displayed her subtle sense of humor and even used her little mistakes in English to her advantage. She endeared herself to her American audience by affecting a coy humility. As an example, when MacKenzie asked her how she felt about winning an Oscar with Red Buttons, who also received one for his role in *Sayonara*, she smiled sweetly and said she was very surprised—"because I do not think they give two Oscar in same family." Then she went on to deliver a stunning version, sung in a mixture of English and Japanese, of "How Deep is the Ocean?" She used some Japanese in her patter and singing, and became, in the eyes of Americans, the epitome of Japanese femininity.

When she appeared on Broadway in 1958 in the Rogers and Hammerstein musical *Flower Drum Song* and sang her beautiful rendition of "A Hundred Million Miracles," a *Time* reviewer wrote, "When Miyoshi Umeki glides on stage to star in her first Broadway show, her first four words capture the house. She is American by solemn determination, but she still lives in the ordered, traditional world of her tight little island home."

Yet the meteor was about to fall. Her last film, released in 1962, was *A Girl Named Tamiko*, starring Laurence Harvey. That movie, too, opens with a temple (Todaiji in Nara), a shrine (Toshogu

Shrine in Nikko) and swift-footed ladies in kimonos.

Parts for Asians were so limited in Hollywood films that Miyoshi turned to television. Her most prominent part was as Mrs. Livingston, the housekeeper in the popular sitcom, *The Courtship of Eddie's Father*. The very first show of the series, in 1969, was titled, "Mrs. Livingston, I Presume."

Asians were typecast and stereotyped. And Miyoshi played her role in that game with consummate craft, though ever bitter that the doors to the world of "normal" acting in film were closed to her. Having become an American citizen, she retired from show business and, for some twenty years, lived in Los Angeles and ran a dance studio in North Hollywood. She then left the city behind and moved to Hawaii. She shunned all publicity, and, for a time, few in Hollywood knew where she was or whether she was alive or dead. Eventually she went to live with her son and grandchildren in the small town of Licking, Missouri.

For Americans, the postwar decades were the brass age of empire, with the White House playing trumpets and horns, and the Pentagon beating drums. They envisaged themselves as being on top of the world, the conductors of sway, with all others below dancing happily to the tune. Americans owned or controlled the canvases, the paints, the brushes, the galleries and the critics. All the rest existed to provide a few extra exotic colors, only to fill in the few remaining blanks with them: the color of foreignness, of variation, of everything considered ancient and destined to disappear in the shadows of a lofty American-designed dream that rose above all else and scraped the very sky with fire.

Umeki Miyoshi possessed colossal talents as an actor, singer and dancer. But in the end, there was no place for those gifts to blossom in her "tight little island home"—or so she believed—and there was no room for them to grow and flourish in her big wide-open adopted home. All she wanted to do was play the parts that suited her talents, not her ethnicity. She died in 2007, age seventy-eight, and is buried in Boone Creek Cemetery in Licking, Missouri, together with her second husband, Randall Hood, who died in

1976. The only personal marking on the gravestone is the single given name "Miyoshi."

One of Japan's greatest film directors, Ozu Yasujiro, has left us with some words that resonate across hemispheres and generations. When I think of the wisdom of these words, I feel all the more that, in my bones, I, too, am Japanese, though the United States is the country of my birth and upbringing, and Australia is the country of my citizenship. Is that a contradiction? Perhaps it is on paper, but not in my mind. I still believe that it is possible to harvest the riches of your ethnicity and present the gifts given to you by your nationality and yet become somebody else—something else— whatever the society around you may insist you are.

Self-definition is the only definition.

Despite their setbacks, Umeki Miyoshi, Mimura Akira, Taro Yashima and Mako never ceased to be Japanese in the amazing gifts they presented to their adopted country, the United States of America.

They are my role models.

I will leave the final words on the role of an artist and the importance of individual responsibility to two iconic artists.

The first, Ozu Yasujiro, wrote, "Follow the popular in things that are of no consequence. Follow morality in things that are of great importance. Follow yourself in art."

The second motto has been passed down to us by the remarkable poet Akashi Kaijin. It tells us, as I interpret it, that the way in which we view our past as a part of our present and take responsibility for our future rests with us: "If you yourself do not burn like the fish who live in the depths of the sea, there will be no light anywhere."

Akashi Kaijin, a native of Numazu in Shizuoka Prefecture, was diagnosed with Hansen's disease when he was twenty-six years old, passing away age thirty-seven in 1939.

THE FIRE ON THE SHORE

44

The Railway Man, the Father and the Son

The war still wouldn't let go of me.

On March 11, 2012, I found myself in Morioka, the prefectural capital of Iwate in Tohoku, about to deliver the keynote address at a very special assembly. This was the first anniversary of the Great East Japan Earthquake, a magnitude nine seismic event causing a tsunami that reached in some points nearly to forty meters above sea level and killing, including those still missing, upwards of 18,400 people. The resultant nuclear accident at the Fukushima Daiichi Nuclear Plant created the worst radiation damage to Japan since the fallout from the atom bombs in and around Hiroshima and Nagasaki.

The venue for the speech was the majestic Iwate Prefecture Public Hall, a building commissioned in 1923, to celebrate the marriage of Crown Prince Hirohito, and completed in 1927. I arrived early, was led into a spacious drawing room and left there. High ceilings, old radiators lining the walls and the dark oak furniture created the harmonious Japanese-cum-Western atmosphere of public and domestic buildings of the early Showa era. Hatoyama Yukio, the ex–Prime Minister of Japan, who was to give the official greetings for the event, was waiting in the adjoining room.

An hour before the ceremonies were to commence there was a knock at the door, and one of the officials of the event entered. He said that there was someone who wanted to speak with me.

"I'm sorry," I said. "I usually do speak with everyone, but actually I'm a little nervous, and I think I had better prepare for my speech."

The official bowed and left, shutting the door. I had given many speeches all around the country—some to the entire student body, faculty and staff of large schools, as well as to groups of senior executives, and others—but this particular speech in Morioka, to an audience of about eight hundred people, many of them relatives and friends of victims of the disaster of the previous year, was an awesome challenge, that is, awesome in the old sense of the word, meaning daunting and frightening. There was a knock at the door again and the same official appeared.

"This man seems to be insistent that he must see you, Mr. Pulvers. He says that you changed his life."

OMG, I thought, that's all I needed an hour before the most daunting and frightening speech of my life. I figured, however, that a diversion might be just the kind of thing that could assuage my nervousness.

"Please let him in."

A man in his mid-seventies entered carrying a large shopping bag.

"Thank you very much for seeing me," he said, bowing.

"Thank you very much for coming," I said, bowing back and gesturing for him to sit down.

He produced some materials from the shopping bag and laid them on the oak table. I immediately recognized the original program pamphlet of *Merry Christmas, Mr. Lawrence* with the photographs of the four main actors in military costume on the cover: David Bowie, Sakamoto Ryuichi, Kitano Takeshi (then known as Beat Takeshi) and Tom Conti.

"Oh, you've got a very rare program," I said.

"Yes, and you changed my life. This movie changed my life."

"Well, it was hardly me. I was only a small part of it. It was Oshima Nagisa who made the film."

The man's name was Komai Osamu. He was born in Morioka and had lived there nearly his entire life.

"Sakamoto Ryuichi played Capt. Yonoi in the film, the cruel commander of the POW camp," he said. "Well, my own father was just such a commander in real life. He was at the POW camp at Kanchanaburi in Thailand, the notorious camp that played such a major part in the building of the Thai-Burma Railway."

Komai Osamu and I spoke for the entire hour, and it was a good thing in the end, for it took my mind off my speech. I had decided to begin the speech, as I always do, with some jokes. This approach comes from my Jewish background. Jokes always break the ice if they work, and the ice at formal Japanese events is often as thick as plate glass. Of course, if they don't work it becomes a chilling disaster for all concerned. On the other hand, Japanese speakers traditionally begin speeches by apologizing for not being worthy of appearing before such an "august audience." My old and now sadly departed friend, the masterful interpreter Muramatsu Masumi, told me that he often began speeches by saying, "I apologize for not telling a joke." This best-of-both-worlds approach always got a laugh and broke the ice in one, if you will, crack. Luckily the audience at the Iwate Prefecture Public Hall in Morioka on the anniversary of the great natural disaster responded to my initial jokes with laughter. I was moved to tears when a lady came up to me after the speech and said, "I lost my son a year ago today, and today is the first time I have laughed since. Thank you!"

Since that day in 2012, I have made the trip to Iwate more than a dozen times, forming a warm friendship with Komai Osamu. He had come that day to tell me about his father.

His father was Komai Mitsuo, born in the Tohoku city of Sendai, Miyagi Prefecture, on April 28, 1904. From age three, Mitsuo was raised in Morioka by an uncle who owned a shoe store. As a youth, he loved literature, and when he married, it was to his high school sweetheart, Yaeko, who shared his passion for the written word.

In 1929, Mitsuo landed a job in Osaka with the transportation company Kokusai Tsuun, which in 1937 changed its name to Nihon Tsuun, or Nittsu, now the gigantic international communications firm. In 1932, Mitsuo volunteered for the army and left the company. The year before, Japanese troops had invaded China, and by 1932, the puppet state of Manchukuo had been established. The young office worker must have felt a patriotic call to arms, although, after being trained for a year and reaching the rank of second lieutenant, he returned to civilian life.

On February 26, 1939, Komai Mitsuo re-enlisted and was sent to present-day North Korea, before again returning to civilian life and his family in 1941. As a reservist, though, he was called to arms in 1942, and when he left at that time it would be the last that four-year-old Osamu would see of his father.

"I don't remember what he looked like," Osamu said to me. "I have never even dreamed once of his face."

His father was sent to the Dutch East Indies (present-day Indonesia) in 1943, and from there to Thailand where, with the rank of captain, he was made second in command of the prisoner-of-war camp at Kanchanaburi. In the meantime, Yaeko was making preparations to evacuate from Osaka to her hometown of Morioka with their three little children, one of whom was Osamu.

It was an incident at the POW camp in September 1943 that changed Capt. Komai Mitsuo's life and the lives of his family in Japan after the war. At that time, the Japanese military was overseeing the construction of a railway from Bangkok to Rangoon—the notorious Thai-Burma Railway. More than 100,000 of the 240,000 Asian and Allied prisoners used as virtual slaves died as a result of disease and the merciless treatment meted out to them by brutal guards and officers. The POW camp in Kanchanaburi was near a railway bridge. A fictionalized recreation of the story of the bridge's construction formed the basis of David Lean's *The Bridge on the River Kwai*.

According to evidence presented to the postwar war crimes trial, members of the especially feared Kempeitai (Military Police Corps) in the camp discovered that some British prisoners had a radio and a map in their possession. The prisoners had taken the radio apart and dispersed the parts among themselves. Some of these parts had been discovered by guards, but the prisoners had laughed them off as "lucky charms" and were allowed to keep them. Batteries, in packages labeled "canary seeds," were smuggled into the camp. When the existence of the radio and map became known to the Japanese officers at the camp, the ringleaders were hauled in and interrogated. In all, eight British officers were beaten and tortured. Capt. Komai, having been ordered by his superior officer to take charge of the investigation, actively participated in the torture.

Normally, prisoners deemed to have been behind such a plot would have faced a military tribunal. The Japanese armed services had elaborate procedures for such trials, even in the field. Those procedures were not followed in this case. As a result of gruesome torture, two officers, Capt. Jack Hawley and Lt. Stanley Armitage, died. Another, Lt. Eric Lomax, who had drawn up the map, escaped death but had severe bruising and two broken arms.

Documents from the Military Court for the Trial of War Criminals conducted in Singapore in 1946 list all the crimes that the six Japanese soldiers—one of them Capt. Komai Mitsuo—committed at Kanchanaburi in September 1943. The six were tried in that military court for those crimes. Did Capt. Komai, Osamu's father, know that what he was doing would constitute a war crime? Or was he only acting out of a perverse sense of patriotic duty in making the British soldiers pay for the crime—punishable by death—of spying?

Osamu once showed me a postcard, the last one his father sent to his mother, dated March 27, 1945, and postmarked from somewhere in Kyushu. (Addresses naturally never appeared on such postcards during the war in order to protect secrecy of location.) Writing from Kyushu, Capt. Komai fears that his children will not remember what he looks like and he assures his wife that she should not worry about him. But the somber tone of the postcard suggests that he is far from assured himself as to the progress of the war and what his fate might be. From Kyushu, he returned to the front.

After the war, Capt. Komai was arrested and held in Singapore's Changi Prison, which was built in 1936 by the British and which was the place where some 3,000 civilians had been incarcerated by the Japanese occupiers during the war. (Approximately 50,000 POWs, mainly British and Australian, were also held near the prison, and they too are usually said to have been "held at Changi.") The charge sheet of the military tribunal accuses the six Japanese of inflicting "severe suffering and injuries" on the eight British officers, two of whom "met with their death in custody." Of the six Japanese, only Capt. Komai pleaded guilty, and on February 7, 1946, he and his co-defendant Sgt.-Maj. Iijima Nobuo were sentenced to death. The other four were sentenced to between one day and life in prison.

On March 14, 1946, at 10:02 a.m., Capt. Komai was hanged. The Imperial War Museum in London has footage that I have seen, taken by the British Armed Forces Film Unit, of Capt. Komai being led up the steps to the gallows.

One of the British officers accusing Capt. Komai Mitsuo of war crimes was Lt. Eric Lomax himself. Then 24, Lomax was a Signal Corps engineer from Edinburgh who had been captured when Britain's "impregnable fortress" of Singapore fell to the Japanese in February 1942. He was eventually transported to Thailand where he ended up at the camp in Kanchanaburi. While at the camp, Lt. Lomax conspired with fellow prisoners to hide the radio. In addition, he drew the map that, if sent to Allied troops fighting the Japanese, could have provided valuable intelligence for a possible invasion of the camp. It is a miracle that he survived the torture, which included hours of beatings, waterboarding and exposure to the elements. These "interrogations" are what killed his two fellow officers.

"My father's trial and execution had an enormous effect on the life of my family after the war," Osamu told me when we met in Tokyo. "My mother never spoke of my father's fate, and I had no idea what my father had done until I was in high school. Apparently, my mother had been telling my teachers in primary and middle school, 'Osamu's father was executed as a war criminal, so there is no knowing what he might get up to. If he does anything, please beat him.' When I was finally told this by a high school teacher, I was in shock."

Years passed during which Osamu continued to pay dearly for his father's transgressions. Companies he applied to for employment failed him at the interview stage when they learned about what his father had done. He and his family were treated like common criminals by officialdom, despite Japan being the country that sent his father to war in the first place. It was only after many years that he set out to discover more about his father, the only one of the six codefendants at the military tribunal in Singapore to plead guilty. His seeing *Merry Christmas, Mr. Lawrence* in 1983 had apparently become a spur to his interest in getting to know more about his father.

At least his father had taken responsibility for his actions, and had not attempted to hide behind the excuse of "just following orders," nor had he resorted to the blatant postwar blame-shifting that characterized the conduct of virtually all Japanese, military and civilian, accused of transgressions during the war. In addition, he had paid the ultimate price. How many fathers of the Japanese people who were condemning Osamu and his family were also guilty of brutality during the war? And how many got off scot-free by cunningly deflecting guilt onto others?

Osamu then heard of a book titled *The Railway Man*. It was published in 1995 by Eric Lomax and tells the story of his wartime experiences, including his detention in the POW camp and his torture at the hands of his captors. Osamu vowed to meet Eric Lomax and apologize for the actions of his father.

Former Lt. Lomax, who passed away in 2012, had himself come to terms with his bitter memories when he had met Nagase Takashi, the man who had interpreted for him and his captors during sessions of torture. Nagase, who returned to Japan in July 1946 to become a teacher of English, spent years atoning for his guilt and striving to make amends with former victims of Japanese torture. When Nagase finally met Lomax in 1993, he apologized over and over again.

"After our meeting I felt I'd come to some kind of peace and resolution," said Lomax of the encounter with Nagase. "Forgiveness is possible when someone is ready to accept forgiveness. At some time the hating has to stop."

It was through Nagase's good offices that Komai Osamu made contact with his father's victim. It wasn't so easy, however, for Lomax to meet the son of his torturer face to face. It took six years before he would accede to do it. He was apparently terrified that Osamu would stab him for denouncing his father. Osamu traveled to Lomax's home in Berwick-upon-Tweed, the northernmost town in England, just across the river from Scotland. They met there on June 30, 2007.

"He stared at my face in silence," Osamu said to me. "He told me it was very hard for him to understand why the son of the man who tortured him had come to apologize. I told him that I had suffered all my life for my father's crimes and that, as a Japanese, I wanted to apologize from the bottom of my heart—and this appeared to move him to understand."

"What his father did had become an obsession with him which had built up over fifty years," Lomax told *The Berwick Advertiser* newspaper on July 4, 2007. "Continuing to hate gets you nowhere. It just damages you as an individual. You have to put things in their place, otherwise your whole life is dominated by hatefulness and you are the one to continue to suffer."

Nagase Takashi, the former interpreter, passed away at age 93 in June 2011. Komai Osamu kept in contact with Eric Lomax up to the time of Lomax's death, and when Lomax's wife Patti came to Japan for the first time on the occasion of the Tokyo premiere of the film version of *The Railway Man*, Osamu stood on stage with her and they spoke warmly of each other. As Oshima Nagisa said to me of *Merry Christmas, Mr. Lawrence*, there is "an unbreakable bond" between victim and victimizer.

Capt. Komai wrote a postcard to his wife Yaeko during the war containing two lines written in katakana: "Last night I dreamed of little Osamu and I was so happy." Katakana is the script that prewar children learned first. Perhaps he hoped his little boy would be able to read his words.

My dear friend Komai Osamu, now over eighty and very ill, cannot forget seeing his own name written on a postcard sent from the front three quarters of a century ago.

45

March 11, 2011, at 2:46:18:1

Exactly one year to the day before I first met Komai Osamu I was in Tokyo. March 11, 2011, was a cold day with relatively low humidity for Tokyo at 34 percent. The low was 2.9 degrees Celsius and the high, 10.9 degrees.

I was dressed up for an important meeting. I had been called into the Naikakufu, or Cabinet Office, the hub of national government policy. At 3:00 p.m., I was to give a presentation to senior bureaucrats there on the subject of cultural diplomacy, that is, how Japan can use its culture in all its forms to its advantage on the world stage. I had served on Prime Minister Koizumi Junichiro's Cultural Diplomacy Task Force and gone a number of times for meetings to the Kantei, or Prime Minister's Official Residence, in Nagatacho. Even though the Naikakufu was located across the street from it, I had never taken notice of the building and made a point to arrive early so as to be on time.

By two-thirty I was already standing outside the building. I announced myself to the guards in the guardhouse at the entrance and they said, "Please go in." But I told them that I didn't want to be too early. I decided to take a walk around the block.

One block behind the Naikakufu is the building of the Tokyo office of Iwate Prefecture. The glass-fronted cabinet attached to the outside wall was adorned with a poster featuring Jodogahama and its lovely seascape. The beach at Jodogahama is a short drive from the port town of Miyako where I had been twice in the past, the last time being 1982 with Susan. I sighed as I thought how nice it would be to return to that beautiful spot with her.

I arrived back in front of the Naikakufu building at 2:42.

"Would you like to go in now?" asked a female guard.

"No, thank you. I think I'll wait five more minutes."

I turned around to gaze at the Official Residence of the prime minister, then the head of the Democratic Party of Japan (and a graduate of Tokyo Institute of Technology where I was teaching, Kan Naoto.) Suddenly—at 2:46 and 18.1 seconds (the Japanese are very precise about time)—the ground began to sway violently. I grasped the concrete post that I happened to be standing beside. The ground swayed even more violently. It was like standing on a Japanese *ukisanbashi*, or floating pier. "Oh, is this the big one?" I thought as I looked over to the nearby skyscrapers at Kasumigaseki. They were leaning and rocking, but not in the same direction. It looked like they might lean so far as to collide with each other. It was a scene out of a Georg Grosz painting, with tall buildings creating angles pointing every which way. Was this a moving picture of the collapse of capitalism, as Grosz had meant his image to depict? The land continued to shake and undulate for several minutes before gradually becoming still again.

"You may go in now," said the female guard, calmly. (Who is better than the Japanese at masking emotions?)

I arrived at a very large upstairs room. One wall was plastered with plasma screens. As I entered, the screens were showing the sea from above. A long white line of crested waves was making its way to the shore. It was a few minutes after three o'clock. The tsunami was traveling at several hundred kilometers an hour. There was no way of telling from the aerial shot how high those walls of water were. In fact, there was not a trace of panic or heightened anxiety in the room filled with Japan's highest-level bureaucratic policymakers.

One thing that surprised me was that my mobile phone wasn't working. No one's was. The overloaded system had shut down. It was ironic, because I had acquired the phone primarily to use in case of an earthquake. But the landlines seemed to be working. I turned to a section chief.

"Would it be possible to borrow the phone and call my wife in Sydney?" I asked him.

"Sure. Go ahead," he replied, pointing to the phone.

I reached Susan on her mobile. She had heard that the earthquake had struck and had been frantically trying to get me on my mobile. I explained the situation and said that I would try to call her in the evening.

The people at the Naikakufu decided to go ahead with the presentation. As I look back at it, this is an indication that the effects of the earthquake were underestimated in the hour after it struck. The presentation lasted an hour through a series of hefty aftershocks.

"Where are you going now?" asked one of the officials.

"There's a talk on at the Japan Foundation at Yotsuya 4-chome starting at 4:45."

"I think the trains are out," she said.

"Oh dear. Would it be possible to get a taxi?"

The section chief was standing nearby.

"I don't think so. You can use my car," he said.

"Oh, that is so kind of you. Thank you."

But when I left the building's front entrance and looked around the streets for the first time, I saw hundreds of people walking in every direction. There was an eeriness in the air that I had never sensed before in Tokyo. The rear passenger door of the car opened automatically, I put one foot in and turned to the section chief who had come down to the entrance to see me off.

"Actually," I said, "would it be possible to take this car to my home?"

"Where do you live?"

"Near Ikegami Station."

The section chief paused for a moment, said, "That's fine," to me, then instructed his driver to be back by 6:30 at the latest. It was 4:15. The trip to Ikegami, given normal circumstances, would take about forty minutes.

As we turned onto a main thoroughfare I saw literally thousands of people walking. Not one of them was using a mobile phone, so I knew that mine was still useless. When we passed a station, there were hundreds, perhaps thousands, of people milling about its entrance. The trains were not running. The roads were congested with traffic. The driver was looking increasingly worried. Then his phone rang.

"This is a satellite phone," he said, picking it up. "Yes. Yes. Yes, sir. I understand."

He turned to me.

"I am afraid that I will have to let you off here."

"No, of course, I understand. Where are we?"

"See that station? It's Gotanda."

We had covered about eight kilometers.

"Could I just ask you to check your *navi* and tell me how far it is to Ikegami?"

He punched at the little screen with his index finger as he drew up to the curb by Gotanda Station.

"It's exactly five kilometers."

Ah, five kilometers. That shouldn't take me more than about an hour and fifteen minutes, I thought.

"Please thank the section chief very much for me."

Luckily, I was wearing the long white Donegal tweed overcoat that I had bought in Dublin in 1997, and my best shoes. It was turning very cold. I started to walk along the highway amid a crowd of people so dense that there wasn't room to swing your arms. I felt sorry for women in high heels and people who might be disabled. For all of the hype in Japan about "unique Japanese preparedness," the Hanshin earthquake of 1995 and the Tohoku earthquake and tsunami of 2011 showed that this alleged "steeling of the spirit" indicates no more preparedness in concrete terms than it did when the same "indomitable" spirit was bandied about during World War II. Preparation requires meticulous contingency planning, not blind faith in your "spirit."

I arrived at Ikegami Station a few minutes after six, went directly to the supermarket, bought bread and cheese and headed for home. As yet there was no panic buying taking place at the supermarket. That would be witnessed all over Tokyo the following day when staples like bread and bottled water were sold out.

I switched on the television, and the colossal scale of the natural

disaster dawned on me. Later that evening I phoned Susan from
the pay phone in the park in front of my home. Needless to say, the
earthquake and tsunami were dominating the news in Australia as
they were all over the world. The very next night I stood in the little
park and on my mobile phone, which was by then working, filed a
report on the disaster for Australia's ABC Radio National.

46

The Devastation at Rikuzentakata

On October 11, 2011, exactly seven months to the day after the
tsunami struck the coastline of the eastern seaboard prefectures
of Tohoku, I found myself standing on the shore at Rikuzentakata,
one of the most badly affected towns.

Rikuzentakata became famous around the world for the single
pine tree, among a forest of some 60,000, that had remained
standing despite the wall of water reaching up to the fifth floor of
the Capital Hotel close by the lone pine.

I had gone to Iwate with an NHK TV crew consisting of the
director, cameraman and soundman. We were making a four-
part program about Iwate-born author and poet Miyazawa Kenji,
and our journey took us from Oshu City to Kenji's hometown
of Hanamaki, from the stunningly beautiful high meadows of
Taneyamagahara down to that desolate and devastated coastline.
(Some authors, like Miyazawa Kenji, are referred by their given
name.)

One of the themes of the program revolved around Kenji's vision
of hope for a contented and prosperous Tohoku. After the tragedy
of March 11 had left many areas of this northeastern region of
Japan unlivable, Kenji's message of compassionate sacrifice for the
good of others, as exemplified by the resolute survivors and those
volunteering there, was touching the hearts of millions both in
Japan and far beyond. His poem "Strong in the Rain" became a

rallying call to all people in Japan, helping them to somehow come to terms with the immense loss of life.

As we drove in our van down from Sumida, a village in the mountains of southern Iwate, toward the coast, there was no visible sign of damage until we were some five kilometers from Rikuzentakata. About ten percent of the town's nearly 24,000 residents were lost to the tsunami following the earthquake. Railway tracks, severed like twigs, hung over the Kesen River that flows into the town. Two local JR stations had been inundated by the tsunami that reached a height there of thirteen meters. In the vicinity of Takekoma, a huge cement company tank, about twelve meters high, had been toppled by the giant wave, carried upstream and deposited on the edge of a field. It looked like a gigantic toy abandoned in the wrong place. Telephone poles were leaning out of the ground. They all faced the sea, forced into a steep angle by the water as it made its way back to sea. Mangled rusting cars were strewn where the tsunami had carried them.

Everywhere you could see temporary prefab houses for residents who had lost their homes. At the time, there were 2,168 such dwellings in Rikuzentakata. I caught sight of scores of volunteers on the outskirts of the town. A few policemen were directing traffic here and there. They had come eight hundred kilometers and wore the uniform of the Osaka Prefectural Police.

But nothing prepared me for the shock of coming down the mountain into the town itself. It was gone. The large three-story Maiya Supermarket, gutted. The four-story City Hall building, gutted, its top-story venetian blinds hanging out of glassless windows like collapsed spider webs. The police station, the sports center—where children had taken refuge and died—the museum, the library with enormous stacks of books covered in black sand piled against the wall, the hospital with an abandoned wheelchair amid the rubble—it all comprised a collage of chaos and unimaginable loss. So much was empty and utterly lifeless: objects out of the daily life of the people such as membership cards for a video club, pocket photograph albums and even a blue water pistol stuck out of the mud at the sides of roads. The many birds' nests under the eaves of the few buildings left standing were empty, too. I stood in the sun, looking out toward the sea, and wept.

The old coastline in the bay at Rikuzentakata had been wiped away, and the water now came right up to the walls of the eight-story Capital Hotel. This had been an attractive tourist spot with its vast pine forest and beautiful view of the sea. Now only the single pine tree, dubbed the "miracle pine," remained standing. In fact, along the 230-kilometer coastline north of Chiba Prefecture, two-thirds of the trees had disappeared.

Also washed away were the livelihoods of hundreds of thousands of people in Tohoku. Among the most prized bonito fish of Japan are the *modorigatsuo*, those "returning bonito" that make the journey back south along the coast primarily in the autumn. The nearby town of Kesennuma, very heavily hit by the tsunami, occupied first place in Japan for both the amount and value of bonito caught. But with so many boats lost or damaged, Kesennuma's fishermen would be lucky to land one-fourth of the annual bonito catch. This is only one small example of the hardships that fishermen, farmers and people in all walks of life in Tohoku were experiencing as a result of the tsunami.

For the entire modern period of Japanese history, ever since the Meiji Restoration in 1868, the people of Tohoku have been looked down on by their compatriots in the more prosperous regions to the south. *Donkusai* (slow-witted) and *akanuketeinai* (unrefined, gauche) are two adjectives that have often been used to describe them during a century and a half of Japanese development. Many people in that part of the country are only too aware of their prewar role to supply Tokyo with soldiers from their men, prostitutes from their women, and rice from their farmers.

It became clear to me during that five-day trip to Iwate in October 2011 that the future of Tohoku lies in its reinvention. I realized that to rely solely on financial aid from Tokyo to restore the devastated districts to their former state would only put this neglected region right back where it was before March 11. The circumstances for people whose livelihood were affected are, of course, dire. But the overall impact of damage from the tsunami was not great by national standards. Fukushima, Miyagi and Iwate, the three prefectures with virtually all of the substantial damage, accounted for just four percent of Japan's GDP, and only sections of the economies of those prefectures were struck. The question was not whether to restore or not, but what kind of region would the Japanese wish Tohoku to be and represent.

I devised a phrase while on that trip. It is LBT: Look Beyond Tokyo. This is the only way that Tohoku can survive. In fact, I would go all the way for the people of Tohoku and say LBJ: Look Beyond Japan. Tohoku should reinvent itself as a semi-autonomous region and not rely again on Tokyo for its historical raison d'etre. The opportunities to develop alternative forms of energy in Tohoku are awesome. In addition, this is surely one of the most beautiful regions in Asia. Recrafted tertiary educational institutions could attract many more students from China, Korea, Vietnam and other parts of Asia and the world. Tohoku should consider itself a part of fast-growth Asia, not slow-growing Japan. Tohoku has the people—now seen in their true light as resilient, industrious and mindful of the natural beauty of their homeland—and the cultural amenities to be the Scotland of Asia.

47

Kenji and Tohoku, Humans and Nature

Up on the sweeping plateau at Taneyamagahara, where the rolling meadow angles straight up to the sky, I thought of Miyazawa Kenji, who was inspired by the unique landscape there to write six of his stories. He found more than literary inspiration and solace on that high plain in his native Iwate Prefecture. He knew that the people of Tohoku could aspire to a better life if they came to appreciate the power of nature and all that it promises. Tohoku had been left behind in his lifetime (1896-1933). Iwate was openly called "the Tibet of Japan," a term I heard until the 1980s, when it was deemed prejudicial and became obsolete.

Kenji the agronomist joined with Kenji the poet and Kenji the Buddhist philosopher to fashion a plan for green social design and animal welfare that was decades ahead of his time in any country of the world. His writings could provide the plan to energize Tohoku. Japan proper was already far behind Western democracies in its consciousness of these two issues of critical importance

The triple disaster of the earthquake, tsunami and nuclear contamination of the land and water could be a turning point for Tohoku only if they were given a free hand to reinvent the region as part of a twenty-first-century model of sustainable growth in harmony with nature. This was the message that Miyazawa Kenji, the great poet of Iwate, had sent out to the rest of Japan and the world. He teaches us that no plan of development that destroys the bounty of nature should ever be adopted; no view of humankind that places it above all other forms of life should ever be held.

48

Immunity from Disaster?

The third catastrophe—that of nuclear contamination—posed a problem that was much bigger than all Tohoku. How did such a calamity come about in a country with such sophisticated technology and disciplined management? The answer is that the technology and mindset to prevent the nuclear catastrophe, sophisticated and "determined" as they were, were not at all fit for the scale of the disaster.

Tokyo Electric Power Company (TEPCO)—the owners and operators of the Fukushima Daiichi Nuclear Plant with its four reactors (plus two more not far away)—had considered such an earthquake and tsunami to be *soteigai*, or outside the realm of predictability. This despite the fact that the very same region was struck in 1896 and 1933 by two massive tsunami that reached heights comparable to the one in 2011. The 1896 Sanriku earthquake and tsunami killed more than 22,000 people, surpassing by several thousand the death toll in 2011. The 2011 catastrophe was well within the realm of predictability. But if you believed that it wasn't, you would not need to apply the means to prevent your reactors from collapsing into meltdown. As for disciplined management, anyone familiar with the culture of the Japanese knows that Japanese "discipline" implies the unquestioning allegiance of workers on the ground to decisions made, some of them for expedient political reasons, by the managers above them. Some engineers in TEPCO, as well as experts in the universities, knew full well what dangers were lurking in the location and operation of the plant. They were brushed aside and denied a voice in both the company ear and the public eye.

One person who has spoken out since the disaster is the prime minister at the time, Kan Naoto. Prime Minister Kan published a book in October 2012 revealing the inside story. Published in paperback by Gentosha, *Toden Fukushima genpatsu jiko sori toshite kangaeta koto* (My thoughts as prime minister on the TEPCO Fukushima nuclear plant accident), this book is a highly revealing document of the crucial events as witnessed and written by the person who was at the very center of the decision-making process in Japan. Kan believed TEPCO to be the root of the accident's cause and the concomitant damage it continues to spread in the region—on land and in the sea.

As the true nature of the disaster unfolded in the weeks and months following the earthquake and tsunami, Kan came to see that no one would be safe in Japan until all of the country's nuclear plants were shut down and decommissioned. How and why he came to this conclusion is the paramount theme of the book. The book does not purport to be an apologia for himself.

"It is not for politicians to judge the value of their work and actions as politicians," he wrote in the foreword. "I have no course but to trust that judgment to history."

He goes on to speak of the catastrophe that befell the Chernobyl nuclear power plant in the U.S.S.R. (present-day Ukraine) in April 1986, having studied its aftermath in the accident reports, adding, "But I hadn't dreamt such a thing could occur in Japan."

Even a prime minister with a science background had been a victim of the Japanese myth of preparedness. Perhaps the greatest lesson to be learned from the Fukushima disaster—and one that, it seems, has still not been thoroughly learned—is that few in Japan had dreamt of the possibility of such an occurrence in their country. Yet immunity was a pipe dream, no more reliable than the pipes that carried water to cool the nuclear fuel rods in the reactors. This mentality of devious and blatant hubris was not part of the problem: it *was*, and still *is*, the problem itself. And another nuclear disaster cannot be ruled out in the Japan of today.

Kan, a graduate of the applied physics department at Tokyo Institute of Technology, was, from the standpoint of prior scientific knowledge, the right person in the right place at that terrible time. He wrote:

> When I heard that the plant had lost all electricity after the earthquake and tsunami, and that the ability to cool down the reactors had been lost, I felt my face freeze in shock. I knew that what followed was meltdowns. . . . The Nuclear and Industrial Safety Agency is responsible for dealing with nuclear accidents, and yet they could give me nothing in the way of explanation or an estimation of what might transpire. . . . So I had no choice but to establish a system in the Prime Minister's Official Residence at a very early stage to gather information.

Then, in the early hours of March 15, Kan was told of TEPCO's intention to abandon the site of the accident. Again, Kan's words:

> The first week after the accident was a nightmare. The consequences kept escalating. At 8:00 p.m. the first night,

Reactor No. 1 experienced a meltdown. . . . The next afternoon a hydrogen explosion occurred there. Reactor No. 3 went into meltdown on March 13, and on March 14, it, too, had a hydrogen explosion. I was at TEPCO headquarters at 6:00 a.m. on March 15 when it was reported that a loud boom had been heard coming from Reactor No. 2. . . . I began to think that we might be facing the worst-case scenario.

The worst-case scenario that haunted the prime minister was a domino effect of meltdowns inside reactors and fuel-rod pools as repair and maintenance became progressively too dangerous to undertake. The nightmare's terrorizing eventuality was the spread of radiation south, leading to the evacuation of tens of millions of people from the greater Tokyo zone and the relocation of the organs of government.

TEPCO officials have insistently denied that they were preparing to abandon the stricken plant, admitting only to planning a partial retreat from its most critically affected areas. With the powerful pro-nuclear lobby in business and government backing them, their spin on the story—including the false claim of "meddling" by the prime minister, which they falsely suggest stymied necessary action—gained credence in the media. This befuddling of the facts of the story—fake news as has not been seen on this scale in Japan since the war propaganda machine was shut down—has been a key strategic element in the nuclear industry's relentless campaign to blur responsibility and to re-legitimize nuclear power generation in the seismically active islands of Japan.

The record is unequivocal: TEPCO found itself unable to control events as they took one turn after another for the worse; and had the prime minister not intervened to consolidate decision-making and expedite emergency measures, a pall of radiation may very well have descended over the entire Kanto region, making greater Tokyo unlivable. Kan chronicled the events:

It was at 3:00 a.m. when Minister of Economy, Trade and

Industry Kaeda Banri came to the Residence with the news that Shimizu Masataka, president of TEPCO, had put in a request to withdraw from the nuclear plant site. If I (had let this happen), fifty million people would have to be evacuated within a few weeks. . . . The very announcement to evacuate would result in mass panic.

He goes into great detail in his book regarding the simulation of the nightmare scenario, explaining that it was to prevent, at whatever cost, the nuclear disaster from spinning out of control that he took personal charge of its management. In Japanese, it isn't the "buck" that goes around, stopping in front of the person who must take responsibility; it's the washtub (*tarai*). Kan grabbed it, contaminated water and all, as it was being passed around and around by TEPCO officials, making sure their own hands showed no contamination from touching it.

As for those officials, it served their purposes—past, present and future—to perpetrate a notion that the prime minister was the one who continued to contaminate the water. The purposeful blurring of the lines of responsibility by the company and the media is an example of just about the most Japanese of Japanese traits there is. The working principle here is the Japanese word *nasuritsukeru*, a convenient term that means "shifting the blame for one's own misdeeds to others." It worked after the war so well that some of the very same people who executed Japan's wartime strategy were back in the seats of power with only a relatively short "leave of absence."

Kan pinpoints the source of the problem in his book.

"This was an enemy created by the Japanese themselves, that a major nuclear accident will not occur," he writes. "This was a premise established throughout Japanese society, a premise that allowed fifty-four reactors to be built. The law, the entire system of government, politics, economics, even the culture was acting under this set premise. Its conclusion was that we don't need to prepare for such a thing. It was this attitude that led to a situation in which no one was able to deal with an accident that could occur."

The aftermath of TEPCO's accident is still very much with us and will continue to be until the entire truth of what happened in Fukushima in 2011 is recognized by the people in power in Japan today. The aftermath is, in a sense, more terrifying than the disaster itself; for it is nothing more than a lead-up to further disasters of a similar or greater scale that may be awaiting us.

In the weeks and months following the accident the prime minister became convinced that "there is no such thing as safe nuclear energy. The risk of the state collapsing as a result of an accident is just too great." Before the accident there had been a plan to increase the number of reactors by at least fourteen by 2030. By the end of March 2011, Kan had resolved to scrap those plans entirely. But he could not resist the onslaught of flak produced by the big guns in industry and their fellow-travelers in the media. Support for him in his own party, the Democratic Party of Japan, eroded. On August 26, 2011, a mere five months after the earthquake, he was obliged to resign. The paradigm of a new energy strategy created by him was buried in the contaminated soils of the northeastern Tohoku region of Honshu, with a new guard standing watch, their backs to the past.

I have dwelt on Kan Naoto's retelling of events not only to chronicle them, but to illuminate the specifically Japanese cultural elements of national character that exacerbated the destructive effects of those elements. To illustrate this in a historical context I want to tell you a story about Shiba Ryotaro, the great author of historical novels.

49

"Run 'em Down!"

Shiba Ryotaro was a student of the Mongolian language at Osaka University of Foreign Languages when, at the end of 1943, he was drafted into the army. Then aged twenty, he received a "provisional graduation qualification" (the actual certificate was issued the following year) and found himself in Manchuria, which was at that time the Japanese puppet state of Manchukuo.

After he entered the Army School at Siping—where, already exhibiting literary proclivities, he founded a haiku club among the ranks—he was assigned to tank duty. Though he excelled more with traditional tanka poems than tanks, he was sent to Mudanjiang, in what is now Heilongjiang Province in northeastern China, and made platoon commander of a tank unit. Writing years later he recalled putting a question to his commanding officer.

"If the enemy lands here," he said, "we'll have to take the tanks south. But the roads are really narrow. What do we do if horse-drawn carts are coming the other way?"

"The officer stared at me in silence for a while," wrote Shiba, "and then gave his answer. 'Run 'em down!'"

I bring up this incident from long ago because it characterized the attitude toward forward planning that pervaded this country's military forces during World War II. That attitude is eerily pervasive today in the government and corporate culture of Japan.

It is customary in Japan at the end of each year to choose a word that best describes the esprit of that year. My choice for the years since 2011 is, hands down, *musekinin*.

Musekinin means "irresponsibility." But the Japanese word is somewhat stronger in tone than the English one—more akin to "a total absence of responsibility," or "a lack of a sense of liability."

No matter that the Great East Japan Earthquake and tsunami of March 11, 2011, was followed by events that led to multiple reactor meltdowns. The generation of nuclear power has once again become the Japanese government's official policy. As with the millions of Asian victims of Japanese aggression prior to the end of World War II in 1945, the policy adopted "after the event" is to mollify victims with ambiguous and insincere apologies and wait until the last one dies. This is the approach taken by the Japanese government toward the victims of the nuclear calamity at Fukushima. The same "run 'em down" mindset is again, basically, not far from being the mindset of the corporate bosses in the nuclear industry—or, if not run 'em down, then run 'em out—which is what they did to the people of the radiation-affected districts of Fukushima Prefecture without proper care for their welfare or future.

In this way, politicians, bureaucrats and the corporate elite are evading responsibility for both the lethargy of innovation in the planning of Japan's economy and the contamination of its land, air and water, and what both of these have meant for people's livelihoods. They have not apologized in any meaningful way nor have they shown any true sense of responsibility for these two catastrophes of mismanagement and cover-up regarding the real causes of the nuclear disaster, namely their own incompetence. Their solution is to return to the *status quo ante*, dig in their heels, pick up their antiquated weapons—the only tools at their disposal—and carry on fighting. It's World War II all over again, fought out not on the battlefields of Asia and the Pacific but on the fallow and contaminated fields of Tohoku. This is what is meant by *musekinin* as we approach what may be the point of no return that this country faces into the third decade of our century.

But then, another key word emerged in 2017. This word is *sontaku*.

Sontaku is an old word that means "conjecture." But its new usage indicates an attitude and action adopted and taken by an underling to please a superior without that superior having specifically directed it. I call it "preemptive sycophancy." More and more often in the realms of corporations and bureaucracies, not to mention the media, people are adjusting their behavior by either making false statements or no statements at all in order that those above them might be pleased. Needless to say, *sontaku* is not only a Japanese phenomenon; it has been practiced in offices in every country of the world and in every era. Perhaps it's only more blatantly obvious in Japan because it is an integral part of the culture of what is called "the flower of silence."

There was a reason for my referencing the nuclear story with incidents from the war, for the wartime mindset of organized irresponsibility is alive and kicking in today's Japan.

Way back in 1946, writing in the May issue of the magazine *Sekai* (World), Maruyama Masao, the most brilliant political scientist of the postwar period, referred to the military mindset as one that protected "the organization" above all else. What he meant was that all appeals to the organization for rationality or logic on the basis of objective analysis of a real situation are rejected in the interests of the decisions taken by the organization—be it an army, a government agency or an electric power company. And so, though you are facing a catastrophe, such as total defeat in war or the probability of another nuclear accident occurring, you continue to ignore factual data that contradict the organization's set plan. If you are defeated, you simply go on to ignore your victims and glorify those who persevered in the name of "the cause."

Just as the bankrupt ideology of communism doomed rational economic and social planning in the old Soviet Union to failure, just as the ideology of anti-communism doomed the United States to the committing of war crimes (without apology or compensation) in Southeast Asia, so the ideology of organizational irresponsibility and the hypocritical shirking of liability are dooming Japan to moral, economic and social decline today. This time it is not the peoples of Asia and the Pacific but the populace of Japan who will be run into the ground, where they will be expected to stay—docile, dejected and defeated—until the white gloves of the next election's candidates appear before their eyes and their temporary presence is required in the voting booth.

50

A World with One Shore

There are many root causes for this mindset of organized irresponsibility that has remained steadfast so many years after the defeat in a war, though, by all rights, it should have been buried once and for all in the war's wake.

My dearest friend, the late playwright Inoue Hisashi, believed that it was the failure to link the wartime responsibility to the emperor that was at the core of the problem of irresponsibility.

"If the emperor, who was at the top of the chain of command, did not have to apologize for the defeat and take responsibility for Japan's cruel war in Asia and the Pacific," he told me in December 1974, "then why should any Japanese feel the necessity to take responsibility for anything?"

In other words, you can acknowledge that the invasion of the Asian mainland was a horrific blunder; you can admit that not those individuals in charge but "the ambiguous culture of Japan" was at fault for the radioactive contamination that has ruined hundreds of thousands of lives; but no one must be *compelled* to take final responsibility for these transgressions. We should all now put these "tragedies" behind us and move happily toward the future.

The trouble is that there is no way in the world you can avoid igniting another disastrous blaze if you do not go back and pick up the charred fragments in the fire you set and conveniently left behind you. Those fragments must be studied and examined assiduously, just as experts in the fire department do so to determine the cause of a fire.

Do we the people have any recourse other than to stand by the side of the road and watch as the tanks roll on, crushing anything in their way? Are we ordinary people doomed to perform our little *sontaku* behaviors, keeping silent so as not to displease or inconvenience those above us? Will people stand up and force their commanders to accept liability for the ruined land and the decimated population left behind?

These questions arise not only in the context of the aftermath of calamities created by Japanese but also of those created by any other nationality. If we continue to pass the washtub of water that we ourselves contaminated to others—be they our contemporaries or our descendants—then what will we do when our leaders drag us smack into the middle of another catastrophe on the road ahead of us? Will we be able to claim we mistook the deadly flames destined to engulf us for the comforting glow of a campfire over our horizon?

When do we scream "STOP!"? Why do we continue to fall for the aggressive posturing of our leaders, as if it truly represented strength of conscience and virtue? As someone who writes, I just wish I knew the answers to these two questions.

There is a Japanese phrase that comes to my mind. It is *taigan no kaji*. *Taigan* means the opposite shore. *Kaji* means fire. This phrase denotes that something is of little or no concern to you. There is a fire that you cannot refuse to see. But it is not where you are, so you can be indifferent to its cause or effect. Or worse, you can feed it, allow it to devour others far away, telling yourself in a delusion of self-righteousness that by doing so you are preventing it from jumping the river—or the ocean—and landing on your shore.

In our world, intimately interconnected as it is, all fires burn on our shores no matter how far away they are from us in distance or time. If you cause miseries to others far away, you are bound, in the twenty-first century, to see the very same miseries fall, with full force, onto your own head.

Today's world has only one single shore, and we are all on it.

KENJI'S NET

51

The Man Out of Step

When Miyazawa Kenji died on September 21, 1933 he was an obscure self-published author of what were considered, by the few who read them, fantasy tales for children. In December 1924, a collection of his stories under the title of one of them, *Chumon no oi ryoriten* (*The Restaurant of Many Orders*), had been published by Kogensha in Morioka. (The lovely old buildings of Kogensha still stand in the district of the city now named after Kenji's imaginary country of Ihatov. Ihatov is an Esperanto-like rendering of Iwate.) Kenji's beliefs and preoccupations could not have been more detached from those of his fellow Japanese—and fellow humans around the world—in his day.

This was an era of fanatical nationalism and impassioned self-scrutiny. Japan had set itself on the course of imperial expansion after its 1895 victory in the Sino-Japanese War and was unable to curb its ambitions. The military in particular nurtured grandiose ambitions of a pan-Asian empire with Japan at the pinnacle of the pyramid of power.

On March 1, 1932, the year before Kenji died, Japan formally established the puppet state of Manchukuo in northern China, and on May 15, Prime Minister Inukai Tsuyoshi was assassinated by right-wing extremists and reactionary elements in the army and navy. Another target was Charlie Chaplin, who had been scheduled to be with the prime minister that day but went to watch sumo instead. The objective of the officers who killed the prime minister was clear: to assert military power over civilian authority. This was to become the main theme of the decade, and it was without a doubt the supremacy of military power over civilian that provided the impetus to go farther into Asia and attack the United States at Pearl Harbor on, to note the date in Japan, December 8, 1941.

In that era of chauvinism and Japanocentrism, author and poet, natural scientist and Buddhist philosopher Miyazawa Kenji was writing his works in which the words "Japan" and "the Japanese" make almost no appearance. His obsession was that of ours now: how humans can live in harmony with other animals, plants and the inorganic world and still generate the energy and productivity necessary to provide an adequate and satisfying life for all people.

"There will be no individual happiness anywhere until all people in the world are happy," is one of his mottos. Idealistic, yes. An unattainable goal, certainly. But Kenji practiced what he preached and worked tirelessly, to the detriment of his own health, for the farmers of his native Iwate. He was a vegetarian from age twenty-one in a country where even today there are few. He felt he was ready, like a character in one of his stories, to go right up to the sun, steal its sunspots and bring them back to Earth if that would solve the energy problems of the planet. He was totally out of step with his compatriots who were marching together, with increasing determination, toward confrontation with the then existing empires of the world. And yet his very steps are the ones we today seem reluctant to take—the steps into a world where we create progress without decimating the organic and inorganic realms that sustain us.

If we are all interconnected, breathing the same air, drinking the same water, communicating with the same devices, relying on the same satellites, then how do we turn those connections from a medium of contamination and destruction to one of compassion and caring?

I found the answer to that all-important question in the writings of Miyazawa Kenji and in my lifelong immersion into Japanese culture.

52

Kenji's Net

The world today certainly depends on the net to keep it together. Kenji, too, had his own net, and one far more cosmic in scale than the one we all use today.

In his short story "Indra's Net," Kenji sees all things as being interlinked by threads. These threads connect not only person to person but all things, organic and inorganic. The universe itself is traversed and permeated by a net of interdependence. If one thread breaks, wherever it may be, all others are affected.

The drops of dew on the net form a mirror in which we can see ourselves. This reflection is, in turn, reflected countless times in the drops of dew behind, to the sides and in front of us. You can see yourself in your dew-mirror, and in the reflection, you also see what is reflected in the dew-mirror behind you. Everything in front of you is reflected in it. In the curvature of the dewdrop you can see what is above and below you and what is to your left and right.

Kenji's net of threads and mirrors exists not only in space but in time as well. In the dewdrop mirrors you can peer far into the past and far into the future. Underlying Kenji's poetry is the notion that you cannot describe a place faithfully if you do not know what transpired there in the distant past and what is likely to happen there in the future. Kenji's "now" encompasses all time and all space. As far as I know, there is no other poet like him.

Kenji's net comes, in concept, directly from India. Indra's net is a Buddhist metaphor whose creation dates back at least twelve hundred years. Kenji personalized that metaphor in his story, and it is the personalization that points a way—like the needle of a moral compass—that each of us may take. He begins the story, as he does some other stories of his, with a lone traveler exhausted by the arduous journey to find himself:

It seemed then that I had collapsed, out of utter exhaustion, on a bed of green grass and wind.

In that faint of autumn wind I exchanged bows, courteous to a fault, with my tin-colored shadow.

Then, I stepped alone onto a dark cowberry carpet and traveled about the Tsela Plateau.

The story goes on to describe of vision of paradise as seen from Tsela Pass in northern India:

The cowberry boasted red fruit.

The white sky blanketed the entire plateau. It was a cold white, whiter than kaolin china.

The rarefied air sang in a high-pitched whirr, no doubt due to the sun making its lonely way beyond the white porcelain clouds. The sun had already sunk below the black barbed ridges in the west, creaking in the dim light of a late afternoon.

I looked around, gasping like a fish.

Wherever I looked, there wasn't even a shadow of a bird, nor was there so much as a trace of any gentle beast.

"What on earth am I visiting here in the upper reaches of the atmosphere, moving around in this air that cuts through me?"

I asked this of myself.

Kenji aspired to be an ascetic whose guiding principle was *kinyoku* (abstinence, the control of worldly passion). In his prose and poems, he often plunges himself into the most physically and mentally trying circumstances, where he confronts his real self and examines it. When he gets to the Tsela Pass (which is described as "part of the galaxy itself") he encounters an angel shooting through the sky "at ten kilometers in the blink of an eye." And yet at the same time it isn't moving at all: "It isn't even budging. It's soaring ahead so far without moving, without changing place, without changing form."

Then the narrator realizes that what he senses externally before him is a part of his own internal makeup: "There's something really funny here! I thought to myself, standing there. This celestial space seems to be right beside my sensations."

It is there that he comes into contact with Indra's net:

> I looked up at the sky. The zenith was now azure blue, and from it to the four corners of the pale edges of the sky, Indra's spectral net vibrated radiantly as if burning, its fibers more fine than a spider's web, its construction more elaborate than that of hypha, all blending together transparently, purely, in a billion intermingled parts.

The wind is drumming. But as with the motion of the angel that is both fluid and static at the same time, the sound of the drum is both heard and silent:

> Impervious to human striking, the drums pounded out a sound with all their might. And while those countless heavenly drums called out, they seemed to be making no sound at the same time. I watched it all for so long that my eyes clouded over and all I could do was stagger about.

In the end . . .

> I vaguely recalled my own figure collapsed deep into the green grass and the wind.

This story is an elaborate and exquisitely lyrical metaphor of a universe in which we are both ceaselessly aware of our place and helplessly ignorant of what it means to us.

Miyazawa Kenji posed a question to us that we are only just beginning to pose to ourselves and, possibly, may just be able to answer: What is our place in the universe?

He must certainly be the world's only author who described

himself as a single illumination of light. The actual lines, the very first in the preface poem of his book *Haru to shura* (*Spring and Ashura*), are again a self-definition, this time as a ray of light.

> *The phenomenon called I*
> *Is a single blue illumination*
> *This ray of light comes from karma's alternating current lamp . . .*
> *Flickering unceasingly, restlessly*
> *Together with the sights of the land and all else*

Among his poems, perhaps this preface best describes his take on life. This take is all-encompassing. He does not view human life, or any other form of life, for that matter, as separate from the rocks, mountains, rivers, the light or the wind. This is what he means by "Together with the sights of the land and all else."

While his vision is poetic and perhaps difficult to discern, his message is clear: that humans are only one tiny unit in the vast schema of life, and that we are not above all other elements but rather exist on the very same plane. The destruction of any of those elements causes the threads of the net to tear and snap, and we fall together with all else.

53

The Water Letters

Inoue Hisashi, who was born in Iwate's neighboring prefecture of Yamagata in the year after Kenji's death, wrote a play for recitation titled *Mizu no tegami* (*The Water Letters*). I was fortunate to have had the opportunity to translate it for presentation at the International PEN Congress held in Tokyo in September 2010. Sadly, Hisashi had passed away in April that year. It is in this work that he outlines the notion of us all being in the same boat.

Hisashi was not preoccupied as Kenji was with nature and its significance to humanity. He was an indoor man, a bookworm who read more voraciously than anyone I have ever known. But late in his life, as a by-product of his ardent interest in the production of rice in Japan and the plight of rice farmers (he had this in common with Kenji), Hisashi turned to the natural environment as it affected the lives and livelihoods of people around the world.

The Water Letters is a compilation of letters read to the people of Yamagata. It urges them to link the fate of the water in their own river, the Mogami, with the state of the waters of the world.

In the play, the people reading letters about how water affects them are the following: A brother and sister in Uzbekistan who are forced to leave their village because the Aral Sea is drying up; an old man bemoaning "the endless stretch of mud and the feeble flow" of his beloved Colorado River in the United States; a twelve-year-old Chinese boy who is scared because the Yellow River "just vanishes away the closer it gets to the sea"; and a girl in Mexico City whose school is teetering on its foundations because the government has been pumping up too much underground water for the city's twenty million inhabitants. In addition, the audience hears from a man who lives in the Maldives, the island state in the Indian Ocean threatened by rising sea levels; a woman in Venice researching the sinking of her city; two little children in Chad who must walk twenty-two kilometers a day to fetch and bring home two pails of water from a well; and a university student in Paris who decries the toll that acid rain is taking on the city's statues. "What about Japan?" the student asks the audience. "Are the bronze statues of Yamagata also corroding away?" Hisashi linked the people of Japan with people around the world.

"Earth is the planet of water," he writes in the play. "Our planet is blessed by water. We are given life by its powers. But more than that, we were born of water and that's why we are water ourselves."

In the mid-Edo period, Hayashi Shihei, a scholar from Sendai, wrote, "The water of the Sumida River (in Tokyo) is linked to the water of the Thames," succinctly stating even at a time when Japan was a country closed off to the world that it is water that interconnects us wherever we are. The message of both Inoue Hisashi and Hayashi Shihei is this: there is no way that we can cut ourselves off from our interconnectedness. With *The Water Letters*, Hisashi was identifying totally with the author that—as he told me many times—he most loved, Miyazawa Kenji.

There are many Japanese creative people who have their feet firmly planted in their native soil but whose vision spans the globe. We know that Henrik Ibsen speaks for us despite the fact that some of his plays are located squarely in provincial Norway. We see ourselves in Chekhov's supremely Russian characters.

So it is with many Japanese artists whose depiction of the people and places around them takes on a universal significance. The dewdrop mirror of Japanese art and literature is in front of us all.

54

Oshima Nagisa and Koyama Akiko

Working in 1982 as assistant to director Oshima Nagisa on *Merry Christmas, Mr. Lawrence* and coming to know him well in subsequent years was a supreme joy. He often quoted to me the phrase "the republic of the cinema," as if film were a country and he one of its citizens. He combined the very best moral qualities of the Japanese with a forthright and radical international outlook.

I came to know him well when he visited Australia in 1981 on the occasion of a retrospective of his films presented by the Australian Film Institute. As his interpreter and guide I travelled with him from Melbourne to Canberra and on to Sydney. It was on the plane from Canberra to Sydney that he handed me an early draft of the script of *Merry Christmas, Mr. Lawrence*.

Oshima had a soft spot in his heart for Australia because it was at a film festival in Adelaide that one of his films was shown internationally for the first time. The film was *Shonen* (Boy).

The boy in the title is little Toshio. Toshio, who moves around the country with his unemployed parents, is pushed against moving cars by his father, then used as fodder in a scam to extort cash on the spot from unsuspecting terrified drivers. Believe it or not the story is based on that of a real family. There is even a word in Japanese for people who purposely put themselves or are pushed like that in harm's way: *atariya*. This word also can mean someone who is lucky, because the verb *ataru* also means to hit the mark or be successful. *Atariya* can refer to a lucky batter in baseball, for instance. The pathetic irony denoted by the *atariya* in Oshima's film comes from the former kind of "hit." I saw *Boy*, released in 1969, long before I met its director, and have always considered it one of his three best films, along with *Ai no korida* (In the Realm of the Senses) and *Merry Christmas, Mr. Lawrence.*

Oshima had a remarkable gift for portraying the innocence and special sensitivities of children, as shown in one of his earliest films, a thirty-minute-long work put together from stills shot in Korea, *Yunbogi no nikki* (Yunbogi's diary). He would have preferred to actually film this story of a little Korean slum orphan compelled to work in order to provide for his brother and sisters. But when he went to Korea with his film camera, Korean-Japanese relations were still fraught with animosity and Japanese filmmakers were not permitted to use them. The year was 1965, and though diplomatic relations between the two countries were normalized that year, all Japanese films, music and books were still banned in South Korea. (Not until the late nineties did the Korean government begin to lift some of these bans.)

I think that Oshima may have identified with sad little boys (as did Ozu), for although his mother lived a long life and was dedicated and affectionate, he had lost his father when he was six years old. His father's family had come from Tsushima, the island roughly midway between Japan and Korea, and it was from the name of the island that his surname Oshima is derived.

"Many Japanese people have been critical of my depicting such an awful Japanese phenomenon as that of the *atariya*," he told me on that trip to Australia in 1981. "But love of country is a strange thing. Just puffing out your chest with national pride and telling people how wonderful your country is does not constitute love of country as I see it."

Producing an Oshima film was never easy. While making *Boy* in 1968 he ran out of money. His wife, Koyama Akiko, a famous actress then and now, was forced to go around clothing stores in Shikoku, one of the film's main locations, offering to model kimonos in locally broadcast television commercials.

After Oshima's first stroke in 1996, she devoted her time to his rehabilitation and she herself was struck by caregiver's depression. The depression sent her to hospital and led her to seriously contemplate suicide. But she fought her way out of the depths of depression and published a most beautiful book in 2011, *Onna toshite, joyu toshite* (As a woman, as an actor), in which she wrote the following:

> I want to live valuing each and every day as it comes. That has been my motto ever since the day that my husband, Oshima Nagisa, fell ill in 1996—and it hasn't changed. Faced with my husband's illness I made it a priority to care for him over pursuing my career as an actress. And I have not wavered once from that choice. . . . I consider the family unit to be that of husband and wife. I always told my children, from when they were little, that they were my precious treasures, but that the person I loved more than anyone was their father.

Koyama Akiko arrived at the location of *Merry Christmas, Mr. Lawrence* after we had left Rarotonga in the Cook Islands for New Zealand in September 1982. (The flashback scenes of David Bowie's character, Jack Celliers, were shot in and around Auckland.) Oshima, a most demonstrative man when it came to all his emotions, was naturally very pleased to see her, and the four of us—the Oshimas, Susan and I—rushed to dine together at a fine Auckland restaurant. He in no way conformed to the stereotype of the reserved Japanese.

Merry Christmas, Mr. Lawrence may be specifically about the war in Asia between Japan and the Allies but its messages of the communion between enemies as not only a hate-hate relationship but a love-love one overrides place and time. It is this that I kept in mind while making my own film about enemies thrown together— *Star Sand.*

In 1985, he told me the following:

The first thing I always want to show (in my films) is what's going on inside the individual. The Japanese have always had the sense that wars are things that happen elsewhere, 'on the outside.' Even Hiroshima and Nagasaki. While Japanese people know that atom bombs were dropped on those cities, at the same time they are not truly conscious of it. They live with a self-deception. The fact is that the postwar leaders of Japan were the same people who brought on the war and all its destruction. . . . I am often asked, when I'm overseas, about the reaction to *Merry Christmas, Mr. Lawrence* in Japan. They think that I would be attacked in Japan by the right wing for showing the ugliness of the Japanese. I was not attacked by them, not at all. The reason is that people on the far right in Japan don't go to see movies like they do in the West!

When I made *In the Realm of the Senses*, I wanted to show everything possible that happens between a man and a woman. But it is not only that. It is a story that unfolds in the context of an era. Though it takes place in the 1930s, the film's context is the 1970s. With *Merry Christmas, Mr. Lawrence*, the story may take place in the 1940s, but the film is about the 1980s. You see, we view the past through the prism of our own era. I don't make so-called period films. My films are about now.

Oshima Nagisa came from that generation of artists who felt personally insulted by the indoctrination they were given in school and society during the war. He considered it his mission to redress that insult and hold up a clear mirror to the Japanese people, forcing them to look at themselves in their true light.

We appeared together for a number of years on the television talk show *Asa made no nama terebi* (Live television till morning). He never pulled any punches on air. He broke every taboo in the book, speaking his mind openly. This was possible, of course, because the show was broadcast once a month from midnight to six a.m. on Saturday, outside the framework of normal viewing. Nonetheless, on that show, in all of his public appearances and, primarily, in his films, he had no equals in being incisive, forthright and free-thinking.

"Everyone was angry with the state of affairs," he said to me of his generation. "It's just that I was the person most aware of what was going on. . . . I want to live every moment as a director in the frontline, even if it means being a target for the bullets of my enemies."

How do you tell fact from fiction in poring over the myriad details of your life? It is not as if we make up stories about ourselves out of the blue. There are always real steppingstones crossing a river, some of them large flat and smooth, others small jagged and loosely embedded. We step on all of them, now safe and steady, now about to teeter or fall.

Your task as the author of your life is to turn back, to travel into the past and study each and every stone, getting down on your hands and knees, putting them right against your eyes and your nose and your lips and assaying them for their value to you. There is no use pretending that a stone of one sort was really a different stone, that a stone was in a particular place when it wasn't. It is furthermore dishonest to give one stone a greater value than it intrinsically has.

But the important thing is to include stones whether they represent things that happened to you and people you have met or experiences you have had both in real life and in realms of art. Taken together they make up a record of where you have been and who you are now.

Oshima Nagisa taught me a great deal about going back to look at yourself in the mirror and see yourself for what you are. It is that ability, which we all possess, that allows us to see ourselves for what we have become.

55

A Woman Ahead of Her Times

I never was able to meet Ariyoshi Sawako, though I spoke with her on the phone twice. A meeting would, I think, have taken place had she not passed away at such a young age, fifty-three, on August 30, 1984. (She suffered from insomnia and fatigue, both of which may have contributed to the cause of her early death.)

Her works of fiction and nonfiction took up many social issues that came into prominence in the years after her death. To my mind, she is not only one of the greatest authors of modern Japan, but a woman who should be given recognition around the world for her impassioned feminist outlook on the misery of the disadvantaged.

During her lifetime, Ariyoshi Sawako was a celebrated bestselling novelist whose works were televised and filmed any number of times. She relished the controversy stirred up by the themes she dealt with, themes that were often unpopular at the time.

There is, for instance, her groundbreaking book about China, *Ariyoshi Sawako no Chugoku repoto* (Ariyoshi Sawako's China report), written on the occasion of her fifth trip to that country. With an anthropologist's scruples and a journalist's scrutiny she shared what is called *sando seikatsu*, or "the three living conditions," with the Chinese people. These are "sleeping under the same roof, eating the same food, and doing the same work," conditions that should be prerequisites for any study of a people. The book, full of photos of rural and urban life, describes with sincere sympathy farmers and city dwellers, the latter uprooted, as many of them were, due to the ravages of the Cultural Revolution. She lectured the farmers in the countryside about the dangers of using too much pesticide and forewarned people in Beijing and Shanghai about pollution in general. Ariyoshi's book on China is neither diatribe nor politically motivated reportage. She cared deeply about the people she met, and this comes through clearly in the writing.

"The Chinese people must know about (the pollution problem) as soon as possible," she wrote in this prophetic book published as early as March 1979. "This knowledge must be spread quickly."

Her book titled *Fukugo osen* (Complex pollution) was a pioneering study of the impact, present and future, of chemical fertilizers, detergents, carcinogenic dyes, exhaust fumes from cars and other polluting agents. It was serialized in the *Asahi Shimbun* in 1974 and 1975 and contributed significantly to the rising consciousness in Japan on ecological matters. Ariyoshi was also decades ahead of her time in her treatment of issues relating to Japanese women and the elderly, race relations, and the developing world.

Her prose works that achieved the greatest acclaim were two novels set in her native Wakayama Prefecture. The first of these, published in 1966, was *Hanaoka Seishu no tsuma*, translated as *The Doctor's Wife*. It is historical fiction that treats the relationship between the mother and wife of Hanaoka Seishu (1760-1835), the doctor who experimented with anesthesia long before it was used in most any other country. The book has been televised in six different productions, and the most recent of twenty-four theatrical stagings took place as late as 2017.

Her other bestselling novel whose location is Wakayama is *Ki no kawa*, published as *The River Ki*. Set in the first half of the twentieth century, it traces the lives and fates of three generations of women. Written in 1959 and published by Chuo Koron, it was turned into an epic TV drama by NHK in 1964 and became a feature film in 1966.

But the work of Ariyoshi that caused the greatest controversy was her novel about dementia and the caregiver's burden, *Kokotsu no hito*, known in English as *The Twilight Years*. Set in the 1970s it is the story of Tachibana Akiko who, while holding down a job at a law office, is obliged to care for her senile father-in-law. The father-in-law relies on her for his every need, while his son, Akiko's husband, a typical 1970s salaryman, is too preoccupied with his work to lift a finger of assistance. Though the novel sold a million copies in its first year of publication, the generally reactionary literary establishment turned a cold shoulder to it. Perhaps the graphic details of Akiko having to deal with the old man's incontinence were too much for the wizened literati. Those details were not spared, however, in the brilliant film version shot in 1973 in black and white by veteran director Toyoda Shiro. This book and film stand as stunning documents of Ariyoshi's prescience in dealing with an issue that is at the forefront of concern in all societies of the world.

The Ariyoshi novel that I love best is *Not Because of Color*, or, in the original Japanese, *Hishoku*. I put the titles around this way because Ariyoshi created the English title first then rendered it into the unusual Japanese one. Published in 1964, *Hishoku* is the story of a young Japanese woman who, while working in a cabaret cloakroom, meets an African American G.I. and marries him despite vigorous opposition from her parents. He takes her to New York. Living in Harlem, she encounters racial prejudice toward herself and her children. *Hishoku* is a superb study of race relations, a tale of assimilation and hope, and a novel that is even more relevant to us now than it was when Ariyoshi wrote it more than fifty years ago.

Another Ariyoshi book years ahead of its time is her travelogue of islands on the periphery of Japan, *Nihon no shimajima—ima to mukashi* (The Japanese islands— now and in the past). In this collection of essays, first serialized in *Subaru* magazine in 1980 and 1981, she takes up the story of the disputed rocky outcrops of Takeshima and the Senkaku Islands, proving that she had an eye on history and the shadows it casts on Japan's future. These islands are today the sharpest bone of contention with Japan and Korea (for Takeshima) and Japan and China (for the Senkaku Islands).

After having read a fascinating study of New Guinea that Ariyoshi published in 1968, I phoned her and asked her if she would be interested in coming to Australia to give talks. She asked for some time to think about it. When I phoned her again she said she definitely did not want to go there, as she was critical of Australia's postcolonial policy in New Guinea.

Ariyoshi Sawako was a Catholic who had spent the early years of her childhood in Dutch Indonesia. She traveled widely in her lifetime, enjoying long stints in the United States, at Sarah Lawrence College in New York and the University of Hawaii. She made her first trip to China in 1961 and went so far as to live in a People's Commune. She counted famous Chinese novelist and playwright Lao She among her close friends. Lao was so brutally tortured by the Red Guards that he apparently killed himself—if, indeed, his death wasn't murder. It was his wife, artist Hu Jieqing, who wrote Ariyoshi's obituary in the mass-circulation Chinese government-owned newspaper, *The People's Daily.*

Her death at age fifty-three from a heart attack deprived Japan and the world of an immense and far-seeing talent, one whose legacy begs for rediscovery and reassessment in our issue-conscious era. Like Miyazawa Kenji and Inoue Hisashi, she redefines what it means to be the citizen of a single country in a world with shared problems.

Her wake was held at St. Mary's Cathedral in Tokyo, and a monument to her memory stands in the precincts of the temple Horinouchi Myohoji in Tokyo's Suginami Ward, nor far from where she lived in the postwar years.

56

The Only Woman in the Room

Another indirect encounter with a person who affected my life deeply was Beate Sirota Gordon. Though not a Japanese, Beate, like me, had a Japanese person living inside her. I corresponded with her by email over a number of years.

I have written a play, which has yet to be produced, called *The Long Black Line*. Among other things, the title is a metaphor for genetic inheritance. All my adult life, I have been fascinated to a fault with this long thin black line crossing centuries and stretching back into former places to connect with ancestors. Beate Sirota Gordon, I sensed from our correspondence, was all too aware of these invisible lines that reach us in our life wherever we are.

Beate Sirota was already well known around the entire country of Japan (by her maiden name) when I contacted her in the first years of the century. I had read her book, *The Only Woman in the Room*, and, once YouTube was accessible, was avidly watching her appearances and speeches of recent years. I was impressed with her command of Japanese, a language of her childhood that she had not forgotten. My impulse was perhaps different from other people who sought her out. I wanted to know how she felt about the Japanese, a people who had treated her parents with untoward cruelty. Since she was Jewish with roots in East Central Europe like me, perhaps I wanted to see where the long black line would lead to.

Beate Sirota is the woman known for composing, in 1946, Article Twenty-Four of the Japanese Constitution establishing full rights for women in all matters dealing with marriage and family.

But the story of how she came to Japan begins long before then and traces back to the town of her paternal ancestors' birth.

Kamianets-Podilskyi lies just north of the Moldova border in Ukraine, at the crossroads of Polish, Ukrainian, Russian and Ottoman Turkish cultures. This is where her father, Leo Sirota, was born into a Jewish family. (Sirota means "orphan" and is not an uncommon Jewish name.) The Sirotas moved to Kiev, the Ukrainian capital, at the end of the nineteenth century. Leo was one of five children, all artistically talented. The three brothers fled the anti-Semitism that overtook Russian life in the early years of the twentieth century. (The Kiev Pogrom of 1905 was particularly vicious, killing approximately one hundred Jews.) They went their separate ways—Pierre to Paris, Wiktor to Warsaw and Leo to

Vienna, where Beate was born in 1923. The fate of Beate's uncles Pierre and Wiktor was tragic. Pierre became a highly successful impresario in Paris, was arrested and sent to Auschwitz, where he perished in 1944. Wiktor, who won acclaim as a conductor in Warsaw, was arrested for political activities and never heard of again. His son, Igor, took part in the D-Day landings in Normandy but was killed in action on August 20, 1944. Leo turned out to be the lucky one: he was detained but neither tortured nor killed.

In 1929, Leo Sirota, by then a famous pianist and teacher, was invited to assume a teaching position at the Imperial Academy of Music in Setagaya Ward, Tokyo, inspiring a number of musicians who would come to prominence after World War II. Beate entered the Lutheran German School in the Omori district of Tokyo, transferring to the American school for her last two years of secondary education.

"Everything was O.K. (at the German school)," she wrote me, "until (Nazi leader Joseph) Goebbels decided to send Nazi teachers to the diaspora to teach the 'Auslands-Deutsche' about the Third Reich. We had to learn to say 'Heil Hitler,' sing the 'Horst-Wessel Lied,' etc., etc. A Hitler Jugend and a Bund Deutscher Maedchen were formed. I, being Jewish, was not invited to join. Slowly I started to learn about discrimination."

The war truncated Leo Sirota's brilliant career as teacher and performer in Japan. In 1939, he and his wife Augustine sent Beate, their only child, to study at Mills College in Oakland, California. She was not in Japan to witness the ostracizing of her parents, who were compelled to leave Tokyo and take up residence in Karuizawa in the mountains of Nagano Prefecture.

I was particularly curious to know how she learned to speak fluent Japanese.

"My parents spoke Russian, German, French and English," she wrote me. "I used some Russian at home with them but (generally) German and English. I learned Japanese well because I played with Japanese children and used Japanese on a daily basis. I always had many Japanese friends."

Leo Sirota was adored by his Japanese students. I've seen home movies of the Sirotas under the cherry blossoms at Ueno, by the old Imperial Hotel and at their home near Nogi Shrine. They provide a portrait of a family both assimilated into Japanese culture and one making an immense contribution to it.

When the war ended, Beate, working in New York as a researcher for *Time* magazine, was anxious to return to Japan as quickly as possible to see her parents, who had spent the war years under "village arrest" in Karuizawa. Being one of the very few non-Japanese in the United States who spoke and read fluent Japanese, she landed a job as a civilian attached to the U.S. Army.

When she arrived in Japan in the winter of 1945, she found that the family home had been burned to the ground in the bombing. In Tokyo during the Occupation she worked as a translator for General Headquarters (GHQ), the central secretariat of the Supreme Commander of the Allied Powers (SCAP); and, by what she herself describes as "a stroke of luck," she was assigned to a team of twenty Americans tasked with composing—in the space of ten days—the new Japanese Constitution.

"I was just twenty-two and, needless to say, I had never written a constitution before!" she wrote me. "But because I was the only woman working on the civil rights section, the job of writing what became Article Twenty-Four came to me."

It is a matter of record that the powerful enforcer in SCAP, Maj. Gen. Charles Willoughby, whom SCAP chief Gen. Douglas MacArthur called "my lovable fascist," was not well disposed toward Beate. Willoughby looked upon all progressives as pro-communist.

"Gen. Willoughby bothered me on a personal basis," she wrote me in an email, "not on a professional basis. He wrote memos about me which were completely false and he also attacked my father. One can get these memos now through the Freedom of Information Act, but I don't want to see them. It's too painful."

For many years, she kept her pivotal role in the writing of Article Twenty-Four to herself. For one thing, there was a twenty-five-year U.S. government ban on speaking about it. After that the Japanese authorities were not keen on advertising the fact that their Constitution had been "handed down" to them by Occupation forces.

After Lt. Col. Charles L. Kades, under whom Beate had worked, and a man she greatly admired, spoke in public of her contribution, she decided to reveal her story to the world. Kades, who had been a New Deal lawyer in Washington, was put in charge of drafting a constitution for the democratic rebirth of Japan, a task which he and his staff accomplished with stunning alacrity. Kades took Beate under his wing, and she gratefully acknowledged his mentoring. He died at age ninety in June 1996, before Beate achieved recognition in Japan in the last fifteen years of her own life.

I wanted to know the extent of her connections with Japan as a child, and this is what she shared:

> I did not have a Jewish upbringing. I had a governess after I was born in Vienna, and she was Catholic and apparently took me to church unbeknown to my mother. I do not remember anything about my life in Vienna. I left Vienna when I was five-and-a-half years old, and the culture shock I received upon arrival at the Kobe docks was such that it erased all memory of Vienna. I had never seen an Asian before, and the sight of all those Japanese men and women, black-haired and black-eyed, with a different color of skin than mine, caused me to ask my mother whether they were all brothers and sisters. My mother, shocked by this question, became motivated to integrate me into Japanese society.
>
> I played with our neighbors' children, visited their homes, learned Japanese games, watched them do homework and practice the koto and the piano, as well as their lessons in flower arrangement and Japanese dance. According to my father, I learned Japanese in three months. Since I was so young, I don't think that this was so astonishing, since the vocabulary of a five-and-a-half-year-old is not that extensive. I was a curiosity

for the Japanese. I had dark brown very curly hair which I wore short, I wore shorts in the summer, and to many Japanese I looked like a boy, so much so that some Japanese newspapers, when writing about my pianist-father, illustrated the article with a photo of me that read 'Beate-san, Leo Sirota's son.' I enjoyed myself thoroughly. The Japanese liked children very much and were very tolerant. They were ready to help in any way they could.

My feelings about the war were certainly conflicted. But knowing the Japanese army and living in Nogizaka . . . I had seen the soldiers marching by with wooden boxes holding the remains of their dead comrades. I had also seen women embroidering scarves with long-life symbols and giving them to the soldiers going to war. I also knew the strict discipline of the Japanese Army and how they absolutely obeyed their superior officers. The soldiers were mostly uneducated men from the countryside. I felt different about the German soldiers, who I thought were more sophisticated and worldly and should have known better and should have shown opposition to the military actions of their superiors. Of course, I wanted the U.S. to win against Japan, but I also felt sorry for the ordinary Japanese soldier.

My father came to Tokyo from Karuizawa to meet me. He looked gaunt and undernourished, and had many wrinkles on his face. My mother did not come because undernourishment had caused her to swell up and she was ill in bed. So I went with my father to Karuizawa. It was a tearful but joyful reunion. My parents, having suffered during their village arrest, did not want to stay on in Japan, even though the Minister of Education himself came to ask him! But my parents said that during the war years they experienced many kindnesses from their former students who, although forbidden to do so by the Kempeitai (military police), brought food and other necessities to my parents at night.

After her book, *The Only Woman in the Room*, came out in 1997 she returned often to Japan to give speeches to students and women's groups.

"The women of Japan," she wrote me, "have done extremely well. They have gone to court; many have been elected not only to the Diet but to local legislatures; they are really peace-loving and ready to fight for peace. They are strong, they persevere. . . . It has only been sixty years—I am surprised at how far they have come."

Beate Sirota Gordon, who passed away at age eighty-nine in 2012, was certainly a person who lived her life on her own terms, regardless of the confines that nationality and ethnicity place around us, making us live in what amounts to an invisible pale of settlement.

57

The Real Milky Way Train

When we are moved by a work of art—reading a poem, gazing at a painting, listening to a piece of music, standing before a stunning work of architecture—we say that our heart skips a beat. The organ that is our heart hopefully does not actually skip a beat. Arhythmia is solely a metaphor. Rather what we experience is the passing through of a Japanese *ma*, a pause in time. This pause in time during which "we forget ourselves" presents as a physical phenomenon.

This *ma* is what all artists strive to create in the senses of the person watching or listening or, if preparing food, smelling, tasting . . . or, if fashioning fabric, seeing, touching. The longer the perceived, sensed or felt *ma*, the greater the power of the art. The artists' dearest ambition is to create a *ma* that goes on and on, into which observers lose themselves to the art.

Japanese artists are particularly adept at creating *ma*. The tea ceremony not so much makes your heart skip a beat as slows it down and calms it. The Noh theater, with its unique slow movements and lyrical messages, redefines time itself by interspacing *ma* inside *ma*. Even its pauses have pauses! And a traditional Japanese meal redesigns the rhythms of eating by presenting small dish after small dish, each to be admired and savored with the eye and nose before consumption. Everything about Japanese art says, "Take your time!"

To take a poetic form like the haiku or tanka and ensconce a microcosm of the world in just a few syllables—seventeen for the haiku, thirty-one for the tanka—is a Japanese way of showing you how to live long in a short span of time. This seeming paradox was brought home to me in April 2014 when I took my daughter Sophie, who was twenty-seven at the time, to Iwate for a trip on the SL Ginga.

The SL Ginga is a steam-locomotive four-car train recreating the world of Miyazawa Kenji. *Ginga* means galaxy, specifically in this case our galaxy, the Milky Way. The train's theme comes from Kenji's masterpiece, *Ginga tetsudo no yoru* (*Night on the Milky Way Train*), a novel he wrote in the 1920s about a train that courses through the heavens along what the Japanese call *amanogawa*, or the Celestial River, the white stripe crossing the sky that we call "the Milky Way."

I had been asked by Japan Railways to take charge of "Kenji's presence" in the train. The overall design of the train was in the hands of the brilliant designer from Yamagata Okuyama Ken. I wrote a profile of Kenji and commentaries on his significance for us today, and selected excerpts of stories and poems symbolic of elements of his worldview: that we humans are but a minuscule part of, equal to and no better than all other parts of all creation. I turned these messages into posters on the walls of the SL Ginga.

Now, the trip between Kenji's hometown of Hanamaki and Kamaishi on the Pacific coast of Tohoku is a mere ninety kilometers. The ordinary train of the Kamaishi Line covers it in a leisurely ninety minutes. But the SL Ginga takes nearly four-and-a-half hours to traverse the distance. Sophie and I had come up on the Shinkansen from Tokyo to Hanamaki, a distance of more than 500 kilometers, in about two-and-a-half hours, and now we were taking two hours longer to travel less than one-fifth the distance. The landscape outside the SL Ginga was moving slowly past us and yet stopped still, like Kenji's angels. My daughter and I were on a trip through the niche-like spaces in Indra's net.

It is not an exaggeration to say that the journey on the SL Ginga with Sophie was one of the most profoundly moving experiences of my life. (She, like our other three children, was brought up to love Kenji's writing.) We were together in this four-and-a-half-hour-long *ma*. In our world today that puts such a premium on speed, there must be room for an anti-broadband of things. We can find ourselves and look at ourselves in the elongated pauses between the beats of our heart. And the SL Ginga is the only moving train in the world with its own planetarium. A show lasts about ten minutes and takes the passengers "as far as they can go" (to quote Kenji) along the Celestial River. It is as if the train were moving both on the earth and above it at the same time.

58

In the Tub with Takuboku

My life in Japan has been a series of these elongated intervals in the spaces between one instant and another.

In October 2014, I took one of my many trips to Iwate, going for the first time to Shibutami, the village where Ishikawa Takuboku had spent his childhood. His primary school is still there, and his classroom is preserved in the state it was in when he attended the school in the 1890s. This visit spurred me to contemplate translating his tanka with the publication of a bilingual edition in mind.

I have always felt that the best way to delve into the mind of writers is to translate their works. Needless to say, we are severely limited in this by the very few languages we know well enough to accomplish it. Translating someone's work is like getting into a Japanese bath with them and doing what is called *hadaka no tsukiai.* The literal meaning of this is "naked association and friendship" but it actually means "heart-to-heart contact." I have been extremely fortunate in my life to be able to sit in this figurative hot tub alongside, among others, Nikolai Gogol, Anna Akhmatova, Osip Mandelstam and Sergei Esenin; Stanislaw Ignacy Witkiewicz and (surely the poet with the most wonderful name) Konstanty Ildefons Galczynski; and a host of Japanese authors and poets from a span of eras.

But Takuboku was resisting. I couldn't even get him to walk through the split *noren* half-curtains that adorn the lintel of the door into the bathing area let alone plunge into the water with me! There was so much information, nuance and emotional messaging going on in his tanka, I had thought it impossible to do them justice in English. Translations from the past are generally correct from a textual point of view but tend to read in English as misty, abstract and pseudo-"Oriental" landscapes lost in a wisp of words. They often leave out subject or verb. The poems hang in the air. This quality presumed to capture the symbolic redolence of the original. But to me this was always a misreading of the original qualities. Yes, the originals are evocative and redolent. But these very qualities must be clearly stated in a translation for them to evoke those effects. This may sound paradoxical: you need to be clear and concrete in order to be vague and suggestive. The reverberations enter the heart only after the poem is taken into the mind. The primary criterion for a good translation is that the translated work reads well. The reader of the translated work should be moved in a similar way as the reader of the original, experiencing the same depths of emotion. Whatever the effect, it all has to make perfect sense.

Takuboku's tanka contain very concrete messages. He was after all a professional journalist and astute chronicler of his times. They are masterful because they are so crystal clear, like perfectly cut little diamonds, the light radiating in a number of directions from their facets. Needless to say, this does not mean that they are not often vague, ambiguous and beautifully suggestive. They are packed with nuanced connotations of a linguistic and emotive nature. Any translation would have to capture these two seemingly contradictory qualities: concreteness and suggestiveness.

It was another one of those miraculous *ma*, almost a revelation, that awakened me to the way to capture this.

The leaves of the trees in Iwate Park, located on the impressive former grounds of the old Kozukata Castle in Morioka, had turned. The brightness and clarity of the day seemed to magnify the yellows and oranges and the stubborn greens draping the branches. A stone poem monument to Takuboku stands beside one of the trees. Wherever you go in Japan you see these *shihi*, or poem monuments, commemorating verse that was either written at or about that spot.

This particular spot had great significance for Takuboku. He was fifteen years old and a student at Morioka Middle School in 1901. (Ten years later, Miyazawa Kenji attended the same school; Japan's two greatest modern poets were born ten years apart and some fifty kilometers from each other in provincial Iwate.) Takuboku, a rebellious teenager and later a feisty polemical adult, left class, allegedly through a window, and walked to Iwate Park to sit under a tree. The tree by the poem monument now is a younger generation of that tree.

On that bright clear October day in 2014, I sat myself below the tree. The inscription on the monument, carved in the hand of Takuboku's lifelong friend, the linguist and scholar Kindaichi Kyosuke, is of the poem Takuboku was inspired to write there. Perhaps that inspiration was still lingering in the same air 113 years later.

Then I was struck! The Japanese word for it is *satori*, or spiritual awakening, enlightenment, sudden comprehension, revelation . . . epiphany. I realized that translating Takuboku was possible if his tanka were limited to three lines in English. And I felt strongly that they needed to be composed of a grammatical sentence or two and given a title. The title was a translator's subterfuge, a devious way to draw the reader into the poem and sneak in more information at the same time. Just as a country can have an invisible fifth column, my translations would have, in the title, a not-so-invisible fourth line.

I translated the poem carved into the stone monument then and there, and continued to translate poem after poem at hotel rooms in Iwate and down to Tokyo. For the first time in my life I was able to stay four days in a suite at the Imperial Hotel in Tokyo, thanks to a major Japanese company, Hitachi, that had asked me to give a speech to some 3,000 people for them. The suite had a large desk by the window. I sat for hours there immersed in translation. What happy moments those were! One day I passed one of the kimono-clad housekeepers on the floor of suites.

"I noticed that you were reading Takuboku," she said.

"Yes. Do you like Takuboku?"

"Oh yes! He really speaks to me."

She put her finger on his popularity. Takuboku, who died from tuberculosis age twenty-six and was a committed social revolutionary, is the eternally young rebel of Japanese letters.

I contacted one of my editors, Abe Harumasa, at Kawade Shobo. He was editing a book that I had written with my old friend, essayist and translator Yomota Inuhiko, about what it means to be Jewish in the twenty-first century. (Yomota's contribution covered Jewish philosophy and Middle Eastern geopolitics; I wrote about the contribution of Jews to the cultures of Europe and the United States. Our book, *Konnichi wa, yudayajin desu* (Hello, I'm Jewish) came out in November of that year.) I proposed a book of Takuboku's tanka in the original Japanese with English translation accompanied by notes for each poem and extensive commentary on his life, times and psychology. Abe was immediately receptive, and the book saw the light of day in April 2015, a half year after I was struck by muses in the open air under a tree in a Morioka park.

The tanka that Takuboku wrote under that tree in 1901 goes like this . . .

In the Ruins of Kozukata Castle
I dozed off in the weeds
As the sky seized
My fifteen-year-old heart.

The last line of the original is so simple and yet mellifluous in Japanese: *juugo no kokoro*. The repetition of the five "o" sounds preceded by the long "u" creates the kind of assonance that Harvard professor Jacobson called "pure lyricism." (To illustrate this, he had used the poem by Alexander Blok about "a girl singing in a church choir . . . about all the ships that sailed to sea." He extracted the Russian vowels and strung them together like musical fabric on a clothesline.) Mulling over this poem by Takuboku while sitting on the spot where he once was, I may have been sensing, in one of those long wordless pauses, what he was feeling as a fifteen-year-old boy on a similar day more than a century ago.

The society that Takuboku took an active interest in—that of Meiji Japan—had found itself in swift political flux. The key word for the era was "polemics." Intellectuals and socially conscious people were actively involved in a nationwide discussion, played out in all aspects of the culture—literature, theater, graphic arts, journalism—as to what the nature of future Japanese society should be. Basically, it is the same discussion that continues today not only in Japan but in many countries: should society be open to ideas on the basis of their true merit, creating a fluid situation that leads to the betterment of all classes? Or should the body polity be unified in thought and action behind one ethnic or ideological or religious idea, an idea that presumably makes the nation "stronger" and more successful at engaging in conflicts with other countries?

As we all know, Japan chose the latter scenario, and the brilliant and multi-faceted culture of the late Meiji era and the Taisho era that followed it was flung into the gutter and stamped on with thick-soled mud- and blood-smeared boots. Had Japanese people chosen to take the former path of open-ended development and freedom of expression, the country, I believe, would have produced a culture that would have continued to dazzle the world in all forms of cultural and social expression.

Of course, it was not only Japan that abandoned freedom for the trumped-up glories of unity. Germany and the Soviet Union did the same. Germany lost thousands of creative liberal people who chose expatriation. They also lost many of their most talented scientists, some of whom went to the United States and worked on the development of the atom bomb. Russia lost—primarily by murdering them—some of the greatest writers and other intellectuals that the modern world had known.

It is clear that Takuboku identified in his writing with those people who wanted to fervently reform Japanese society. Sadly, in his own eyes, he lacked the resolve to commit himself to any movement. Perhaps "resolve" is not the right word. Perhaps he was simply like most people in any country. They sympathize with the reformers but are too bogged down in the troubles of their own everyday life to be able to extricate themselves from them.

I fear, alas, that I am much like Takuboku in the temperament of his "passive activism." But Takuboku was also like a man caught in quicksand, not sinking further down but yet unable to get out. He pulls on his own hair, hoping that this will somehow extricate him. But it just causes further pain and anguish, with the result that he remains where he is, struggling just to keep his arms and feet moving, to "keep afloat."

Takuboku identified with the downtrodden because he saw himself as one of them. In *Romaji nikki* (*The Romaji Diary*), a chronicle of his thoughts and actions written in Japanese in Roman letters, he writes of his desperation for money. Life for him, with a wife, daughter and mother to support, was a constant struggle for survival. He could look back, however, to a much more comfortable childhood, with his father being chief priest at a temple. Perhaps his desperation at being poor was exacerbated by memories of the idyll of childhood.

In today's Japan, with the ever-widening gap between the haves and the have-nots, this struggle has become a reality for more and more people. The lack of job security that plagued Takuboku's life, the necessity for him to move from place to place wherever there was a job to be had, the anxiety caused by the fact that a person could be fired at the drop of a hat for "not fitting in" or for arguing against injustice, the introduction of restrictions on freedom, the oppression of people seen by the government as "radical" . . . these aspects of Takuboku's times are all too familiar to us in Japan today. This is what makes Takuboku our contemporary. And though he may have found himself unable to act, he participated in the polemics through his writing, demonstrating to us the importance of free expression, of dialogue and argument, of commitment in the public arena to asserting the rights of all people.

There are two crucial historical events occurring in Takuboku's lifetime that affected him deeply. The first is the attempt on the part of Tanaka Shozo to hand a petition to Emperor Meiji to do something about the toxic waste produced by the Ashio Copper Mine that was polluting the waters at farms downstream in Tochigi Prefecture. Though Takuboku was only fifteen at the time of this incident (December 1901), it impacted his consciousness sufficiently for him to write a tanka about the affair.

Tanaka Shozo was one of the world's first ecological pioneers, a significant social thinker who formulated clear principles to show the vital importance of protecting nature from manmade pollution and a progressive intellectual agitator who, as editor of the *Tochigi Shimbun* (the present-day *Shimono Shimbun*), propagated the works of John Stuart Mill and Jeremy Bentham. He was elected to the Diet in 1890, which itself shows that Japanese democracy was sufficiently developed to accommodate such a visionary in the establishment, such as it was in those days.

I was reminded of the 1901 petition to the emperor when Diet member Yamamoto Taro handed an anti-nuclear letter to the emperor in 2013, exactly a century after the death of Tanaka Shozo, and I was dismayed at the vilification poured on Yamamoto by the media for his ignoring protocol. Not much has changed in a century. Perhaps in some ways Meiji Japan was even more tolerant of dissent than today's Japan.

Tanaka Shozo once said, "A true civilization does not destroy mountains, defile rivers, tear apart villages or murder people." This certainly rings true today.

If any quotation from the Meiji era proves that the issues in which Takuboku and his contemporaries were deeply and personally involved are no different from those that affect us today, this one does. A society without vigorous polemics that reach the public through various forms of media, art and social intercourse is a society destined to stagnate. If only Japan had heeded the wisdom of Tanaka's motto; if only all countries of the world would do likewise today!

The second incident affecting Takuboku, to an even greater degree, was that involving the socialist author, translator and journalist Kotoku Shusui, who was arrested for treason on false charges and executed together with others on January 24, 1911. This date has to be seen as marking the beginning of the decline of Japanese democracy, a decline that took Japan down the dark spiral staircase ending in the depths of defeat in war on August 15, 1945.

The cause and fate of Kotoku Shusui had a huge impact on Takuboku. For one thing Takuboku was much older then than he had been when encountering the cause of Tanaka Shozo back in 1901. For another, Tanaka, unlike Kotoku Shusui, was certainly not executed and had been allowed to continue writing.

Both Kotoku Shusui and Takuboku were enamored of the writings of the Russian scientist, philosopher and anarchist Pyotr Kropotkin. Like Kotoku Shusui, Takuboku had read Kropotkin's work in English. On June 15, 1911, less than half a year after the execution, Takuboku wrote a long poem bemoaning the lack of activism in Japan.

But the ideal of an activist poet was one that by nature and circumstance he could not fulfill. He found himself unable to become an active protester, and he had pangs of conscience over this personal shortcoming. Even so, his honesty shines through in his writing, in which he admits his shortcomings and yet continues to support progressive people through it.

As far as his work as teacher and journalist was concerned, Takuboku traveled to Tokyo, Otaru, Hakodate, Sapporo and Kushiro. But he was not able to secure long-term employment on a decent salary. Takuboku and his family lived, of necessity, a very frugal life. Sometimes, when he did receive a lump sum from a publisher, it didn't last long. His son was born in October 1910. On the day of the birth, he was paid twenty yen (about a month's wage) by the publisher of his tanka collection, *Ichiaku no suna* (*A Handful of Sand*). But the boy died on the twenty-seventh of that month and the royalty went to pay for the funeral.

Sometimes his own feisty personality was the problem. When he was at the *Otaru Nippo* in 1907, a disagreement led to the business manager of that daily newspaper physically striking him. He soon resigned, despite his dire financial situation.

The great lesson that we learn from the life and writing of Takuboku is this: a society either creates a place for its creative people to be freely active in the way they see fit, or that society will go into decline and cease to prosper.

One of Takuboku's most famous tanka is "Labor." Here we see the struggle and the toll it takes on his psyche:

However long I work
Life remains a trial.
I just stare into my palms.

Another is "Revolution":

Nothing seems to disconcert my wife and friends
More than my going on about revolution
Even when struck down by illness.

Takuboku moved around a good deal in his short life, living and working in various cities in Hokkaido and Tokyo. Like Kenji he was obsessed with trains and experienced similar slips in time on them. Though they were both activists in their own way, the two poets are vastly different in their answers to life's questions: Kenji's answers were spiritual; Takuboku's were political.

But this tanka by Takuboku seems so Kenji-esque that it may very well have sent a ray of light into Kenji's mind that later came out in the scene of *Night on the Milky Way Train* where the passengers alight at a station in the sky before a radiant cosmic clock . . .

On a Train
I glimpsed out the window on a rainy night
To catch the clock at a station
Stopped in the woods.

I don't know if it is the train or the clock that is stopped in the woods, or both. That is the perfect image to describe the feeling you get when you travel, for the time being. Sometimes I feel that this is what I have been striving to do my entire life: catching a working clock stopped for as long as it will allow me to see it that way.

59

Ito Daisuki! (I Love Ito!)

From the very beginning of my life in Japan, I sought out those aspects of Japanese culture that I felt had true universal value. They were often couched in obscure aesthetic terminology or expressed in terms of allegedly "untranslatable" linguistic references that were assumed to make a subject "uniquely Japanese."

The Japanese themselves were masters at cultural obfuscation and provincial, if innocent, trickery. One young Japanese fellow back in the late sixties assured me that though he had never seen a Noh play, Noh was in his blood and as a Japanese he understood it far better than I ever could. I was also told countless times that I would never understand the "real meaning" of many Japanese words because "only a native Japanese is capable of understanding this sort of thing." One word I recall being mentioned was *nasake*. In English, we have wonderful equivalents: compassion, mercy, pity, kindness and charity, to name a few.

The Japanese are not skilled at recognizing universality in their native culture. For decades, they assumed that its value was limited to them, that it had little applicability outside the context of the Japanese way of life. Nothing could be farther from the truth . . . and, thank goodness, that tendency toward obfuscation and feigned mystery has become a thing of the past.

Even though Japanese cinema is one aspect of the culture that has traveled well, there is one film director who has been neglected in the world outside Japan. Directors like Kurosawa, Ozu, Mizoguchi and Oshima have gained reputations as masters of world cinema. Many other directors, long deceased or currently working, are also given retrospectives or festival screenings. But I rarely hear the name of Ito Daisuke outside Japan. His films took me into a realm of openly expressed emotion that many people do not associate with the Japanese.

In July 1959, Japan's leading film magazine, *Kinema Junpo*, published a list of what it hailed as "the best ten Japanese films of all time." This list included works by Naruse Mikio, as well as the young but by then amply acclaimed Kurosawa Akira. Ozu Yasujiro's *Umarete wa mita keredo* (*I Was Born But . . .*) came in third; Mizoguchi Kenji's *Gion no kyodai* (*Sisters of the Gion*), second. But the work considered in 1959 to be the best Japanese film of all time was *Chuji tabi nikki* (*A Diary of Chuji's Travels*), which was actually a trilogy of silent films made in 1927 by director Ito Daisuke.

Born in 1898 in the beautiful castle town of Uwajima in Shikoku's Ehime Prefecture, Ito Daisuke attended middle school in Matsuyama. When his father died in 1916 he was, as an only son, obliged to give up his studies and go to work. But an encounter with the famous playwright and director Osanai Kaoru, a leading light in the new theater movement in Japan, led Ito to Tokyo, where he aspired to be an actor. Being suave and good looking, the stage would have seemed an apt choice for him. Yet it was as a scriptwriter that he found his first success.

After much of Tokyo was destroyed in the Great Kanto Earthquake of September 1, 1923, and the fires that raged in the following days, Ito moved to Kyoto and joined the Nikkatsu studio. At the time, Kyoto rivaled Tokyo as a center of filmmaking, particularly the cranking out of *jidaigeki* (period dramas) that Japanese audiences craved. He directed his first *jidaigeki* in 1926, and made eight of them in 1927, including the Chuji trilogy.

The trilogy was an instant success with the film-going public and marked Ito out as the most skilled practitioner of the genre. As with Abel Gance, the great French silent film director who in many ways resembles him, Ito was markedly influenced by D.W. Griffith, the American pioneer of epic screen dramas. Ito became known for his use of the moving camera, so much so that he was given the nickname "Ido Daisuki," a pun on his name that means "He just loves to move." But if you look at Ito's silent films, what sets his technique apart isn't just that he largely spurned the fixed camera shots prevalent in the cinema of the day. He also skillfully employed tracking shots, follow shots from the side with what appears to be a hand-held camera, vertical movement and circling shots. Together with his very tight editing, all this transforms garden-variety fight scenes into an art form—and it was those scenes in period dramas that became the emblem of Japanese cinema of his day and beyond.

A major complication occurred with the seeming loss of all of the prints of his masterpiece, the Chuji trilogy. So, younger readers of *Kinema Junpo* in 1959 would have had to take its editors' word as to the supreme merit of this work. Then in 1992, a miracle occurred, when a good portion of the trilogy turned up after a couple in Hiroshima "discovered" some cans of film that had been stacked outside [!] on their veranda. The film was restored and digitalized.

We can now see why the magazine editors gave it the premium

award and why the lead actor, Okochi Denjiro, was considered a legend in his own time. Watching this film, I was overwhelmed not only by Ito's classic fight scenes but also by the subtlety of the romantic encounters in it. When Chuji and the beguiling ingénue flirt with each other amid enormous barrels for making sake turned on their side, an atmosphere of intimacy and tenderness is created, heightened by the silence of the medium.

Ito was one of the many directors around the world who did not readily make the transition to the talkie. (Japan entered the talkie era in 1931, but Ito didn't make his first one until four years later.) In addition, he was an iconoclast whose heroes are outlaws and rebels. As such he had trouble adjusting to the growing censorship and restrictions that were being placed on film as Japan marched, with high steps, toward a repressive fascism in politics and the arts.

It wasn't until 1948 that Ito made his true comeback. The censors of the Allied Occupation's GHQ did not look favorably upon the *jidaigeki* or anything that smacked of prewar moral codes. The comeback came with his brilliant take on the mores and warmth of Osaka life—*Osho* (*The Chess Master*).

Osaka is a city whose people are much more forthright about their emotions than the people of Tokyo. (If Tokyo is London, Osaka is Liverpool. It even has a colorful dialect, a kind of Japanese Scouse.) A true son of Osaka, the chess master wears his heart conspicuously on his sleeve, a trait that many non-Japanese believe to be "un-Japanese." Two remakes of this film followed the 1948 production, the first starring one of Japan's most brilliant actors, Mikuni Rentaro. I have seen all three, and the original version, with Bando Tsumasaburo, known in Japan as "Bantsuma," is incomparably dramatic and moving.

Osho is the story of Sakata Sankichi, a master of shogi, the board game often referred to as Japanese chess. His all-consuming love of the game leads him to pawn not only his (and his wife's) worldly goods, but also his daughter's kimono and the ancestors' Buddhist altar. His wife threatens to walk out, but Sakata manages to salvage the marriage by winning at his game and reclaiming the altar. Sakata is a loser in life, but one who lives it to the fullest. The ending, poignant and deeply illustrative of the *ninjo* (human warmth) typical of the people of Osaka, has brought tears to my eyes every time I've seen the film.

Ito directed ninety-five films in all and he scripted a whopping 200. Director Watanabe Mamoru has said, "It is fair to say that Japanese cinema began with Ito Daisuke." He was both an incorrigible rebel and a technical master whose philosophy was, "Let us seethe with both the wisdom and the fighting spirit that smashes the conventional frame."

There is a Japanese phrase, *reigan nesshu*, which means, "Keep a cool eye but a passionate hand." Ito Daisuke revised this to *netsugan nesshu*: "Keep a passionate eye and a passionate hand." It is these words, engraved in his own hand, that adorn his tombstone in the precincts of Rengeiji, a temple in the Omuro district of Kyoto, not far from where he and his wife Asako, who is interred with him, lived.

When confronted with his nickname of "Just loves to move," he countered, "It's not just a camera technique in use. It represents the dashing of my heart (*kokoro no shisso*)."

What more telling words could there possibly be than "the dashing of my heart" to describe the life and work of this stunning filmmaker . . . and to symbolize what all creative people are searching for in themselves?

60

Until My Heart Breaks in Two

As the years passed in Japan, I felt greater and more intense affinities with Japanese creative artists, practitioners of craft and performers of drama. I thought of the Japanese as a theatrical people and expanded on this theme in my memoir *If There Were No Japan*. Some of the theatrics come from the past, some from the present.

I felt in the marrow of my bones that everything I had done up till my arrival in Japan in 1967—my upbringing in Los Angeles, my studying Russian and Polish, my travels in Europe—was all done for the purpose of preparing myself to go to Japan. This was the result; and the result is what gives the time leading up to it its meaning.

I sought out Japanese creative people, both from the past and the present, who were confronted in their life with stark choices, as I was. The home that author Hayashi Fumiko built at a location a short train ride from Shinjuku took me back an era and allowed me to have the kind of heart-to-heart contact with the spirit of the flamboyant hot-blooded woman who was just such an author.

In 1939, Hayashi bought a plot of land in the Ochiai district of central Tokyo's Shinjuku Ward. She had commissioned the architect Yamaguchi Bunzo to design a home for herself, her husband, mother and son. The house was completed in 1941, but she didn't truly settle into life there until after the war.

Immaculately preserved in every detail, including its lovely tranquil garden, the building is now the Hayashi Fumiko Memorial Hall run as a museum by Shinjuku Ward. I have been going there for well over twenty years in all seasons. It provides a fascinating look into the life of this writer who resurrected her success in the postwar years.

If you compare the treatment dealt out in the immediate postwar period to Japanese writers who supported their nation's military aggression in World War II with that meted out to similarly inclined writers in Europe, the Japanese literary collaborators seem to have gotten off lightly. Of course, there were exceptions, such as the gung-ho novelist Hino Ashihei. After the war, Hino was publicly vilified for his aggressive support of the war effort, and though he tried to make amends by touting progressive causes, he took his own life, by poison, out of unassuaged guilt. But generally, writers who had enthusiastically waved the flag and rattled the saber during the fifteen-year-long war in Asia and the Pacific sifted through holes in the national consciousness back into the routine of ordinary life. Many, indeed, continued to publish as if nothing had happened.

In France, the novelist Robert Brasillach was executed after Gen. Charles de Gaulle, then prime minister in the French Provisional Government, ignored his pleas for clemency. While in Norway in 1947, Nobel Prize-winning author Knut Hamsun was put through a grueling trial for collaborating with the Nazis, despite the fact that he was by then nearly ninety years old.

Why were the Japanese less vindictive about their literary figures—and they were legion—who supported the invasion of mainland Asia, leading millions of ordinary Japanese citizens to believe that their cause was just and righteous?

The case of Hayashi Fumiko may help answer this question nearly seven decades after her death, at the age of forty-seven, on June 28, 1951.

For one thing Hayashi's background and upbringing go a long way to explaining the kind of novelist she turned into, as well as illuminating the nature of her preoccupations and obsessions.

Hayashi's father was a shady itinerant peddler who did not own up to his paternity of her. She spent her early childhood in Nagasaki, Sasebo, Shimonoseki and Kagoshima (her mother's hometown), among other cities, before moving to Onomichi in Hiroshima Prefecture at the age of thirteen. By eighteen she was writing prose and poetry for the local newspaper. The next year she followed a lover to Tokyo. Perhaps incensed by her father's betrayal, Hayashi was a pioneering feminist who believed that women had just as much right as men to pursue their romantic interests as they saw fit. This became one of the recurring themes of her fiction. It was this indomitably feminist aspect of her writing that attracted me to her in the beginning.

Hayashi took on a series of rough menial jobs in the capital and, for a time, was homeless. But in 1928, she began to publish, in what would be twenty installments, her novel *Horoki* (*The Diary of a Vagabond*), which came out in book form in 1930. This fascinating autobiographical novel became an instant hit, selling more than

500,000 copies. It has also been filmed three times, most famously by Naruse Mikio in 1962, with another early Japanese feminist, superstar Tanaka Kinuyo, in the lead.

Hayashi soon made a reputation for herself as a travel writer. In 1931, she went to Korea—then a colony of Japan—as well as to Russia and France, before moving on to London for a short while and returning to Japan in the early summer of 1932.

The trip that started her on her journey as an embedded journalist with the imperial Japanese forces was one for the *Tokyo Nichi Nichi Shimbun* (today's *Mainichi Shimbun*) in January 1938 to Nanjing (then Nanking), where her country's military had just brutally ravaged the population in what has come to be called the Nanking Massacre. After that, in 1940, Hayashi was again a safe and trusted embedded reporter with Japanese forces in Manchuria and Korea. For eight months in 1942 and 1943 she found herself in Vietnam, Singapore, Java and Borneo, all places under the control of Imperial Japan. Finally, in 1944, she returned to Japan and immediately evacuated, with her elderly mother and her adopted toddler son to a remote hot-spring village in Nagano Prefecture.

Hayashi Fumiko was never openly apologetic, neither during the war nor after it, about her role in the war effort, despite her having been the first Japanese woman of note to be in Nanking after the 1937–38 massacre and the first to enter Hankow (present-day Wuhan) with the invading Japanese troops in 1938. She could not claim that she hadn't witnessed atrocities. There was no basis on which she might credibly plead innocence. She knew everything there was to know about the brutality of the Japanese military. So why then was she effectively exonerated by the public after the war? Is this another example of Japan's convenient amnesia?

Let's look more closely, for an answer, at her writing. She had joined the so-called Pen Corps, following the troops in their bootsteps. Her *Hokugan butai* (North Shore Corps) was published by Chuo Koron in 1939, describing life on the Chinese front. There is next to nothing in it about the actual fighting. Rather it takes up, in documentary-like fashion, the routine personal trials of individual soldiers. Of course, this too makes her an apologist for the war effort. Her personalized approach, virtually devoid of tactical details about battles, appealed to readers and augmented their sympathies for their fighting men. But it also had the effect of mitigating for a less vindictive attitude toward her once the war was over. Unlike Hino Ashihei, she hadn't waved the flag in people's faces.

But, I believe it was her sincere efforts to redeem herself through her fiction after the war that saved her from a humiliation that she no doubt expected. This form of "silent guilt" characterized the postwar attitude of the entire nation. One didn't need to beat one's chest in repentance. In fact, Japanese people are normally wary of public displays of contrition. Too many guilty parties made an instantaneous about-face in an effort to rejig their public image from one of patriotic militarist to avid peacemaker.

Hayashi Fumiko's choice was to segue herself into a champion of the downtrodden victims of war, particularly women and children. She wrote tirelessly and eloquently after the war about women who were victims of the war's brutality. Reinventing herself in the public eye was her way of repenting, and her compatriots interpreted this as an apology and took her back into their hearts.

As a matter of fact, by the end of 1943, she had become disillusioned with the war effort and ceased to write about it. In Nagano in 1944, she jotted this down: "I now see writing about reality today in the face of every obstacle and impediment as a personal sin in itself, and in this miserable country existence, unsupported and at wits' end, my only salvation is to write children's stories."

Hayashi Fumiko's postwar success was so remarkable that she was overwhelmed with offers to write from the editors of periodicals and publishers. In many ways, she had become the voice of Japanese women, both those who had supported the violence and those who had suffered under it. The immediate postwar decade was one in which Japanese men, ridden by guilt, were open to the views and active participation of women. (Once Japan began to enter the era of rapid growth in the 1960s, the men took over the reins of power again and relegated women's public roles to tasks on the sidelines.)

Under extreme pressure due to having taken on an overly heavy workload, Hayashi Fumiko died of a heart attack in 1951. So many admirers crowded around the hearse carrying her body that the vehicle could not proceed for some time. Officiating at her funeral was novelist Kawabata Yasunari, who summed up her reputation succinctly: "The deceased often did terrible things to others in order to maintain her literary life," he said, "but in two or three hours she will be reduced to ash. Death extinguishes all sin, so I ask you in your heart to forgive her."

In his play about the life of Hayashi Fumiko, *Taiko tataite fue fuite* (Blow the flute, beat the drums), Inoue Hisashi puts very telling words into the mouth of his heroine. I feel as if she could have said these words in real life and that they represent a certain amount of redemption for her wartime sins. Perhaps the Japanese people who lived with her during a traumatic era sensed this too, which is why they forgave her and writers like her.

Inoue's heroine says, "I humble myself before the readers who danced to my flute and drums. Thanks to that flute and drums there were war widows, there were soldiers who had to be repatriated, there were the orphans of war. And so, to show my deep and apologetic regret to my readers, I must write now about their suffering until my arm falls off, until my heart breaks in two."

That is the Hayashi Fumiko that, despite her personal transgressions, I wanted to intimately know and make a part of my own story. I hadn't supported my country when it prosecuted an unjust war for a decade between 1965 and 1975. But I hadn't opposed it either. I had done nothing active to stop it. Inaction in the face of evil is nothing to boast about.

The distance between Hayashi Fumiko and me was not so different in kind.

61

Bristles on the Heart

Through my friendship with Inoue Hisashi, I was able to meet a remarkable woman, Yonehara Mari. Mari was the elder sister of Hisashi's second wife, Yuri.

I had something very much in common with Mari: our connection with Russia. She was a fluent speaker of Russian and often acted as interpreter for important visitors to Japan, such as Pres. Boris Yeltsin.

Mari was a prize-winning essayist as well as an expert on the Russian language. *Shinzo ni ke ga haeteiru wake* is the intriguing title of a book she published with publishers Kadokawa Shoten. In English, the title would be "That's Why Hair Grows on the Heart."

In this collection of about seventy short essays, she covers a wide variety of topics, most of them gleaned from her experiences as a child growing up overseas and later from having worked as a simultaneous interpreter. The essay that lends the book its quirky title touches on the subtle differences in expression in different languages and how difficult it is for an interpreter, pressed for time, to do them justice. "That's why it is said," she wrote, "that a simultaneous interpreter's heart is covered in bristles."

In a number of the essays she relates stories about her and Yuri's most unusual parents. She tells how she fought with her friends as a little girl over whose father was the greatest, Mari proffering that hers was greatest because "he's in the Communist Party."

"So what's the Communist Party?" shouted back another girl.

"I don't know!" she exclaimed. "But it's the opposite of the Liberal Democratic Party."

Although neither of them had a clue as to what a "party" was, young Mari did know that her father, who was a very portly man, had spent sixteen years hiding "underground." The problem was that she couldn't figure out how such a big man could have remained underground for so long. "It must have been very cramped," she recalls thinking.

Her mother was, as she describes her, "a born critic of everything." Setsubun, the February festival to welcome the harbingers of spring, was not celebrated in the household. (It's like refusing to acknowledge Thanksgiving in America.) During Setsubun people throw beans, proclaiming, "Out with the demons, in with happiness!"

"I don't like this philosophy about demons being sent out and happiness being brought in," said her mother. "We don't throw beans in this house."

When Mari was in kindergarten, her mother was told, "Your daughter is a problem because she doesn't know the meaning of cooperativeness." Her mother denounced the kindergarten and immediately pulled her out of it. Later, when Mari and her little sister Yuri started school, their mother didn't approve of the custom dictating that girls should carry red backpacks and boys, black, so she sent her two small daughters to school with brown ones.

Disgruntled by many aspects of postwar Japan, the girls' parents took them to what was then Czechoslovakia where, from 1959 until 1964, they attended an international school in Prague. It was naturally a Russian-run school, given Czechoslovakia's satellite status in the Soviet bloc. Upon their return to Japan they had trouble fitting in to the Japanese school system.

"I was totally confounded by the tests I was given in my new Japanese school," she relates in the book. "Virtually all of them were multiple-choice questions about facts."

One of the questions she recalled was this:

"In what year was the Kamakura Shogunate established? Choose the correct answer from the list: 1. 1868; 2. 1622; 3. 1497; 4. 1192.

"When I was first confronted with questions like this I couldn't believe it," she wrote, "and thought it was some kind of joke. It's understandable why I thought that. For five years at my school in Prague I had been given only essays and oral exams that tested our grasp of knowledge . . . . In Japan they should have been giving us questions like . . . 'Discuss the economic background of the establishment of the Kamakura Shogunate,' or 'Why was the shogunate established in Kamakura, not in Kyoto?'"

Mari and Yuri were only two of tens of thousands of returnee Japanese who are compelled to adjust to the strictures of "fact-oriented" learning that characterizes Japanese educational methodology. But while most returnees come back to Japan from North America, Western Europe or another country in Asia, Mari and Yuri's narrative is extraordinary.

My favorite essay in this collection is "The Sacred Territories of Work." In this Mari tells of an incident that occurred in the town of Okhotsk in the Russian Far East. She had gone into the post office to buy stamps for a picture postcard. There were two windows at the counter in the post office, one for ordinary mail and the other for special delivery. Though no clerk was at the window for ordinary mail, she stood and waited there.

"Won't do you any good standing there," said the clerk sitting at the special delivery window. "Clerk's off today. Sick."

"Well then, would you please sell me some stamps?"

"What? Are you serious?" retorted the clerk, glaring at her. "No way I could do that. What do you think? I'd never invade another person's territory of work."

"I looked around the post office," she wrote. "The other clerks there were lazing about, chatting with each other and playing chess. As this was the only post office in Okhotsk, I had no choice but to forego sending my picture postcard of the town."

If that had happened to me when I bought my condoms in Leningrad in 1965 my life might have been changed forever.

After finishing her secondary schooling in Japan, Mari went on to major in Russian at Tokyo University of Foreign Studies, topping it off with an MA in Russian Literature from the University of Tokyo. Her spoken and written Russian were spectacular. She translated her brother-in-law Inoue Hisashi's play about Hiroshima, *Chichi to kuraseba*, into Russian. (This is another thing we had in common: I translated it into English, under the title *The Face of Jizo*.) Mari's talents did not stop there. She wrote brilliant and insightful nonfiction that won her major prizes, including the Yomiuri Literary Prize, the Kodansha Essay Prize, the prestigious Oya Soichi Nonfiction Prize and the Bunkamura Deux Magots Literature Award.

After her sister married Hisashi, Mari moved close to where they lived in that old city of temples near Tokyo—Kamakura. But then, at the height of her powers as an author and interpreter, she was diagnosed with ovarian cancer. She went through several months in agony and passed away in May 2006, age fifty-six.

Mari was still healthy when I spoke with her two years earlier. I had gone to Ishigaki Island in the Yaeyama Islands in the far south of Okinawa Prefecture to give a public talk, and the sponsors, the city of Ishigaki, asked me if I could recommend someone suitable for the following year. I immediately suggested Yonehara Mari. They were delighted. I phoned her up right away.

"Mari? It's Roger. Have you ever been to Ishigaki Island down in Okinawa?"

"No, I haven't," she said.

"Look, would you like to go?"

There was a long pause.

"Well, uh, it's very kind of you, but, you know . . . ."

"Oh no. Not with me!"

I explained the situation, and she was kind enough to agree to give the talk. It wasn't long after her trip there that she received her diagnosis. I never had the chance to ask her how she liked Ishigaki, or, for that matter, many other things that I still wanted to know—about life in Prague in the early sixties; about how it felt to be a returnee from a country that did not conform in the minds of Japanese to the usual places people came back home from; and about whether Japan will really someday become a cosmopolitan nation where tolerance and openness to varied lifestyles rule the day.

After she died, when I read her book about bristles on the heart, and her other books, I felt I had truly known her and seen what a wonderful and fulfilled life she had led—and what a difference she made to the life of people in Japan.

62

Sakamoto Ryuichi and Fukushima

My long friendship with Sakamoto Ryuichi is another treasure in my life.

Ryuichi and I first met on Rarotonga in the Cook Islands in late July 1982. I felt like the intruder as I introduced him to David Bowie on a blindingly sunny Rarotonga beach. The two consummate musicians were, after all, linked to each other in a world of their own.

I flash forward in my mind from the Cook Islands in July 1982 to Oxford in October 2011. I went to Oxford where, at Hertford College, Ryuichi was to appear with acclaimed actor Yoshinaga Sayuri in a concert of music and poetry linking the disasters of Hiroshima and Nagasaki to the calamity of Fukushima. Yoshinaga read poetry written by children who were victims of those nuclear catastrophes, while Sakamoto played pieces on the piano, including some from the score of *Merry Christmas, Mr. Lawrence*. The event was extraordinary. It was filmed by NHK for broadcasting back home in Japan.

"It is a total illusion," Ryuichi told me after the concert, "to think that nuclear energy can be peaceful. What happened at Fukushima is the same as what people in Hiroshima and Nagasaki experienced, except that this time the Japanese people brought it on entirely by themselves."

In 2012, he reaffirmed his beliefs publicly in the June 15 edition of the *Asahi Shimbun*:

Keeping silent after Fukushima is barbaric. I have for a long time felt troubled by the way things are decided in Japan, based on 'the mood of the moment' rather than on solid logic. There is no real discussion on the principles that underlie issues. Now Prime Minister Noda Yasuhiko has exacerbated my disquiet. Noda has painstakingly referred to his desire to defend people's lifestyles. Yet I wonder who exactly he has in mind when he talks about 'the people.'

Nuclear contamination is not the first social issue that Ryuichi has deeply involved himself in. He has worked to preserve forests and encourage tree planting to offset carbon emissions. After the U.S. invasion of Iraq in March 2003, he started an internet project called Chain Music, which he has vowed to keep going until all U.S. troops leave that country and the war has ended. Chain Music—like a chain letter—links musicians dedicated to "building a musical memorial to the desire for peace." He has also associated himself with the campaigns Zero Landmine and stop-rokkasho— the first being self-evident in its focus, the latter referring to a nuclear-reprocessing plant under construction in the village of Rokkasho in the Tohoku prefecture of Aomori.

Ryuichi was turned on to serious music from an early age. In 1963, when he was eleven, he was already studying composition, a field in which he earned an MA at Tokyo National University of Fine Arts and Music. By 1978 he was prominent in the seminal electronic music band he co-founded, Yellow Magic Orchestra (YMO), which took the Japanese and Western rock and pop music scenes by storm for several years and whose influence is widely credited in much of today's popular music.

There has never been much of a music protest movement in Japan as there has been, for instance, in the United States. Modern folk music in the U.S. has been profoundly inspired by issues relating to the oppression of the working classes and the brutalities of war. From Woody Guthrie to Joan Baez and Bruce Springsteen the message has been embedded in the music. In Japan, *enka* (traditional popular songs) did flirt with social and political issues before World War II. But since 1945, that genre has done little more than drip with tears and maudlin sop. Things changed briefly in the 1960s with the release in 1965 of "Shinda otoko no nokoshita mono wa" ("What the Dead Man Left"). That anti-Vietnam War song, with lyrics by poet Tanikawa Shuntaro and music by Takemitsu Toru, was taken up by the protest movement in Japan and sung by many artists. A decade later, in 1974, Japan's most popular postwar singer, Misora Hibari, went to the city of Hiroshima and, at the first Hiroshima Peace Music Festival, sang "Ippon no enpitsu" ("A Single Pencil"), her song with the haunting lines: "If I had a single pencil/ I would write 'The Morning of August 6'/ If I had a single pencil/ I would write 'Human Life.'" Her theme was that even a single pencil can stop a war, incidentally, a theme taken up by the world educationalist, Malala Yousafzai.

Ryuichi belongs in this tradition. He is at the forefront of protests over the use of nuclear power in Japan, "so that this disaster may never be repeated. . . . Humans and nukes cannot coexist, whether it be for weapons and/or electricity."

"Raise your voice and do not stop raising it," he wrote in the *Asahi*. "Do not give in. Do not lose heart. Be persistent. I believe that this is the only way we will ever change society in the end."

I felt that I was a citizen-for-life of this Japan. It was in this Japan that I felt I was on my own home ground, even if I never would be able to "really" appreciate a Noh play or understand the "Japanese" meaning of compassion, mercy and human kindness.

This was the Japan I witnessed in the 1960s, when young people acted according to the dictates of their social conscience.

63

The Tail of the Lizard

I had the good fortune to meet Nogami Teruyo, the woman who had worked with Kurosawa way back from the time she was a script girl on *Rashomon*.

It was director Koizumi Takashi who introduced us. She was perhaps the person most intimate with Kurosawa's filmmaking and most tolerant of his swinging moods. In his later years, she acted in the role of a virtual producer, going through trying times in the company of the director when they were in Siberia preparing for and filming *Dersu Uzala*. (I invited Nogami to give a talk at the Center for the Study of World Civilizations at Tokyo Institute of Technology when I was head of the center, and she came, together with Koizumi, for what was the double treat of reminiscences of "our time with Kurosawa.")

In 2007, Nogami Teruyo published a memoir under the title *Tokage no shippo* (The tail of the lizard) about four years after the publication of her other volume of reminiscences, *Tenkimachi*, which has appeared in English as *Waiting on the Weather*. The later volume is made up of interviews, and as such is an oral history of the people Nogami worked with and with whom she shared her life.

The main protagonist of these memoirs, aside from Nogami herself, is Kurosawa. We also get perceptive looks into the lives of novelists Shiga Naoya, Ibuse Masuji and Nosaka Akiyuki, as well as film directors like Itami Mansaku, who was her mentor. (She formed a lifelong friendship with Mansaku's son, Itami Juzo when the latter was a very young man, and many fascinating episodes between them are related, as well, in *Waiting on the Weather*.)

Tokage no shippo goes into revealing details on the personality and working methods of Kurosawa. It is hard to overestimate the impact that his winning the Gran Prix at the Venice Film Festival in 1951 (for *Rashomon*) had on both the Japanese film community and the Japanese nation at large. That achievement of international recognition was, I would say, the single most important event in the cultural life of Japan in the first decade after the war. Once again it signaled that it was all right to feel pride in your culture and what it could contribute to the world. It fostered a reaffirmation of faith amid the postwar despondency over Japanese values: that Japanese culture *did*, after all, have worldwide significance.

Nogami offers these insightful comments about the inspiration for the making of *Kumo no sujo* (*Throne of Blood*), Kurosawa's 1957 version of *Macbeth* set in medieval Japan: "The success of *Throne of Blood* was due to the fact that [Kurosawa] introduced a Noh style into it. He had taken refuge during the war in the world of the Japanese classics, haiku, Noh, and the like. He wasn't unique in this, however. At the time, many authors hated militarism and escaped into the study of the classics."

Kurosawa based the makeup of the Lady Macbeth character in the movie on the Noh mask called Shakumi, and was known to hold photos of Noh masks before a mirror and order the makeup accordingly. The astonishing "rain of arrows" at the end of *Throne of Blood*—where the body of actor Mifune Toshiro is pierced by a rush of deadly arrows—is arguably the most dramatic of all the scenes in Japanese cinema. Nogami explains: "When I tell people that we used real arrows in that scene and had no insurance, they just can't believe it. . . . Only Mifune could do a scene like that." (Actually, fishing line was run through the arrows to guide them to fixed spots. The lines had to be kept taut at all times lest the arrows veer and cause a tragedy.)

"The shooting of that scene alone," writes Nogami, "took three days."

What insurance company today would cover the making of such a scene with real arrows? What producer would sanction such a three-day arrow "shoot"? Only a director of Kurosawa's collosal charisma and artistic arrogance could pull it off.

Nogami Teruyo is also the author of the novel *Kabei* on which director Yamada Yoji based his film *Kabei* (*Kabei: Our Mother*). The story of her life, sketched in *Tokage no shippo* is as poignant and dramatic as that film.

Born in May 1927, she grew up primarily in the Tokyo district of Koenji, the location of *Kabei*. Toward the end of the war she was evacuated with her sister to rural Yamaguchi Prefecture, where her great uncle had a home. This is where the story has its origins.

In *Tokage no shippo* we get intriguing glimpses into what life was like in the early Showa era. We see that her father, on leaving home and returning every day, would linger in front of photos of his deceased parents and bow. When he went to Tokyo to enter university he married a distant relative, Murata Ayako, and her family paid his tuition as part of the marriage bargain. In the year that her parents married, 1923, the Great Kanto Earthquake struck the Tokyo region. This—and the rise of fascism leading up to the war—is the backdrop for the early years of Nogami's life. On her deathbed in January 1954, her mother sat up and said worryingly: "When I die, I don't think we have enough zabuton (individual floor cushions) for the wake." Three years later, her father, who had been a committed socialist all his life, died of liver cancer.

Nogami says of herself, "I am a real child of the Showa era." Reading her book is indeed like reliving that period. She was elated when the war ended. "No more air raids," she writes, "and now you could turn on the lights to your heart's content."

Prewar Japan, rural and urban, the war at home, the postwar recovery and the renaissance in Japanese culture as seen through the lens of Kurosawa Akira, not to mention intimate portraits of major creators of that culture . . . it's recorded in the words of a primary witness of history. The cover of the book attests to the author's keen wit. Drawn by Nogami herself, the cover art depicts a lizard with a cane in one paw. The lizard's tail has been sliced off, and the reptile is glaring back at the severed end—as, perhaps, Nogami looks back at her past—remarking, "Farewell, tail. Thanks for all your trouble."

And a fitting end it is to a part of this tale too, about Japan's past that continues to live—as if it still existed just as it was—inside me.

THE AMERICAN IN ME

64

The Leaving of Los Angeles

The war in Vietnam was the war of my generation and, by rights, it should have been the well-deserved and resounding defeat of my generation.

But we Americans were too focused on the threat of communism and too intent on flogging our version of liberty in every corner of the globe to admit that a "third world" country with the GDP of a small U.S. state could send us packing. We should have felt ashamed, disgraced and humiliated in a similar way that the Japanese and the Germans did. Shame, disgrace and humiliation might have helped us recover our humanity. They might have stayed the hand that reached out again to ruin the lives of millions of people in the Middle East under the very same guises of "truth, justice and the American way."

This is not to say that many Americans did not feel contrite after the war ended in 1975. They lived for a time with the so-called Vietnam Syndrome. Define this as "temporarily felt pangs of conscience leading to a healthy, if brief, bout of introspection." Instead of admitting ignominious defeat and making just reparations for it at home and in Vietnam, Cambodia and Laos, Americans just sat down on their carefully edged lawns and licked their wounds, waiting for someone to parade down their street and fire them up with the kind of rhetoric that would get the blood racing again. This is what substitutes for atonement and healing in the United States of America.

The spuiker of salve came along in the person of an amiable actor named Ronald Reagan. What is Reaganism, if not "the ideology of soothe" based on the belief that all the world's people desire, in their hearts, to be Americans—or, at least, to be like Americans. It was this unquestioning faith in American moral superiority based on a misreading of postwar history that restored American pride without the diversion of repentance.

America is always in need of a devil whose presence justifies the nation's self-styled holier-than-thou exclusiveness. The Soviets had provided that presence until their corrupt empire collapsed of its own weight and a string of new demons in the Middle East replaced them in the scriptures of American foreign policy.

"We're doing the worst thing to you, we're depriving you of an enemy," said eminent Russian political scientist and diplomat Georgi Arbatov to American journalists when his country was in the throes of perestroika. Founder of the USA and Canadian Institute in Moscow, Arbatov's witty remark stands as an apt one-sentence summary of the American bogeyman syndrome.

I was long gone from my country by the Reagan years, yet my own wounds would not heal. I hadn't made a gesture of protest, save for the handy one of leaving. Did I picture myself as a kind of latter-day Bertolt Brecht? Hardly. For one thing, I don't have sufficient self-love to measure up to Brecht. But I did write a play titled *Bertolt Brecht Leaves Los Angeles*, and I did have his evasive action of emigration firmly in mind as a solution to my, if hardly my country's, problems.

No country cares about a single individual's leaving, unless you are an Andrzej Wajda and can use emigration as a lever to confound your country's leaders. Brecht had no such clout when he left Germany in February 1933. I was not even a language teacher when I left the United States for good in 1967, but I understood Brecht's rationales implicitly. Brecht would have asked himself— why be at home when the knock comes at the door? There would be no knock on my door but there would be a heavy draft—the U.S. military draft—coming through it to chill me to the bone. Why stay in Los Angeles and wait for that? Most artists migrate seeking the light to see and the air to breathe freely. I look back at *Bertolt Brecht Leaves Los Angeles*, a musical, as my best play, though it has had only one production, more than forty years ago in Melbourne. (The beautiful music was composed by German migrant to Australia Felix Werder, who himself had been in Berlin in the 1920s.) The play comes under the category of "wishful autobiography." I suppose I wanted to see my own leaving of Los Angeles as a statement—Brecht's was; mine wasn't. For me it was simply an easy way out.

65

The Embassy of North Vietnam

My one chance to take a personal stand, however modest, came about in 1974. I was living in Canberra, teaching Japanese at the Australian National University and writing fiction and plays. In December 1973, I received a grant of $150 from the National Capital Development Commission (NCDC), the government bureau in charge of planning in the capital, to stage a play in Garema Place, the main outdoor square in the nation's capital.

Well, *The Fat Lady*, featuring three characters from a circus, including a politically radical transvestite, played in Garema Place one fine afternoon, drawing not only a large crowd, mostly of mums and kids ("no dear, it's not exactly like Pinocchio") but also the drama critic from *The Canberra Times*. To this day I cherish, in an album, photos of the play and audience, as well as a clipping of that newspaper's review, headlined "Gutter Humour in Garema Place."

In 1973, $150 carried significant purchasing power. The first bottle of wine that I bought in Australia, in August 1972, was an excellent 1968 Stanley Leasingham Cabernet Shiraz. It cost $1.69. The $150 grant could have taken me a long way to having an admirable wine cellar. It was the first money I'd ever made from my plays in Australia, and I was determined to do something more positive with it than putting down seven dozen-plus bottles of fine wine.

So I wrote a letter to the Embassy of the Democratic Republic of Vietnam offering the money to that country "to be used in hospitals and schools destroyed by United States bombing." North Vietnam maintained an embassy in Canberra at the time, despite Australia's "all the way with LBJ" orientation.

On January 16, 1974, I received a letter from Nguyen Dang Khoa, under whose name were the words "diplomat in charge of the Embassy."

"We thank you very much for your letter dated January 14, 1974," he wrote in the letter that I now have before me. "Your lofty sentiments and kind gesture toward the Vietnamese people are greatly appreciated. We inform you that the contribution to healing the wounds of war in the Democratic Republic of Vietnam can be sent to our embassy in Canberra at any time which is convenient for you."

A couple of days later I arrived at the door of the embassy with a $150 check in hand. I pressed the doorbell and glanced across the street. That is when the venetian blind in the house opposite was lifted into a V. I could see the lens of a camera poised between it and the blind below it. I flashed my "Smile of the Year" in the direction of the blinds, the embassy door opened and I entered.

Was I naively aiding and abetting the enemy? Did my money really go to a hospital or a school? I don't know. I am certainly not making any claim whatsoever to having done something altruistic or in any way heroic. I simply wanted the money I made from my writing to help victims of my country's attacks on them.

I have been lucky in life. I have never been forced to make that despicable choice facing people who live in a zone of belligerency, either of domestic or foreign origin: support a war you do not believe in or be seen as a traitor and face the consequences.

But the lesson I have taken from those ugly years of the U.S.-led war is that each person's individual response to injustice does matter, and that putting your guilt behind you without at least acknowledging it is a sure-fire way to blunder, again and again, into the criminal trap of further unjustified aggression. As someone born, raised and educated in the United States, I share that guilt and, wherever I go, still carry it inside me. That, too, is the American in me.

I learned another thing from that war: I came to realize how very hard it is for individuals to actively oppose belligerence when their nation is on a warpath. Until you are faced with the dilemma of stark personal choice—"Are you with us or against us?"—it is easy to speak out, give a few bucks for a good cause and fancy yourself on the side of the righteous.

66

Peaceful Circumstances? Back to Japan in the 1960s

What was Japan like when I arrived there for the first time?

I saw a country embroiled in social and political controversies, very much unlike the Japan that people of a younger generation than mine were to experience in the heady bubble years of the 1980s and the so-called lost decades that succeeded them right up to the present day.

In 2015, I completed a novel titled *Peaceful Circumstances*. This novel is about a naïve and beautiful white American girl from L.A. who, while spending her junior year abroad in Tokyo, falls in love with a black American soldier about to be sent from his American base in Tokyo to Vietnam. It is set in 1968 with the radical student movement as social backdrop.

Japan in 1968 was bursting with pride and hopeful anticipation to build on its burgeoning prosperity. The brilliantly successful Tokyo Olympics were already four years in the past, and people had started taking the Shinkansen bullet train—such a marvel when it began operation in 1964—for granted. In April of 1968 Japan's first skyscraper, the thirty-six-story Kasumigaseki Building, was completed. Novelist Kawabata Yasunari was awarded the Nobel Prize for Literature, and Dr. Wada Juro of Sapporo Medical College performed Japan's first heart transplant. (Sadly, the eighteen-year-old patient lived for only eighty-three days.) The average monthly wage for a university graduate was just a bit over 30,000 yen, but a beer cost only 130 yen, and for 660 yen (less than two American dollars) you could have both the morning and evening editions of the *Asahi Shimbun* delivered to your home for a month.

In 1968, everyone wanted all three of the so-called 3Cs: car, cooler and color television. These had steadily come within the reach of the average household, though a state-of-the-art Sony color TV then set people back the hefty sum of 120,000 yen (the equivalent of about five times that sum now). Five celebrity personalities were elected to the House of Councilors on July 7, 1968: novelist Ishihara Shintaro, comedian Aoshima Yukio, writer Kon Toko, volleyball coach Daimatsu Hirobumi and comedian "Knock" Yokoyama. The Agency for Cultural Affairs (Bunkacho) was established in June. Japan may have not have been No. 1, but it had officially become, as far as GDP went, No. 2 in the world. The goal of the leaders of post-feudal Meiji-era Japan "to catch up with and overtake the West" had been, despite the catastrophe of World War II, largely achieved, and by peaceful means, to boot.

The then Agriculture and Forestry Minister Kuraishi Tadao blasted Japan's so-called peace Constitution when he exclaimed in February 1968, "With its ridiculous Constitution, Japan is no more than a concubine."

I do hate these metaphors that equate states with the enslavement or demeaning of women. As for agriculture, the Central Union of Agricultural Cooperatives (Nokyo) had an iron hold over the lives of farmers, keeping them tied tightly to its lines of credit. Nokyo was hand-in-glove with the ruling Liberal Democratic Party, giving conservative politicians a rock-solid rural base that only began to crumble in the late 2000s.

The student movement, with a broad spectrum of support throughout the community, was agitating on campuses. On March 28, 1968, students took over the Yasuda Auditorium at the University of Tokyo and halted the graduation ceremony. When mothers with sons and daughters at the university sent their children caramels, so gaining the nickname "Caramel Mamas," someone put up a poster, on November 23, reading, "Don't Stop Us Now, Mummy!" Most critically, the entrance exams for 1969 were aborted, dealing a blow to the university's immediate future.

The three top movies of 1968 took up serious themes of persecution and war: Imamura Shohei's *Kamigami no fukaki yokubo* (*The Profound Desire of the Gods*), Okamoto Kihachi's *Nikudan* (*The Human Bullet*), and Oshima Nagisa's *Koshikei* (*Death by Hanging*). Intellectual ferment, expressed and widely followed in the thick monthly magazines, was evident not only on campuses and in theaters, but also in the nation's living rooms.

On March 27, 1968, a research committee of the then Ministry of Health and Welfare revealed that *Itai Itai* (Ouch Ouch) Disease, a condition that attacks the bones and often kills, was caused by cadmium poisoning, and that pollution by mining companies was to blame. Along with the recognition of the industrial causes of Minamata Disease, a grave neurological disorder brought about by the ingestion of mercury, this marked the first consciousness in Japan of the effects of wanton industrialization on the environment and the health of the nation.

Many things were yet to come. In 1968, disabled people and minority groups of all sorts had to grin and bear the ignorance of the general population toward their plight and the active public biases expressed against them. Women were blatantly discriminated against in the workplace and openly harassed, without consequence to the perpetrators; children were bullied with impunity. Japanese society was anything but victim-friendly.

Yet despite all this, back in 1968 there was not only a sense of hope in the air but also a dogged idealism: that Japan could create an equitable and fair society; that the new prosperity would be shared; that young people would have a voice in their future.

Young people of today looking back to the Japan of the 1960s would see the same ultraconservative cliques in power that wield ultimate influence now. They would no doubt be dismayed by the lack of concern then for the disabled, for minorities, and for the environment. But they would be wrong to conclude that their counterparts were apathetic and uncommitted to radical social change. In fact, the entire Japanese society had a social dynamism in 1968 that it pitifully lacks today.

The 1960s had started with a resounding bang.

The government under Prime Minister Kishi Nobusuke, the grandfather of Abe Shinzo, was determined to upgrade military ties with the United States by signing the Treaty of Mutual Cooperation and Security, known in Japan as Anpo. Demonstrations broke out, primarily in Tokyo, under the banner of the Zengakuren (All-Japan League of Student Unions), garnering a good deal of sympathy among the general populace. It was these demonstrations that made Zengakuren famous, laying the groundwork for student-movement agitation for the rest of the decade.

The anti-Anpo struggle came to a head, on June 15, 1960, when University of Tokyo student Kanba Michiko was killed in a clash with riot police in front of the Diet building. Though the legislation to ratify the treaty was pushed through, a scheduled visit to Japan by U.S. President Dwight D. Eisenhower had to be canceled, and Kishi was compelled to resign.

Tokyo was, meanwhile, undergoing a huge transformation in the buildup to its hosting of the 1964 Summer Olympics. This was symbolized by the completion of new freeways and the amazing Shinkansen, the first high-speed train of its kind in the world. These transformations reverberated through society at large, as Japanese people finally began to believe that the ravages (and guilt) of the war years could be put behind them. Until then, for instance, they were not in the custom of eating out at restaurants as a family. This was to become the norm during the "decade of the Tokyo Olympics," introducing a new emphasis on family life.

The artistic scene was exploding. A new generation of filmmakers, led by iconoclastic and radical director Oshima Nagisa, was calling the integrity of some of Japan's hallowed social institutions into question. In films such as the 1960 *Seishun zankoku monogatari* (*Cruel Story of Youth*) and the 1969 *Shinjuku dorobo nikki* (*Diary of a Shinjuku Thief*) Oshima took up themes of young love and youth violence, portraying them as rebellions against the staid, suffocating mores of the older generation that had failed to socially reform Japan. Kobayashi Masaki, in his monumental nine-and-a-half-hour-long trilogy, *Ningen no joken* (*The Human Condition*), told the real story of Japan's war and its effect on those forced to fight it. This epic, released between 1959 and 1961 as six films, stands as one of the world's greatest antiwar works of art, as well as representing a heartfelt and powerful apology for Japan's role in World War II.

The so-called *angura* (underground theater movement) was well under way by mid-decade. Kara Juro's stunning and passionate plays, performed in a huge red tent, redefined the relationship between actor and audience, and brought a kind of poetic nihilism onto the stage. Betsuyaku Minoru wrote *Zo* (*The Elephant*), his play about the stubborn unwillingness of a *hibakusha* (radiation victim) to lie down and die. Though kept in bed by the medical staff of a hospital, he protests the discrimination dealt him by his own society after the war. Terayama Shuji was creating metaphorical surrealistic dramatic works at his Shibuya space, Tenjo Sajiki, that would awe audiences on his tours of Europe. As for literature, the brightest star was surely Mishima Yukio, and while he was no leftie, he was a radical. His rightwing poses and eloquent defenses of a romanticized vision of traditional male-worshipping Japan contributed to the turbulent polemics of the decade.

In every aspect of the arts—from those above to music and design—the atmosphere itself was vibrating. Audiences and viewers *expected* innovation. This was a decade when Japan wanted least of all to rest on its laurels. Those laurels were being regrown and nurtured by brilliant young artists who had chiefly been brought up and inculcated with the democratic ideals of the 1950s.

It certainly looked as if a new social model was being formed in Japan, one in which polemics flourished and a fairer and more aware community of citizens was being fostered. It was, in a way, Meiji all over again, without the militaristic chauvinism.

But things began to turn by the end of 1967.

Uchigeba and the Radical Student Movement

The tremors of unrest around the world were shaking Japan.

The war in Vietnam was sparking mass demonstrations there too. In October 1967, a student was killed at Haneda Airport during a Zengakuren protest against a visit by Prime Minister Sato Eisaku to South Vietnam. (Sato was, by the way, Abe Shinzo's great-uncle.) Less than a year later 3,000 people, many of them workers, demonstrated at Osaka Airport against the U.S. military's use of the facilities there.

By May 1968, more than a million people were marching in Paris as the French government briefly teetered. The Dubcek government in Czechoslovakia was putting a humanitarian face on communism until, in August that year, the Soviet Union invaded and ripped that face to shreds. Demonstrations in the U.S. were unsettling the establishment in both political parties.

Many Japanese people recognized that, by 1968, with a century having passed since the Meiji Restoration, the economy was booming, accompanied by bizarre predictions of Japan becoming No. 1 in the world; and that it was time to reform Japanese society along truly democratic lines, creating a viable two-party system and social welfare structure.

But, it wasn't to be, for two reasons.

The arch-conservative government of Sato Eisaku, re-elected in February 1967 and then again in January 1970, had a message for the Japanese people: you've never had it so good. That was true. But the establishment's reasoning was that this required further sacrifice on the part of the people and the continued suppression of both individual freedom and liberalized social welfare in the interests of eternal industrial growth. The people eventually bought this line: economic growth at the expense of personal freedom and broad-based social welfare. (China is marching on this path in a more extreme manner. There is no doubt that, in essence, their model comes economically from Japan and politically from the old Soviet Union.)

The second reason for the collapse of the 1960s' dream of a more open and socially tolerant Japan was the internecine struggles within the student movement itself.

It was obvious from the start of the 1970s that the radical student movement was self-destructing at a rapid rate. While the antiwar movements in the West were increasingly effective in focusing attention on the cruelties perpetrated by the United States in Southeast Asia, the Japanese protest movement was rent by factional strife, symbolized by the word *uchigeba*, or violent in-fighting. While student activists in Europe and the United States were becoming conscious of threats to the environment and the needs of the underprivileged, their counterparts in Japan were hung up on ideological struggles among Marxist and neo-Marxist factions.

In May 1969, left-leaning students held a debate with Mishima Yukio on the University of Tokyo's Komaba campus. This debate marked the peak of the 1960s' polemic. Yet the debate, which had gone long over time, turned into a philosophical and aesthetic confrontation, culminating in Mishima's professed adoration for the emperor as Japan's supreme national symbol, a symbol the ideology-bent anti-imperial students were never going to accept.

The death knell for the student movement was sounded on February 28, 1972, when police, after a ten-day standoff, stormed the mountain retreat where members of the Japanese Red Army had holed up with a hostage, the wife of the retreat's manager. The Red Army members had gone to the Asama Sanso retreat in Nagano Prefecture after sentencing some of their comrades in a kangaroo court and murdering them. Japanese television was at the scene televising the standoff and the dramatic freeing of the hostage in the kind of prolonged news coverage never before seen in Japan.

With the Asama Sanso Incident, as it became known, the radical student movement that had matured in the 1960s, enjoying the wide support of the general public, collapsed. The interest the Japanese people had in social issues, whether concerned with the welfare of the underprivileged or ecological deterioration, was gradually snuffed out. Similarly, the social polemics of the sixties, nurtured in virtually every art form, no longer dominated the national debate. The thick magazines that had carried in-depth articles on politics and art were slowly losing their readership, and the high status of serious literature, so popular in Japan since the war's end, was beginning to go into decline.

68

The Accumulation of Little Happinesses and the Downfall of the Japanese Economy

The political dumbing down of Japanese society began not, as many critics say, in the 1990s, but two decades before, when some Japanese people started to turn away from issues and problems in order to concentrate on, for lack of a better word, lifestyle.

This pursuit of a lavish lifestyle implied a studied disregard for social needs, which the media and government were, in any case, all too happy to ignore. A new banner of Japanese communal, and hence personal, aspiration was hoisted high into the air: the banner of affluence. The primary goal now seemed to be the accumulation of little happinesses through the pursuit of wealth. Get your hands on as many of the iconic 10,000-yen notes as you could and the nation was bound to follow obediently at your heels.

Did this differ in any way from the aspiration of Americans? Not much. But Americans had a media largely unfettered by the invisible links of government control. The Japanese media ceased to provide a sounding board for a new social model that could be ready to take over when people would aspire to a life not solely dedicated to conspicuous consumption.

Looking back, one event of the early 1970s struck fear into the hearts of the Japanese, and that fear led them to be all the more cautious and circumspect of liberal social ideals. That event was the oil shock of 1973.

Arab members of OPEC instigated policies that would quadruple the price of oil, and Japan, utterly dependent on oil imports, went into shock. There was a nationwide rush to buy toilet paper after word spread that it would be in short supply, with some people hoarding enough to last for years.

The lessons were clear: prosperity is not guaranteed; there must be no let-up on personal application and sacrificial enterprise if Japan is to be safe from manipulation by outside forces. On the one hand the 1970 World's Fair, or Expo, in Osaka had been an unmitigated success, with visitor numbers topping sixty-four million. Japanese people were clearly still fascinated by foreign customs. But their fascination went little further than a penchant for the outer trappings of culture such as fashion and cuisine. The trendy lifestyle fashions that dominated the 1980s were just that—fashions. European models of welfare politics and social design did not get so much as a look-in.

The Liberal Democratic Party, entrenched in power for what then seemed for good, was determined to forge a Japanese solution to gain world prestige and power. This solution had no place for "soft" issues such as welfare and ecology. Instead, the construction of dams, roads and bridges, whether needed or not, was pursued with a vengeance. These were seen as prestige projects that would stand as sources of pride for the Japanese. No matter that most Japanese were living in tiny "rabbit hutch" apartments, that the needs of the disabled were being roundly neglected or that the country's natural beauty was being systematically buried under millions of tons of concrete. As long as GDP went up, the government could convince the people that their personal efforts were worth the sacrifice. Don't worry about the other guy, just look after yourself, your family and your company, and Japan will regain its "rightful place" in the world community. China beware!

Japan in fact witnessed unprecedented prosperity in the 1980s, but it was a prosperity solely for the rich and opportunistic, and it was to be short lived and ultimately destructive of economic equality, political discourse and social experimentation.

These are the elements of the postwar model that brought the Japanese economy to its knees. Again, China beware!

69

Jishuku, or Self-censorship

As for the media, it has not been easy, with my European-ingrained belief in the freedom of word and image, to live and work within the Japanese system.

This is not due to censorship or other restrictions on freedom of speech, though there is much of that in Japan. It is due to the Japanese people's penchant for *jishuku*, or self-censorship. The Japanese people don't really need people on top to tell them to restrict self-expression. They are quite happy to do it themselves. Restriction and self-curtailment *are* the self-expression of the Japanese. (This is the root of all *sontaku*, the contemporary version of *jishuku*.)

I remember well returning from Sydney to Tokyo in early January 1989. It was a few days after the death of Hirohito, the Showa emperor, on the seventh of that month. I rode the Narita Express train into town and took a taxi from Tokyo Station to a television studio to take part in a talk show.

It was early evening. The city was deserted. It looked like Melbourne in a scene from *On the Beach*. The *jishuku* mood that had overtaken Japan during the emperor's prolonged illness was still in force. It had virtually shut down nighttime Tokyo. In Japan, you're not allowed to have fun when the national—or corporate, or institutional, or neighborhood—mood doesn't "call" for it. All bad things—and all good things, as well—must be shared, or seen to be shared.

The *jishuku* mood that overtook Japan between the announcement, in September 1988, of the Showa emperor's illness and his death the following January gave an inkling of what the country was like during the war.

Many city lights were dimmed or shut off and a good deal of innocent merrymaking was discouraged and frowned upon. At that time, the Chunichi Dragons baseball team had won their Central League playoffs, but decided not to pour beer over their heads or hold a victory parade. Singer/songwriter Inoue Yosui's persuasive television commercial for Nissan cars included the line, "Is everybody fine?" The commercial continued to run, but that line was muted out. The popular singer Itsuki Hiroshi canceled his wedding reception, and many people across the country followed suit and canceled theirs too. In short it was considered improper and un-Japanese to be seen to be celebrating when the emperor was in discomfort and pain. No government directive was issued, no bureaucratic regulation promulgated. Businesses suffered seriously. But it was the people of Japan who eagerly accommodated. They just felt they should lie low. The harmony of the community was, for nearly four months, restrained by a shared feeling of what is—and is not—socially "becoming."

Certainly, many in the West have historically shared just such a sense of common impropriety. It may even be said that the Japanese adopted their notion of what is "becoming" from Victorian England. When her beloved Prince Albert died in 1861, Queen Victoria went into deep mourning. It was from this time that jet jewelry became popular all over Britain. It was as if an entire nation was obliged, by custom, to go into mourning with her. People did it willingly. It was part and parcel of being British at the time.

I have had personal media run-ins with *jishuku* as well.

In the 1980s I did a weekly spot on FM radio in Tokyo. When there were heavy rains in Nagasaki I was told, before going on air, "Don't mention the weather." If a plane crashed somewhere, I was "asked" to exercise self-control: "Nothing about air travel today."

Any talk deemed "unbecoming" was a no-no. I was required to practice self-restraint for my own good. Had I spoken on air about the wrong thing at the wrong time I would have found myself off the air and out on my ear.

The wartime era took the "self" out of self-censorship, and Japanese society was subjected to the oppressiveness of military diktat. Civilian authorities cowered before the men in starch. The censors at the Ministry of the Interior, aware of the immense propaganda value of film, strengthened their hand when it came to the medium. As it happens in others countries as well, prudishness is turned into a semi-legal obligation and becomes a vile form of mass harassment.

When Kurosawa Akira submitted his script for *Ichiban utsukushiku* (*The Most Beautiful*) in 1944, the censors found one specific line in its notes obscene. The director was puzzled as to why a scene about a girls' corps of volunteers leaving the factory gate was deemed obscene. The censors told him that the use of the word *mon* (gate) suggested female genitalia. (And this is the same government of the time that condoned the mass enslavement of women in brothels spread around Japanese-controlled regions of Asia and the Pacific!) The fundamentalism of the military ideology, akin to that of certain religions, held sway over Japan during the war years. It is no wonder the postwar era saw a liberation from puritanical values that found unfettered expression in every art form.

The Japanese media are known for their cowering faint-heartedness. Examples of genuine investigative journalism in Japan are as rare as hens' dentures, and the only big scoops you see are at the nation's ice-cream parlors. People often blame the bureaucrats and the politicians for creating restrictive rules in Japanese society. But in reality, the restraint that the media exercise in Japan is largely self-imposed and self-inflicted. The desirable state would be one in which the people could afford to be more liberal minded while retaining the admirable aspects of self-discipline that make them courteous and admirably self-effacing. The opening up of the society, however, depends more on the people liberating themselves than them waiting for the government to do it for them. The trouble is that the meek population of Japan waits and waits for some superior force to act on their behalf.

Miyazawa Kenji, though known in Japan for his deep understanding of the motives of evildoers—he wished to negate their presence not by fighting with them but by embracing them tightly—was moved to write the following about art, though his words can apply to the media as well: "If art merely repeats itself or misrepresents the truth, if it becomes nothing more than an escape for the incompetent and the cowardly, then I say, 'Smash it to bits!'"

Though the Japanese may present themselves as docile and apathetic, an active iconoclasm is also an innate sensibility in their tradition. As a society, they keep their anger pent up and under wraps. But once it is let out they can be formidable protesters. I saw it in the 1960s, and I believe it is going to be seen again in Japan in the future.

This volcanic social phenomenon is one source of the fire in Japanese originality, its lava waiting to burst forth. I was drawn to that fire below the surface from age twenty-three and still feel its heat more than fifty years later.

70

Predicting Your Future

My parents bought their first television set in 1952, when I was eight years old. It was a ten-inch Admiral.

Those were relatively early days for the new exciting medium, and it wasn't long before my friends and I were glued to the screen. We had two television heroes. One was a little boy named Beany, who wore a little beanie. The show was called *Time for Beany*, and its characters, beside the little boy full of chutzpah and beans, were all cleverly drawn, especially the gigantic fop to Beany's antics,

Cecil the Seasick Sea Serpent. Albert Einstein, it is said, adored the show that in its first year was broadcast only in Los Angeles before going nationwide. Einstein apparently once walked out of an important meeting so as not to miss it.

The other of my favorite programs was *Criswell Predicts*. Criswell, or "The Amazing Criswell" as he was known in Hollywood, was Jeron Criswell King, a handsome chap with a blond spitcurl, a deep voice and a raven's stare. He was allegedly staring through the television camera into the future. To a little boy with a fertile imagination, his weekly predictions were a thrill. As it was with the bumps on a pillar and the bend of a venetian blind, I have a crystal-clear vision of the details of a particular show in 1953 that has remained with me ever since.

"Ten years from now, by 1963," intoned Criswell, peering at the nine-year-old me right through the glass of the TV screen, "we will all be traveling around Los Angeles in helicopters, men will be wearing capes over their shoulders, and women will wear lipstick in rectangular shape instead of following the lines of their lips."

In what was my first act of journalism, I wrote these three predictions down in 1953, fully expecting them to come true and prove that Criswell was indeed amazing. By 1963, I was a university student and I had lost my notes. But I hadn't forgotten Criswell's predictions. I looked around the campus of UCLA, where I was an undergraduate. No helicopters in the air except one from the LAPD, the Los Angeles Police Department, hovering high above Royce Hall. No capes on men or women. And the women who were wearing lipstick did not have mouths like the side of a matchbox. "Criswell Predicts" may have been off the air by the end of the 1950s (what's amazing is that he lasted that long), but the man hadn't counted on a little Los Angeleno determined to hold him to his word.

I must admit to some disappointment that "The Amazing Criswell," Hollywood psychic and friend of the stars, was a phony. Ever since then I have taken such predictions of the future with a grain of salt. *Time for Beany*, with its rundown characters and sinkable ship called the "Leakin' Lena," had more in common with reality than the visions of the charismatic Criswell. And it looks like Albert Einstein concurred.

So what good is talk of the future?

Is Kenji's vision of us all being happy, meeting on the far side of the Milky Way, joining hands in a dance around a huge bonfire that can be seen in every corner of the universe, any less fanciful than Criswell's predictions? In fact, it is. It is a vision of Kenji's ideal world. He peers into the drop of dew in front of him to see the past reflected in it, and in that past, he sees the future reflected again in the dewdrop behind him. In this way, all time is encompassed in the present instant; all phenomena—past, present and future, whether occurring where you are or anywhere else—exist in the here and now. Kenji doesn't predict the future. He envisions it as an element of the present. In that sense, the future has already happened. We simply need to open our eyes to recognize it in the lives of the other animals and the sweep of nature that we all share right now.

This was the metaphor that I was looking for: Kenji realism. That you could share in the joys and miseries of all your contemporaries and the delights of nature everywhere. This inspired me and reset the needle of my moral compass, whose movement had become so erratic due to the vagaries of adolescence and the crossing of tangents that had been my life. It was in the writings of Miyazawa Kenji that I discovered my own direction.

71

O Lost! Are We?

I am an immigrant.

Immigrants are like pictures painted first at home, then sent out to other places to hang from then on in their museums. Our pictures may be suitably ignored there, admired or hated by the people there. Some of our pictures remain obscure, perhaps never making it out of the deep bowels of the building. Others may hang in pride of place covering a big space of wall in a much-frequented room.

This was certainly the case of writers like Vladimir Nabokov, James Joyce and Joseph Conrad. Nabokov and Joyce may have rejected their homeland for political or social/personal reasons, but they remained writers of their own land or ethnicity. Conrad, like Samuel Beckett, switched languages and in doing so founded another identity, one detached from that of his former home. (Nabokov, too, had written in English, a foreign language, but he remained a Russian writer.)

As for me—and this implies no comparison of stature whatsoever with the above-mentioned giants of letters—I only wanted to make it out of the bowels of the museum in my new land, Japan, and into a corner of any room whatsoever, however rarely frequented, to remain there until new pictures replaced mine with something more finely expressed and radiant.

Though I gave up my American citizenship and disassociated myself with the country, I am its product. While living in the United States as a teenager, I idolized author Thomas Wolfe. His good Christian upbringing in Asheville, North Carolina in the first decades of the twentieth century could not have been more different from mine half a century later in Jewish Los Angeles. (If you read the book that I believe to be the greatest American classic of the twentieth century, *O Lost: A Story of the Buried Life*, which is the unexpurgated version of his first book, *Look Homeward, Angel*, you will find passages there that were deleted by Wolfe's brilliant but stodgy and puritanical editor Maxwell Perkins. Some passages are virulently anti-religion, while others are explicitly erotic. Wolfe's style, bowdlerized by Perkins, is decidedly non-naturalistic, not so distant in spirit from that of the author he admired and met on three brief occasions, James Joyce.)

Wolfe went to Harvard Graduate School in September 1920, a month before his twentieth birthday. I went there in September 1964, three months after my twentieth. Dear reader, once again I am not making high-handed comparisons for literary purposes. I was convinced, until I read every single biography written about his life, that he had lived in Perkins Hall Room 32, where I took up residence on the Harvard campus. How did I conjure up that "fact"? I have no idea. He had not lived there. But I even told some people how amazing it was that I was actually living in the same room that was occupied by Thomas Wolfe.

My link with Thomas Wolfe was solely one of the spirit. I shared his American spirit of wanting to devour the world, of desiring to touch everything in it, if but once. When he arrived at Harvard he seriously contemplated, it is said, reading every book in the Widener Library. (The library had been established only five years before Wolfe got to it, so it wouldn't have had the millions of volumes it has today. But it was a substantial collection once owned by Harry Elkins Widener and donated to Harvard by his mother Eleanor in memory of her son. Harry, Class of 1907, had died on the Titanic.) I actually entertained the same notion for a few hours one day, wondering whether I should start with "A" or some other letter. This devouring of the lives of others was something that Kenji, in his Japanese way, strove for by enveloping the cosmos in his consciousness. It is akin to attempting to leave your skin in order to get under the skin of others, to become them, if only for an instant.

We definitely do rewrite the past. We do it every day of our life. By truly believing that I was living "in Thomas Wolfe's room" I was rewriting the present so that I could form a vision for and of myself in the future. Along with my belief in "The Amazing Criswell," my own notions of life would have to be scrutinized and re-scrutinized by me if I was ever going to commit them to paper. Or else I would be creating on paper a "story" about myself and others, a story with only a tenuous attachment to truth.

I returned to Boston in September 2000 for the first time since leaving Harvard in June 1965 and made a beeline for Perkins Hall. The old building was still there. I climbed the stairs, worried that the door to Room 32 might be locked. Fortunately, the room—

which was actually two rooms, one with a fireplace and study, the other a bedroom—had been turned into a common room and the door was ajar. I entered. No one was there. I went immediately to the fireplace. I had once looked under the mantelpiece while living there and "seen" the initials "TW" carved into the wood. Naturally I had carved "RP" beside them. The mantelpiece had obviously not been changed since I had been there. I bent down and looked under it. There were no initials at all, no "TW" and no "RP," just a few scratches and gashes under a new coat of paint. The fact is that there had been no "TW" under there, and I had not carved my initials there either, though at one time I had been convinced of it.

What then in the past can be recorded faithfully? Can we reconstruct a life, even the one we know most intimately—our own?

I think we can, but we must do it with great care for the feeling and sensibilities of others. It goes without saying that we must be honest with ourselves. But at the same time, we must scrupulously ensure that our honesty is not a ruse for false modesty, that we are not actually endeavoring to ingratiate ourselves into the good books of our readers by presenting ourselves as eternally well meaning. One thing I have learned from living with the Japanese is that an excessive display of modesty is a sure sign of conceit. We must not ever claim so much as a moment of feeling that we have not felt at the time. Ambition and ego, yes, by all means. But the excessive pushing of that ambition at the expense of others and the conspicuous wearing of that ego on the sleeve so that all and sundry may massage it are two actions that I have never wished to adopt. I would rather my little picture remained somewhere below a dark staircase in the basement of that building than get it up to the Exhibition Hall through the exercise of excessive ambition or the aggrandizement of ego.

That we cannot escape our own view of the world no matter how desperately we strive to share those of others is a fundamental feature of the human condition. Even Miyazawa Kenji, who believed that he was not only himself but all others at the same

time and that we are all mentally and spiritually a part of each
other, could not manage it in real life. Paradoxically, the attempt
only forced him further into himself. His ideal of commonality
was expressed in two lines from the preface to the poem "Spring
and Ashura":

Just as everything forms what is the sum in me
So do all parts become the sum of everything

Despite all this, in his life he felt terrifyingly alone and isolated
from all people around him.

As for Thomas Wolfe, he best expressed the longing for
commonality and its inevitable unattainability in *O Lost*, whose
hero . . .

> . . . knew he would always be . . . caged in that little round of
> skull, imprisoned in that beating and most secret heart. . . .
> Lost. He understood that men were forever strangers to one
> another, that no one ever comes really to know anyone, that
> imprisoned in the dark womb of our mother, we come to life
> without having seen her face, that we are given to her arms a
> stranger, and that, caught in that insoluble prison of being, we
> escape it never, no matter what arms may clasp us, what mouth
> may kiss us, what heart may warm us. Never, never, never,
> never, never.

He ends that paragraph with five "nevers."

But is it so? Can we not touch others by becoming them for an
instant . . . when we read a book, look at a picture, listen to a song,
ride on a slow train through a magical landscape with our own
beloved child?

Those are the instants—and there can be strings of them—of
ma, when time itself stops, in which we are able, blissfully, to forget
ourselves. We all have them. They give us what is best described in
our life as "bliss."

Had I been a German like Brecht in the Germany of the early 1930s, I would surely have left my country. Had I been a Japanese like Mako's father, Taro Yashima, in the Japan of the late 1930s nothing would have kept me in my country. This exemplifies, on the one hand, an aversion to engagement. It may be expressed in terms of individual protest or personal integrity but, in the end, it entails extricating yourself from the location that has been the center of your existence up to then.

I drifted from the United States to Eastern Europe to Japan and then to Australia. This movement in itself was no different from that of hundreds of millions of people who have migrated from one country to another. The only anomalous feature of my choices is that not many people leave the "land of golden opportunity" for good; not many choose to opt out of their tie to "the home of the free."

My choice ended up causing a rift with my parents that was never bridged. To them and their parents the United States offered a pinnacle in life's climb. You could go no higher than America. Why would you choose to live your life on distant plateaus, ever gazing upward toward the American summit far away? It was true for millions of migrants. There was no better place on the face of the Earth.

But you must choose what is best for yourself even if it differs from what is best for others.

72

Our Path in Life—A Walk in the Garden

In January 1996, Susan, the four children and I moved from Tokyo to Kyoto, settling into a lovely old two-story home facing the Kamo River just north of the Botanical Gardens at Shobuencho. Even the name suggested tranquility: Shobuen means "Iris Garden" (*cho* denotes a small quarter of a district). Though I saw no irises in

Shobuencho, the lovely neighborhood boasted many plants and trees.

We had made it a habit to plant Australian native trees in every Japanese home we lived in, and the one at Shobuencho was no exception. Behind it Susan planted a small wattle, Australia's exquisite native plant. Thanks to the rich soil and frequent rains, it soon grew into a gorgeous flowering tree whose radiant yellow flowers brightened up the surroundings.

Gray and white herons were frequent visitors to the river in front of our home. Since the heron makes appearances in *Night on the Milky Way Train*, and since it was the bird on the herald of Lafcadio Hearn's family (hence, apparently, his surname), I thought of them as visitors from a former time.

The little supermarket I shopped at was a three-minute bicycle ride away. On one sweltering day in July 1997, a week before Susan and I were to take the four children to the U.K. for a month-long drive around that country, I stopped the bicycle at the head of a little gravel and dirt path behind our home.

One of those moments of heightened consciousness overtook me. Another *ma*, an interval in which you take in every single detail around you, a kind of mini-cosmic consciousness. It certainly seemed to be. It must have been the light. It was angling down in all directions through a small bamboo grove by the side of the path. Random lines and patches of light fell onto the path as if it was a Kandinsky canvas. I said to myself, "Walk the bike down the path and elongate the interval."

I very slowly began to walk my bike, telling myself that the thirty-second-long walk would last my lifetime, that this slow motion was a symbol of my going through my whole life. Of course, I came to the end of the path all too quickly and raced to the supermarket to buy the groceries. Yet that little walk has stood in my mind since then for an entire life's journey. And what a journey through a grid of lines and patches of light it was! I can still hear the soft crunch of the gravel under the tires and feel my face getting warm then cool as I made my way over the long narrow canvas, a moving figure traveling right through a work of art.

Another metaphor of *ma* had struck me in 1968 when I went to the Katsura Detached Villa in Kyoto. This villa, with its five teahouses, has what is called a *kaiyushiki* garden. The *kai* means "around" and the *yu* means "play." But this garden is not designed for playing around. *Kaiyu* means "to wander or range from place to place." So, a *kaiyushiki* garden is a "stroll garden," one that is designed to be walked around at your own pace. (Another famous stroll garden in Kyoto is the one at Bokugoan on the grounds of Nanzenji Temple. This is one of my favorite spots in Kyoto, where there is an old aqueduct built to take water to the city from Lake Biwa and from where you can start on a long promenade skirting the eastern mountains along Philosopher's Walk all the way up to the Temple of the Silver Pavilion.)

The stroll garden at Katsura Detached Villa leads you through little landscapes that remind you of the seasons and their passing. This is a trip through transience, a journey that helps you realize that your life is finite and that all things of beauty fade and die out.

If the great gothic cathedrals of Europe instill awe in you and make your little life feel insignificant before a great God, then it is the stroll around the garden of Katsura Detached Villa that inspires you with the notion, in the opening lines of *The Tale of Heike*, that "all is vanity and evanescence," that all beauty fades and all life vanishes.

But it was not the stroll garden, nor was it the rustic teahouses, with their gentle reminders of mortality, that sank into my consciousness back then. It was the stepping-stones of the garden. Of various sizes and shapes, they are placed not so much to allow ease of progress for the pedestrian as to provide them with pure aesthetic pleasure. Again, this is the aesthetic of evanescence at work. You are taking a step. But it is not leading you in a straight line. Each step reminds you that your life is taking a turn, however imperceptible, and each turn represents a moment in the present where the future can be glimpsed simultaneously.

What is the direction of these stepping-stones? Where are they leading you? It is impossible to tell. They lead nowhere, and they seem to come back to the place you were before.

It is December 2000. In a month, we are putting Kyoto behind us and moving to Sydney. We are walking south along the bank of the Kamo River. There are no herons on the little islands in the middle of the river. The sky is gray and featureless. You can't even see the sun. The so-called Hangi cherry blossom trees that line the river beside the Botanical Gardens are leafless. Their limp branches hang down like hair. The trees will blossom as they do every year sometime in May, later than most of Kyoto's cherry blossom trees.

We all stop for a moment. There are stepping-stones here too, taking you from one bank of the river to the other. The four children step onto the stones one by one. I am standing beside Susan watching them. They were all born in Japan and raised there. They speak native fluent Japanese. Our son, the eldest, hops from one stone to another. He is the first across. The three girls follow in the order of their age and are soon on the far bank. They are waiting for their parents with their backs toward us. This is the last time they will live in Japan as children. This was their home, their native country.

"You go, darling," I am saying to Susan.

She walks carefully down the short embankment, steps onto a flat stone and starts to cross the Kamo River. But for some reason she stops right in the middle and turns around.

She is looking at me and not moving. She is perfectly still there, even now.

About the author

Author, playwright, theater/film director and translator, Roger Pulvers' novels include *The Death of Urashima Taro*, *General Yamashita's Treasure*, *Star Sand*, *Liv*, and *The Dream of Lafcadio Hearn*. He has also published numerous works of nonfiction, collected essays and translations from Japanese, Russian and Polish. Roger's plays have been performed extensively in Australia, Japan and the U.S. He has twice directed at the Adelaide Festival of Arts in Australia and at major theaters in Japan. He was assistant to director Oshima Nagisa on *Merry Christmas, Mr. Lawrence*. In 2016 he wrote the screenplay for and directed the film of *Star Sand*, which was released throughout Japan in 2017. Prizes and honors include the Crystal Simorgh Prize for Best Script at the 27th Fajr International Film Festival in Tehran, the Miyazawa Kenji Prize and the Noma Award for the Translation of Japanese Literature.

About the cover

Lucy Pulvers was born in Kyoto, Japan in 1989 and has lived in both Tokyo and Kyoto. She is bilingual in Japanese and English. Lucy has studied at the Julian Ashton Art School in Sydney and was the 2014 Thea Proctor Scholar there. She has been a finalist or semi-finalist in a number of prizes, including the BP Portrait Award in the U.K. Lucy has illustrated various books, and exhibits her work regularly. Her work can be seen at www.pulvers.co

Mount Laurel Library
100 Walt Whitman Avenue
Mount Laurel, NJ 08054-9539
856-234-7319
www.mountlaurellibrary.org

CPSIA information can be obtained
at www.ICGtesting.com
Printed in the USA
LVHW091635130621
690121LV00008B/1610

9 781911 221470